The Joan Palevsky   Imprint in Classical Literature

In honor of beloved Virgil—

"O degli altri poeti onore e lume . . ."

—Dante, *Inferno*

The publisher gratefully acknowledges the generous contribution to this book provided by the Classical Literature Endowment Fund of the University of California Press Foundation, which is supported by a major gift from Joan Palevsky.

The Rhetoric of Conspiracy
in Ancient Athens

The Rhetoric of Conspiracy in Ancient Athens

Joseph Roisman

UNIVERSITY OF CALIFORNIA PRESS
Berkeley   •   Los Angeles   •   London

University of California Press, one of the most distinguished university presses in the United States, enriches lives around the world by advancing scholarship in the humanities, social sciences, and natural sciences. Its activities are supported by the UC Press Foundation and by philanthropic contributions from individuals and institutions. For more information, visit www.ucpress.edu.

University of California Press
Berkeley and Los Angeles, California

University of California Press, Ltd.
London, England

© 2006 by The Regents of the University of California

Library of Congress Cataloging-in-Publication Data

Roisman, Joseph, 1946–.
 The rhetoric of conspiracy in ancient Athens / Joseph Roisman.
  p.   cm.
 Includes bibliographical references and index.
 ISBN -13, 978-0-520-24787-1 (cloth, alk. paper);
 ISBN -10, 0-520-24787-6 (cloth, alk. paper)
  1. Speeches, addresses, etc., Greek—History and criticism.   2. Conspiracies—Greece—Athens—History—To 1500.   3. Rhetoric—Political aspects—Greece—Athens.   4. Politics and literature—Greece—Athens.   5. Athens (Greece)—Politics and government.   6. Conspiracies in literature.   7. Rhetoric, Ancient.   8. Oratory, Ancient.   I. Title.

PA3264.R65   2006
885'.0109358—dc22
2005029593

Manufactured in the United States of America
13 12 11 10 09 08 07 06 05
10 9 8 7 6 5 4 3 2 1

This book is printed on Natures Book, containing 50% post-consumer waste and meets the minimum requirements of ANSI/NISO Z39.48–1992 (R 1997) *(Permanence of Paper)*.

To Hanna, Elad, Shalev, Nava, and Robbie

Can two walk together, except they be agreed?
Amos 3:3

Humpty Dumpty was pushed!
1960s bumper sticker

Contents

Preface xi

Abbreviations xiii

Introduction 1
   The Athenian Conspiracy and Its Vocabulary 2
   Positive Plotting 7

1. Plotting Homicide 11
2. Plotting and Other People's Possessions 19
   Plotting and Contested Inheritances: Isaeus 19
   Plotting and Demosthenes' Inheritance 22
   Collusions to Appropriate Contested Inheritances 27
   Plotting, Desire, and Damage 31
   Plotting Borrowers and Lenders 35
3. Legal Plots and Traps 44
   Plots to Obstruct Litigation: Demosthenes and the Challenge of *Antidosis* 45
   The Choregus's Homicide Trial (Ant. 6). 47
   Framing in Crime: Andocides 51
   Framing in Homicide 54

Legal Traps: Stephanus and Epaenetus	58
Plots and Entrapments: Apollodorus and Nicostratus	62

4. Political Conspiracies: Plots against the City and Its Regime 66
   Plotting in Aristophanes and Thucydides 66
   The Legacy of Oligarchic Conspiracies: Andocides and *Hetaireiai* 69
   The Legacy of Oligarchic Conspiracies: Lysias and the Thirty 72
   Plotting Politicians and Public Officials 85

5. Plotting Legislation and Political Measures 95
   Demosthenes' *Against Aristocrates* (Dem. 23) 96
   Demosthenes' *Against Timocrates* (Dem. 24) 103
   Plotting Motions and Honors 114

6. Foreign and Domestic Plotters 118

7. International Conspiracies 133
   Plotting War: Philip and the Fourth Sacred War 133
   Plotting in International Trade 145

Conclusion: Conspiracy Theories, Ancient and Modern 151

Appendix A. Demosthenes 32. *Against Zenothemis* 161

Appendix B. The Date and Background of Aristocrates' Decree 165

Works Cited 169

General Index 181

Index Locorum 187

Preface

This book is intimately associated with an arduous research project focused on the Athenian rhetoric of manhood, during which I could not help noticing how often the Attic orators referred to plots or conspiracies. The unwise idea of simultaneously collecting information on two different subjects probably contributed to the long period separating the research for and the publication of my book *The Rhetoric of Manhood: Masculinity in the Attic Orators* (Berkeley, 2005). Yet with the orators and modern studies of them still fresh in mind, the work on the present book was made much easier. Although the relationship between the two books is easily recognizable in the frequent references to *The Rhetoric of Manhood* below, this study neither duplicates its predecessor nor is a by-product of it, because the ancient Athenians' tendency to putting conspiratorial constructions on events was not gender-specific. Rather, *The Rhetoric of Conspiracy* is an independent foray into what I regard as an Athenian (and possibly Greek) conspiratorial mind-set, especially the rhetoric that articulated it. Together, however, the two books may enhance our understanding of the values, patterns of thinking, and fears that informed these Athenian speakers and their audiences.

This work's interest in conspiracy makes questions of the speeches' authorship not of a paramount importance; hence the sparse attention given to this subject and the meager use of square brackets to denote dubious authenticity, as opposed to the extensive use of descriptors such as "Demosthenian" and "Lysian" to identify a speaker or a speech.

Unless noted otherwise, all ancient dates in this study are B.C.E. I have used Latin spelling for proper names but transliterated Greek words close to the originals. The use of abbreviations outside the Abbreviations list follows the conventions of the *Oxford Classical Dictionary* and the bibliographical journal *L'Année philologique*. I have used the accessible Loeb Classical Library for the order of Hyperides' speeches and the fragments of the Attic orators.

Finally, it is my pleasant duty to acknowledge my gratitude to Edwin Carawan and the anonymous readers of the University of California Press for their most helpful comments. In a repeated act of kindness, Professor Andrew Stewart suggested the idea for the book cover. I also thank Peter Dreyer and Karen Gillum for their review of the manuscript, and Laura Cerutti, Cindy Fulton, and Rachel Lockman for shepherding it through the publication process. I could have accomplished nothing without the support of my family, to whom I dedicate this book.

Abbreviations

Ancient works and authors frequently cited have been identified by the following abbreviations:

Aes.	Aeschines
And.	Andocides
Ant.	Antiphon
Arist.	Aristotle
Ath. Pol.	[Aristotle's] *Athēnaiōn Politeia* (*Constitution of Athens*)
Dem.	Demosthenes
Din.	Dinarchus
Dion. Hal.	Dionysius of Halicarnassus
EN	Aristotle's *Nicomachean Ethics*
Eur.	Euripides
Fr.	Fragment
Hyp.	Hyperides
Hell.	Xenophon's *Hellenica*
Is.	Isaeus
Isoc.	Isocrates

Lyc.	Lycurgus
Lys.	Lysias
Mem.	Xenophon's *Memorabilia*
Oec.	Xenophon's *Oeconomicus*
Plut.	Plutarch
Pol.	Aristotle's *Politics*
Pr.	Demosthenes' *Prooimia* (*Preambles*)
Rep.	Plato's *Republic*
R&O	*Greek Historical Inscriptions, 404–323 BC*, ed. P. J. Rhodes and R. Osborne (Oxford, 2003)
Rhet.	Aristotle's *Rhetoric*
Thuc.	Thucydides
Tod	*A Selection of Greek Historical Inscriptions*, ed. M. N. Tod (Oxford, 1948)
Xen.	Xenophon

Introduction

Even a cursory reading of the Attic orators turns up a multitude of charges of conspiracy and tales of plotting that involve almost every facet of Athenian life. There are plots against people's lives, property, careers, or reputations, as well as against the public interest, the regime, and in foreign affairs. Athenian conspirators are a highly diverse group and include male and female citizens, resident aliens, slaves, kin, friends, politicians, and businessmen. Outside Athens, foreign powers conspire against the city with the help of local agents. This is not to say that the theme of plotting dominates the oratorical corpus. Its presence is often a function of the circumstances that occasioned the speech, the speaker's belief in the existence of a plot or its rhetorical usefulness, the legal issues involved, his wish to slander an adversary and undermine his case, and various other considerations. For example, speeches involving fraud tend to stress the conspiratorial characteristics of the crime and the offenders. Others, such as Demosthenes' celebrated speech against Meidias, associate the defendant with plotting harm (e.g., Dem. 21.88, 106, 115, 126, 139) but do not expand on his conspiratorial means, perhaps because the orator's wish to highlight Meidias's confrontational and bullying conduct has left limited room for stories of underhanded mischief. Overall, however, plotting appears in most of the speeches in some form or other, and it is therefore unfortunate that the phenomenon of conspiracy charges, their popularity, and their rhetorical, cultural, and psychological significance has received, at best, only scant scholarly attention.

The subject merits investigation for several reasons. It is important to know why charges of conspiracy are so common in the corpus, and what their prevalence tells us about the ancient Athenians and their worldview. Moreover, there is value in assessing the likelihood and validity of the plot scenarios described in the speeches, especially since some of them have been adopted fully or partially by modern scholars, as well as in looking at how these Attic speakers use conspiracy models or *topoi* (commonplaces) to shape their arguments and sometimes their speeches. Lastly, it is of interest to examine to what extent the Athenians' conspiracy theories resemble, or differ from, their modern counterparts. This book attempts to answer all these questions by focusing on the rhetoric of conspiracy in the Attic oratorical corpus, which is one of the most important sources for the social and political history of Athens from around 420 to the 320s.[1]

THE ATHENIAN CONSPIRACY AND ITS VOCABULARY

The English word "conspiracy" is derived from the Latin *conspirare* (lit., "to breath together"), which chiefly means to agree to act together or to combine to perform an evil or criminal act.[2] *Black's Law Dictionary* (2004) defines conspiracy as "an agreement between two or more people to commit an unlawful act, coupled with the intent to achieve the agreement's objective, and (in most states) action or conduct that further the agreement; a combination for an unlawful act." The considerably broader Athenian perception and vocabulary of conspiracy are more inclusive. They include evil plots that are not criminal in character, means, or objective, and ones that are hatched and executed by a single person.

The terms most commonly used in the oratorical corpus for conspiring and colluding are derived from the verb *epibouleuō* (to plot, to design against). Among the somewhat less frequently used verbs, with their derivatives, are: *paraskeuazomai* (lit., to prepare, devise, procure), *kataskeuazomai* (to contrive); *mēkhanaomai* (to contrive, devise); *sunomnumi* (to swear together), *sunistēmi*, and more rarely *suniēmi* and *suntithēmi* (to set or contrive together); *sustasiazō* (to plot,

---

1. For this source, its strengths and shortcomings, see Roisman 2005, 3–6, with bibliography.
2. The original meaning of *conspirare* resembles that of the Greek *sumpneō*, which normally, however, did not denote conspiring. For Latin terminology of political conspiracies, see Hellegouarc'h 1972, esp. 80–109; Pagán 2005, 10–14.

join a *stasis*, or "revolution" or partisan group), and *sunergeō* (to work jointly).³

A speech attributed to Demosthenes that concerns the contested inheritance of the wealthy Hagnias (II) well illustrates the vocabulary of plotting and scheming ([Dem.] 43).⁴ It records an intense legal feud over the estate before it was awarded to a female relative of Hagnias's. According to the speaker, who is the heiress's husband, the other claimants to the estate did not give up at that point, but resorted to evil tricks (*kakotekhnountes*), which they had been practicing for a long time. Two brothers had fabricated (*kataskeuasantes*) a will in an attempt to dispute the heiress's claim and were joined in their contriving (*sunkateskeuazen*) by another person, who served as their witness. Undeterred by the discovery of the fraud and their legal defeat, they persevered. Conspiring (*sunomosantes*) with other men, they made a written pact. All plotting (*epibouleusantes*) together, they each individually challenged the heiress's right to the inheritance before the archon. When the matter reached the court, everything was contrived (*kateskeuasmena*) by them so that they had more time to plead their case than the speaker, who spoke on behalf of her son and could respond to only a few of their lies. Their trickery (*sophisma*) consisted of all telling the same story and corroborating one another's versions. By plotting (*epibouleusantōn*) and supporting one another (*sunagōnizomenōn allēlois*), they deceived and misled the jury through this scheme (*paraskeuēs*) to vote in their favor ([Dem.] 43.1–10; cf. 43.81).

Thus, within a short narrative span, the speaker makes an extensive use of the rich lexicon of conspiracy. Excluding the possibility of his having a weaker claim to the estate, he accounts for his legal defeat as the outcome of a clever scheme that victimized the heiress and the Athenian court and justifies his seeking redress. He portrays himself as standing alone against a group of evildoers and acting in the open, as opposed to their behind-the-scenes machination. He denies the opposition any legitimate motive and complains that its long-term planning, rich experience in the arts of fraud, and expert knowledge of legal procedures (here *diadikasia*) have given it an unfair edge in the contest. Although the dis-

---

3. For *epibouleuō*, and *bouleuō* (to plan, and, more rarely, to plot), in a judicial context: Gagarin 1990. For *paraskeuazomai*, see Wyse 1904, 375, 591; Dover 1974, 26. For the vocabulary of political conspiracy, chiefly *sunomnumi* and *hetairoi/eia* (companions/ship): Calhoun 1913, 5–7; Sartori 1957, 17–33; Aurenche 1974, 15–43. Except for some special cases, I do not in this book discuss plotting in the meaning of planning or doing harm.

4. For the speech and the case, see chapter 2.

puted estate has been subject to five rival claims, the speaker depicts his adversaries as collaborators in the same scheme. He turns their right to speak, each within his allotted time, into an abuse of the system, and the similar grounds they have used to challenge his wife's right to the estate into a well-rehearsed lie.[5] Regardless of whether the speaker's accusations are justified or groundless, the point here is that he thinks that he can credibly challenge the validity of an earlier legal decision with a tale of conspiracy.

As we shall see, other conspiracy tales and charges in the oratorical corpus display similar traits and add new ones. Generally, conspiracy scenarios use the question "Cui bono?" to identify the plotters and their goals. They deduce the plotters' aims and intentions from the results of the alleged scheme, which the plotters execute in the open or behind the scenes. Tales of conspiracy order events and actions in a logical sequence of cause and effect or turn them into pieces of the same puzzle. When necessary, they may even rewrite the past. In reconstructing past conspiracies, speakers often refuse to consider the possibility that chance has played a role in the affair or that the plotters' plans could have failed. The presumption is that the conspirators are practically omnipotent and can will events to fit into their schemes.

In both Assembly and court speeches, plotters resemble one another in character, goals, and modus operandi. They are brazen, shameless, and intimidating. There is nothing about their doings that is unintentional, innocent, or honorable, and even their charitable deeds or declarations of decent intentions conceal a harmful agenda. Their goals are selfish and ultimately basic. They want profit, power, to win a conflict, and similar objectives, which make their use of plotting to attain them likely. They like to operate in contexts that emphasize formal rules of conduct or engagement such as trial or legislation, because rules and regulations give their victims a false sense of security. They are skilled in long-term or complex planning and in predicting human reactions to their actions. They equally excel in taking advantage of opportunities and of their victim's weaknesses. Their being stronger and often more knowledgeable than their opponents violates the ethos of justice and fair contest that ordains that the strong should not plot against the weak (Lys. 24.27). Hence, even an adversary's long and arduous preparations for a speech can be described as plotting (see, e.g., Lys. 7.3). Yet plotters, immoral or formidable though they are, cannot fool the plot detector,

---

5. Cf. Thompson 1976, 29–30, 67.

who is able, often uniquely able, to identify them, uncover their schemes, and, if time and other factors permit, frustrate their plans. His success, however, depends on his ability to persuade his audience in the city's political and judicial institutions that he or they have been plotted against; hence, the significance of the rhetoric of conspiracy.

The allure of this rhetoric is almost self-evident. Plotting conveys premeditation, which makes the alleged plotter undeserving of the lenient treatment accorded to unintentional acts. Since the ancient Greeks' notion of intentionality encompassed one's positive attitude toward an act, regardless of whether one initiated it or not, it facilitated charging opponents with conspiring harm even if they did not inflict it in person. Intentionality also assumes a very strong desire to commit an act, and conspirators are often portrayed as consumed with their plot.[6] Conspiratorial activity, which is often accompanied by other undesirable conduct, maligns an opponent's aims, methods, and character and presents him as a threat to individuals, to the state, and to the community and its values.[7] It also challenges the accused to disprove an allegation, which is more easily made than refuted. Conversely, making charges of conspiracy, especially against the public interest, can earn the accuser popular gratitude for uncovering a hidden threat. In fact, it is advantageous to allege plotting even when the conspiracy is not criminal in nature. This is the case with many nonactionable plots described in this book, in which images of opponents involved in clandestine, tricky activity or of a solitary man facing a coalition of powerful ill-wishers are designed to garner sympathy for the speaker and invoke the notion of fairness that, alongside the laws, was supposed to guide Athenian jurors in a trial.[8] Conspiracy allegations even justify questionable conduct on the part of the victim necessary to defend himself from a plot. They also explain and mitigate one's loss in past conflicts and encourage jurors to intervene in the present trial on one's behalf to correct former injustice and violations of the law, lest they come to be seen as the plotters' accomplices (Lys. 22.17).

It is hard to imagine that conspiratorial charges could yield these and

---

6. For intentionality and responsibility, see Rickert 1989, esp. 71, 128. Cf. also Gagarin 1990 for the Athenian notion of design, which could include what modern readers would have considered an unintentional result.
7. According to Aristotle, conspiring was also a mark of cowardice and effeminacy: *Hist. Anim.* 608a35–b13. Plotting in the company of other undesirable attributes or conducts: e.g., Lys. 14.25–26; Dem. 21.126; 39.34; cf. Ant. 2.2.12.
8. Meyer-Laurin's (1965) antagonizing law and fairness in Athenian trials and prioritizing the former as the jurors' exclusive guideline are too rigid; see Todd 1993, 52–73.

other benefits unless there was in Athens an a priori readiness to believe in the pervasiveness of conspiracies in human affairs, and that both individuals and states had few inhibitions in resorting to them to attain their goals. The orations justify such a premise. They are full of alleged plots to kill, to deceive, to subvert the government, to betray friends and nation, and even to start a war. Does the popularity of plotting charges show a deep-seated anxiety about conspiracies, or even reveal the Athenians as such to be conspiracists, that is, men inclined to construe and be receptive to conspiracy theories that are based on false logic and non-existent evidence? Only a case-by-case analysis of plots in the orations, which this book endeavors to provide, will tell if such a characterization is justified. The learned Eli Sagan, one of the few readers of antiquity to investigate the topic of ancient Athenians' suspicions and anxieties, has, however, already put them through a Freudian analysis and judged them paranoid. Sagan sees all humans developing from an infantile paranoia to paranoid stances of varying intensity, and eventually, with maturity, to prevailing over their paranoid tendencies. Among the clear signs of a paranoid position, which is rooted in a wish to obtain controlling power and in greed, according to Sagan, are a suspicious worldview, an attitude of basic distrust, and a resultant aggression toward others. "Conspirators and traitors are everywhere," and powerful, cunning enemies threaten one from without. Sagan cites Aristophanes' mockery of the popularity of charges of subversions and tyranny in Athens as a proof of paranoid anxiety. He regards democracy as the least paranoid of societies, but also as carrying within itself paranoid inclinations, and characterizes Athens's aggressive foreign policy in the second half of the fifth century as the most paranoid behavior among Greek states. From 403 to 322, however, Sagan sees the city as enjoying a stable democracy, in which politicians peacefully debate what is best for the polis.[9]

I deal with the psychology of Athenian conspiracy in the concluding chapter of this book, where I also list my main differences with Sagan's thesis. Suffice it to say here that if suspicions of internal and external plots are a sign of arrested paranoia, their multiplicity in the speeches of fourth-century Athens contradicts Sagan's idealization of this period as a golden age of mature democracy. The following chap-

9. Sagan 1991, esp. 11–12, 16–17, 24–25. Aristophanes' criticism: *Wasps* 493–502, and chapter 4 below. Sagan's discussion is also inspired by Richard Hofstadter's influential 1967 study, which treats McCarthyism as a paranoid phenomenon. Dodds 1951, 30, 44, 97 n. 98, 253, discusses Greek religious and pathological anxieties.

Introduction 7

ters deal primarily with how and why speakers allege conspiracy and, when possible, test the validity of their allegations. But I shall also examine, when appropriate, whether these charges fit the category of a paranoid position or reflect a different psychological construct. For besides serving as a weapon in a feud, conspiracy tales may function as a device to explain events and results that are otherwise inexplicable, or that are unwelcome. By offering an alternative to chaos, and an explanation for a perceived injustice, conspiracy scenarios help both individuals and groups to reaffirm their value systems, identify the danger or the culprit, and thus offer hope of stopping the wrong or punishing the wrongdoers.[10]

But before examining the merits and characteristics of conspiracy charges in greater detail, it will be useful to discuss cases where the notion of plotting appears in neutral and even positive contexts.

POSITIVE PLOTTING

At times, the Athenians regarded plots and plotters with approval. For example, conspiracies and conspirators in the public interest, such as against the enemies of democracy, were held in high esteem. Harmodius and Aristogeiton, who conspired against tyranny in 514, enjoyed cult status in Athens and were identified with democratic freedom and equality under the law.[11] One of the tyrannicides' would-be imitators was the Athenian Agoratus, who claimed (allegedly false) credit for participating in a plot that had resulted in the assassination of the oligarch Phrynichus in 411 (Lys. 13.72). In Lysias's speech against Eratosthenes, whom he charges with responsibility for the death of his brother under the radical oligarchic regime of the Thirty, the prosecutor urges the jurors of the restored democracy to convict the defendant. He argues that they should not both, on the one hand, design harm (lit., plot: *epibouleuete*) against the Thirty (then resident in Eleusis in Attica) and, on the other hand, let one of them (i.e., Eratosthenes) go when he is present in the city (Lys. 12.80). As in Agoratus's case, plotting is approved of here. The target of the plot often, in fact, determines the attitudes toward it. This is true of

---

10. See Conclusion for a more detailed discussion of this view. Cf. Pagán 2005, e.g., 6, 19, 22, 90, who argues that historians' writing about conspiracies alleviates their readers' fear of them.
11. Esp. Page 1962, nos. 893–96; Thuc. 6.54–59; *Ath. Pol.* 18.2–6. The last two sources are more critical of this conspiracy but also allude to the positive popular perception of the plotters, for which see Fornara 1970; Wohl 1999, 355–59; Fisher 2001, 277–78.

foreign affairs as well. Thus Aeschines "quotes" Demosthenes' boasting that he had plotted and contrived (*sustēsai*) to move the Spartans to rebel against Alexander the Great (Aes. 3.167).[12]

Of course, there is nothing positive about being the target of an inimical plot, but plotting by foreign powers appears to have enjoyed semi-legitimate status.[13] Isocrates uses this attitude in his composition *To Philip* (written in 346), where he harshly criticizes those who accuse Philip of Macedon of plotting and intervening in Greek affairs in order to impose his rule on the Greeks. The logographer thinks that such allegations are foolish and, especially, slanderous. Attributing a plot to attack Greece to the Persian king, he argues, will make the latter seem a man of courage and worth. But ascribing the same designs to Philip, a descendant of Heracles and Greece's benefactor, exposes him to disgrace, anger, and hatred (Isoc. 5.73–77).

Isocrates' different valuation of the same activity is noteworthy for two reasons. Firstly, his positive judgment of the Persians' plots against Greece contradicts his negative depiction of these designs in his *Panegyricus* and the *Panathenaicus*, written around 380 and 342–339 respectively. There, they serve, with other devices, to delineate the Persians' evil character and justify taking up arms against them.[14] Secondly, Isocrates' distinction between worthy and despicable plots reflects the opposing views of plots from within and from without. As opposed to plotting against the Persians, the historical enemy of the Greeks, it is considered shameful for the king to plan evil against fellow Greeks.[15] Isocrates' logic is akin to that of Aeschines, who argues in relation to Philip and Athens that there is nothing wrong or blameworthy if a buyer (Philip) buys inside influence to enhance his interests, but those who are bribed and plot against the polis deserve its wrath. Both Isocrates' and Aeschines' distinctions are primarily designed to augment the culpability of their respective adversaries, Philip's detractors and Demosthenes.[16] And for all we know, Isocrates' reproach against those who blame Philip for plotting against Greece shows not so much his disbelief in such plans

12. See similarly Thuc. 1.33.4; 3.20.1, 82.4, and 6.86.3, 87.5 for different evaluations of plots or plans in accordance with their aims. Cf. Dem. 8.18.
13. A similar attitude seems to have applied to plotting in war. See its neutral meaning in Xen. *Hipparchicus* 9.8–9, and cf. Hesk 2000, 85–142.
14. Isoc. 4.67, 136, 155, 183; 12.102, 159, 163.
15. Isoc. 5.80. The question of how much Isocrates, or others, truly believed in Philip's right to be considered Greek is outside our interest: see, e.g., Green 1996, 21–23.
16. Aes. 3.66; cf. Lys. 12.44; [Dem.] 7.45. The distinction between internal and external plots had also a practical dimension: it was easier to catch and punish local plotters than outside enemies: cf. Dem. 8.32.

as his seeking to influence the Macedonian king to abort them.[17] Yet these logographers' different characterizations of plots—external: praiseworthy or legitimate to reprehensible; domestic: always blameworthy—is an indication of the wide range of devices for interpreting and detecting plots that was available to Athenian speakers.

That range is the focus of the rest of this book. For reasons of convenience, I have divided the conspiracy allegations into the categories of homicide cases, plots involving inheritances and property, legal conspiracies, political plots and those against public interest, and international conspiracies. The classification is too neat, because some plots fit more than one category. It is based, however, on the plots' primary goals and attributes and the contexts in which they are reported. Where proper or possible, I have tried to test the probability and substance of the orators' allegations, occasionally using the conspirator's analytical tools for this purpose, although with the hope of not falling into the enticing trap of conspiratorial logic.

17. *Contra*, Markle 1976, whose dismissal of Isocrates's call in 346 to Philip to use persuasion, not force, to unite the Greeks, as mere propaganda is too stringent and evinces the spell of the propaganda school of interpreting ancient texts. See also Perlman 1973, 110–11; id. 1969. Cf. Sealey 1993, 166.

CHAPTER I

Plotting Homicide

Athenian homicide law distinguished between premeditated killing, which was severely punished, and unintentional killing, or manslaughter, which had good prospects of being pardoned. Both categories of homicide criminalized the killing of a person through an agent or plotting (*buleusis*).[1] Yet, the notion and vocabulary of plotting accommodated charges of premeditated killing especially well, legally and rhetorically, because they presupposed planning to do harm, concealment, unworthy motives, and often taking advantage of the victim's vulnerability. The speechwriter Antiphon, whose extant compositions happen all to involve cases of loss of life, makes effective use of plotting allegations in trials involving both premeditated and unintentional killings.

The speech *Against the Stepmother* (Ant. 1) is delivered by a man who charges his stepmother with poisoning his father through an agent. He reports that his father had had a good friend who intended to put his mistress (*pallakē*) in a brothel. When the speaker's stepmother heard of this, she persuaded the mistress to give both men what she described to her as a love potion that would restore their love for their respective female companions. In actuality, it was a deadly poison, which the mistress mixed in wine she served the two men at the friend's house in the Piraeus.

---

1. Intentional and unintentional killing: Dem. 21.43; MacDowell 1963, passim, esp. 58–60; Gagarin 1981; MacDowell 1990, 258–59; Carawn 1998, 36–49, 68–75, 223–27, 255–60, 356–61. *Bouleusis*: MacDowell 1963, 62–63; Gagarin 1981, 30–37; 1990.

11

Both had died, and the mistress had been executed, and now the speaker asks the Athenian homicide court of the Areopagus to mete out identical justice to his stepmother. The latter, represented by the speaker's stepbrothers, likely argued that she should be exonerated (1.6).[2]

Rather than validating the prosecutor's charge, I shall examine the way he uses conspiratorial notions and terms to support it, and his possible reasons for employing them. The speaker faced a number of difficulties proving his charges, not the least of them being the lack of corroborative testimonies. The allegation that the stepmother had wished to kill her husband had probably originally been made by the mistress (cf. 1.19), but it could easily be dismissed as self-serving, and the mistress was no longer there to repeat it. Equally unsubstantiated was the speaker's claim that his father had told him of the circumstances of his death or instructed him to seek revenge (1.30). He charged the stepmother with having tried once before to give his father poison disguised as a love potion, but he was unable to introduce the testimony of slaves that would incriminate her, he claimed, owing to his adversaries' refusal to hand them over to him for interrogation by torture (Ant. 1.5–12, 20). An additional obstacle was the lack of apparent motives for the stepmother to kill the speaker's father, a point the speaker largely avoids in his speech. Equally unhelpful were the fact that the stepmother had not been at the scene of the alleged crime and the claim that justice had already been done when the mistress was executed. Allegations of conspiracy helped mitigate or even resolve these difficulties, enabling the prosecutor to exclude the possibility of a tragic accident and use logical deduction and arguments from silence, rather than hard proofs, to substantiate the charge that the stepmother had indeed committed murder by proxy.

Accordingly, the prosecutor repeatedly insists that the drug had been administered, not by mistake or without malice, but as an intentional, willful, and premeditated (*ex epiboulēs kai proboulēs*) act. He turns the stepbrothers' reluctance to hand over the slaves for torture into an admission of their mother's guilt, even though the slaves had given no testimony and such refusal was common in Athens.[3] He tries further to reduce the likelihood that his father's death had been accidental by endowing the step-

---

2. For the court: Gagarin 1997, 119; and for the conspiracy involved, cf. Gagarin 1990, 94; 2002, 150. Based on Ant. 1.9 and Aristotle *Magna Moralia* 1188b29–38, scholars have deduced that the woman might have claimed that she had provided the potion to the mistress but had no intention of killing her husband: see Gagarin 1997, 104–21; Carawan 1998, 229–42; Faraone 1999, 114–16. Gagarin 2002, 146–152, however, argues that she must have denied any involvement.

3. Declining a dare to torture in Athens: Thür 1977, esp. 59–60; Todd 1990, 32–36; Gagarin 1996; Johnstone 1999, 85–87; cf. Hunter 1994, 89–95.

mother with a history of contriving (*mēkhanōmenēn*) against his father's life (1.3, 5, 9, 21, 25–27). He also presents her as able both to plan far in advance and to calculate the best opportunity to strike, two basic ingredients of conspiracy tales. He depicts the mistress as the wife's unwitting agent, but also blurs the line between her, the implementer of the scheme, and the wife, its planner.[4] To evoke the jury's apprehension and loathing, he calls the defendant "Clytemnestra," the name of Agamemnon's monstrous wife, who together with her lover successfully plotted the death of her husband (Ant. 1.17). Countering the defense's protests under oath that the woman is innocent, he claims that it is impossible to know what had happened unless one had been present at the planning, and people who plot to kill those close to them do it in secret (1.28). His assertion is a fine example of the perverse logic of conspiracism, in which lack of knowledge suggests the existence of a plot rather than being a reason to doubt it. Indeed, men's ignorance of and lack of control over women's handling of foodstuffs, and the existence of female channels of communication to which men were not privy, added to the plausibility of his accusation.[5]

The popularity and usefulness of the rhetoric of conspiracy in homicide cases is evinced by its use by both prosecutors and defendants. In Antiphon's rhetorical exchanges between prosecutors and defendants in two hypothetical cases of intentional homicide, the defendants, (including an admitted killer), argue that the prosecutors have conspired against them, that they had persuaded a dying slave of one victim to give incriminating testimony, and that the defendants could not have plotted the killing unless the victim had plotted to kill them (Ant. 2.4.3, 7; 4.2.5, 7; cf. 4.4.4–5). Such assertions are often responses in kind to charges of plotting and planning homicide (e.g., 4.3.4).

Antiphon's speech for a Mytilenean man who was accused by the relatives of the Athenian Herodes of killing him (Ant. 5) is an actual case where a defendant uses the rhetoric of conspiracy to answer a murder

---

4. Ant. 1.15–16, 19–20. See note 2 above for the possibility that the defense charged the mistress with planning the murder. See also Arist. *Rhet.* 1.7.13 1364a for a prosecutor who laid the chief blame for a disappointing military campaign once on the speaker, who had advised (planned) it, and then on the general who had implemented the plan; cf. Dem. 19.21. Homicide cases and planning: e.g. Ant. 2.1.1, 2, 5, 6; 2.2.3, 2.8; 2.3.7; 4.4; Lys. 3.28–29, 33–34, 41–43; Din. 1.30; cf. Aes. 2.148; 3.223; [And.] 4.15. Gagarin 1990; 1997, 166–67; and for this case, 2000, 150–52. For premeditated assaults, cf. Lys. 3.15; 4.9–10.

5. Poison was a concealed and furtive weapon, which, according to Just 1989, 268, 265–68, belonged, together with magic, to "feminine art." See also Faraone 1999, esp. 110–19; cf. Ehrenberg 1962, 198, and Gagarin 2003, 205, on love potions. Cf. Foxhall 1996, 151, for suspicion of female networks, though Lys. 1 may not be a good example of their solidarity.

charge.[6] The case revolves around the disappearance of Herodes during a journey from Mytilene on Lesbos to Aenus in Thrace. It is not easy to reconstruct the prosecution's case reliably from the speaker's biased and self-serving presentation of it, but it appears that he was charged with murdering Herodes as a service (either as a favor or for pay) to his friend Lycinus.[7] The defendant denies any involvement in Herodes' fate. He says that he and Herodes happened to have boarded a ship going to Aenus but were forced by a storm to disembark at another Lesbian port and then changed to a different ship, whose decks provided better shelter from the rain. They took to drinking together, and during the night, Herodes disappeared, never to be found again.

As in the case of the stepmother and the mistress, the charge of murder by proxy bolstered a problematic case in which the (alleged) killer and the victim were practically strangers and the former had no apparent motive to kill the latter. As in the case of Ant. 1, the circumstances surrounding the death were not conducive to a charge of premeditated homicide, hence its reconstruction as a death trap. Since conspiracy and coincidence are antithetical, and nothing in a conspiracy scenario is what it seems to be, the prosecution claimed that it was no accident that the two men had sailed on the same ship and later transferred to a different one, and that the defendant had successfully lured Herodes to his death by trickery. Unlike the accuser of the stepmother, however, the prosecutors supported the charge with evidence. They produced the testimony of a slave (by now dead) who had confessed under torture to helping the defendant kill Herodes, as well as a note, allegedly written by the defendant, informing Lycinus of the murder.

The speaker rejects the charges, however, and highlights the nonconspiratorial character of the affair. He insists that his meeting with Herodes was purely accidental and strongly denies that he had any likely motive to commit the crime (5.20–22, 57–60; cf. Lys. 10.5). He responds to the allegation that he had killed Herodes on land and then disposed of his body by throwing it into the sea from a small boat by claiming that he has witnesses to attest that he had never left his ship, and he challenges the prosecutor to explain Herodes' disappearance or find the boat that was used to transport his body (5.26–27, 39–42, 45). But he also attempts to turn the tables on the prosecution with plotting charges of his own. He thus presents the slave's testimony against him as a frame-up,

6. For the case, see Schindel 1979; Edwards and Usher 1985, 23–7, 68–124; Gagarin 1989; 1997, 173–220; 2002, 152–64.
7. Ant. 5.57, 62–63; cf. Lys. 1.44. Carawan 1998, 334–38, however, thinks that Euxitheus was charged with planning the murder rather than executing it.

and his accusers as crafty schemers. To discredit the slave's incriminating testimony, he maintains that the slave had later recanted his story, and that his adversaries had killed him to prevent the speaker from reinterrogating him and finding out the truth (5.34–35, 46). As in the stepson's case, a postulated testimony makes a strong proof. The speaker also asserts that the incriminating note had been planted on the ship by his accusers as part of their machinations, which they had contrived after initially failing to get the slave to testify against him (5.55–56).

The entire plot had been contrived in advance with great skill, the speaker says. The prosecutors had planned their "lies" for a long time and waited until he was away—that is, for the right opportunity, when he was vulnerable—to join in a conspiracy and plot against him (*ex epiboulēs sunethesan tauta kai emēkhanēsanto kat' emou;* 5.25; cf. 19, 35). To further impugn their methods and aims, he describes them as vexatious litigants, or "sycophants" (*sukophantes*), a category of men who often resemble plotters in character and means.[8] Experts in law, but distrusting the merits of their case, they are suing him under the public procedures of *endeixis* and *apagōgē kakourgōn,* which allow them to imprison him before the trial—illegally, he claims—, in the hope of sabotaging his defense, inducing his friends to testify against him in order to save him from suffering, and humiliating him. This procedure also gives them the opportunity to sue him again in a homicide court if they fail to get a conviction in the present trial (5.16–18).[9] In response to the prosecution's ascription of his alleged crime to mercenary motives, he counters that what his adversaries are really after is his father's property or a reward for dropping their suit (5.79–80; cf. 5.10). He then contrasts these conspirators, whom he characterizes as powerful, greedy, tricky, and lacking in any moral inhibition, with his own and his father's victim status. He claims that the prosecutors are recklessly endangering his life and says that he is too young to be experienced in litigation and that his father is too old and has been unfairly slandered (5.1–7, 74–80).

Because unsolved mysteries have always been a hotbed of conspiracy theories, and because a chance encounter is less persuasive as an argument

---

8. For *sukophantes,* see Christ 1998; Rubinstein 2000, 198–212. They will be henceforth termed "sycophants," although the Greek, which denotes abusers of the legal system, has nothing to do with the modern English meaning of the word. Sycophants and plotters: e.g., And. 1.92–99; Dem. 38.3.

9. For the procedural and probable argumentation in this case, see esp. Carawan 1998, 314–50. It is noteworthy that the speaker, who blames the prosecution of devising a ploy to sue him again for homicide, also asks the jury to acquit him, because it will leave the prosecution the option of retrying him under a more proper procedure (5.16, 85).

than a premeditated one, the prosecution's conspiracy charge must have had considerable appeal. The accusers identify the author of the plot, Lycinius, based on the question "Cui bono?" which may be simplistic but also has an attractive logic. They construct a chain of events that followed a preconceived plan, which was quite convoluted, but also appealing to an audience that would rather look for a hidden agenda and link actions in a causal order than leave the death unexplained. The defendant's response is to allege a plot himself in the hope of accommodating that same conspiratorial mind-set. By so doing, he strives to undermine the prosecution's evidence and legal case and to account for their motives and actions. His conspiracy charges also deny the accusers the moral advantage they enjoy as would-be avengers of their relative's death.

Scholars are divided about the speaker's guilt, and it is probably better not to attempt to resolve the mystery of Herodes' disappearance.[10] This is, in fact, the speaker's point in a passage relevant to our subject. Apparently challenged to come up with an alternative explanation for Herodes' death, the speaker adamantly refuses to speculate about the identity of the killer. He argues that murder cases may remain unsolved and warns against the injustice of convicting innocent persons just because they happen to have been near the crime scene (5.64–70). His persuasive efforts illustrate the difficulties of convincing an audience that would rather believe that a conspiracy had taken place than that it had never existed.[11]

Lysias too wrote a speech for a defendant accused of plotting murder, but he has him focus on the legitimacy of his act, rather than hurling charges of conspiracy back at his accusers. *On the Death of Eratosthenes* (Lys. 1), written for Euphiletus, who had killed his wife's lover, Eratosthenes, has been studied extensively as a valuable source of information about adultery in ancient Athens, chiefly in light of Lysias's success in changing the focus of the trial from a charge of plotting to kill Eratosthenes to the legal and moral right of a *kurios*, or head of household, to punish adulterers with death for seducing women under his roof. Yet the speechwriter is very much aware of the damaging effect of the allegations of plotting and tries to refute them, directly and indirectly, throughout the speech.[12] Since we have only the defense's word for what the prose-

---

10. See, e.g., Schindel 1979, esp. 22–41 (favors Euxitheus's innocence); Gagarin 1989, esp. 103–15 (argues for his likely guilt).
11. Gagarin 1989, 99–102, however, thinks that the speaker does not offer an alternative solution to Herodes' disappearance because he cannot better the prosecution's case.
12. For the speech: Roisman 2005, 34–36 and the literature cited in notes 32–33 there. Pertinent to the present discussion are Carey 1989, 60–61, 81–83; Usher 1999, 57; cf. Todd

cution claimed, it is hard to know how the case was presented. It appears, however, that Euphiletus was accused of laying a well-planned trap for Eratosthenes (Lys. 1.40, 42). It was alleged that he had instructed a slave girl, whom Euphiletus describes as the go-between for his wife and her lover, to tell Eratosthenes to come to his house at night (Lys. 1.37). Eratosthenes came unarmed and unprepared for any violent conflict, it was argued, and the defendant dragged him from the street into the house and killed him sacrilegiously next to the hearth, suggesting perhaps that the victim had tried to escape his killer, but was forced in and then sought shelter by the hearth (Lys. 1.27, 42). We do not know what motives, if any, were attributed to the killer, or whether Eratosthenes' adultery was acknowledged, but the prosecution surely tried to show that rather than being the lawful killing of an adulterer caught in the act, this was a case of premeditated murder (Lys. 1.30; cf. Dem. 23.53).

Euphiletus responds by stressing the heinous nature of adultery and men's moral and legal duty to uproot it. In addition to justifying his act, this tactic allows him to present himself not as a plotter but as the victim of a plot concocted by Eratosthenes and his own wife. He describes the former as an experienced and skilled adulterer (1.16), the wife as cunning and resourceful (1.11–14), and himself as a man busy with his own affairs and a trusting husband who had been "completely ignorant of my misfortunes" (1.15).[13] More concretely, he argues that the maid who had informed him of Eratosthenes' visit had done so under compulsion, that on the night of the murder, Eratosthenes had entered his house when he (Euphiletus) was asleep, that he had found Eratosthenes lying naked next to his wife, and that he had killed him in the bedroom; in short, no collusion with the maid, no trap, no enticement or dragging of an unarmed victim inside, and no supplication at the hearth (1.21–28). By emphasizing that he had no other motive for the killing but his wife's infidelity and upholding the law, he tries to combat the accusation of using a legitimate façade to conceal a dishonorable or illegal motive and action, a common allegation against plotters.[14] He

---

2000, 12, 16. Attempts to reconstruct the prosecution's case: Scafuro 1997, 331–32; Gagarin 2003, 202. Euphiletus's countercharging the prosecutors with plotting-related terms such as devising and lying (1.28, 39) can be best described as perfunctory.

13. I cannot share Carey's 1989, 60–61 reconstruction of Euphiletus's character as that of a borderline fool, or Porter's thesis (1997) that regards the speech as too comical and literary to have been given in court. The speaker's trust in his wife only after a testing period, and his careful handling of the news of his wife's affair, evince caution and even cunning: 1.6, 16–21. Gagarin's (2003, 204) claim that the speaker diminishes his wife's role in the affair is not easy to reconcile with Lys. 1.6–14. Euphiletus as victim: Carey 1989, 64.

14. Lys. 1.4, 43–46, and see Lys. 10.5; 11.2; and Ant. 5 above for similar denials of homicide plots by arguing the absence of a likely motive.

also insists that his conduct prior to the murder had not been conducive to a trap. The day and the time of the murder had not been prearranged, but were determined by the adulterer's decision to pay his wife a visit (1.21–22). Otherwise, instead of inviting a friend to dinner on the evening of the murder, which might have deterred the adulterer from coming, he would have gone to his friend's house or, alternatively, would have asked him to stay and help him to take revenge (1.39–40). He would also have alerted his slaves or friends beforehand and during the day to be prepared to accompany him to the fatal encounter, instead of searching frantically for companions, including some who were away at the time, to accompany him and witness the crime and its punishment (1.41–42). These probability-based arguments illustrate the difficulties speakers encountered in proving that there had been no conspiracy and that chance had played a part in what happened. Lastly, and to cover all contingencies, Euphiletus argues that what mattered was not how Eratosthenes had been caught, but that he had committed the crime (1.37–38). Yet sensing that this argument might alienate an audience expecting justice to be served without trickery or deceit, he immediately proceeds to make the aforementioned claims that his actions prior to the murder show that he had not conspired to kill Eratosthenes.[15]

Antiphon's and Lysias's different uses of the rhetoric of conspiracy in homicide cases well illustrate its adaptability to changing circumstances and strategies. Yet in depicting plots, plotters, and their victims, both logographers follow core concepts and motifs that recur in other types of conspiracy in the oratorical corpus. Among others, these include the absence of spontaneity or fortuitousness in human conduct and actions, a heavy reliance on logical connections and deductions to prove and disprove conspiracies, the exposure of plotters who hide behind other men or a misleading front, the assumption that plotters possess overwhelming ability to execute a crime, and the expectation that uncovering the conspiracy will, nevertheless, result in the plotters' punishment for their evil deeds. Largely missing in the plots described here, however, are the greedy desire for more and the wish to obtain controlling power, which Sagan regards as signs of an Athenian paranoid position. Rather than serving as instruments of destruction in conflicts over power, these conspiracy scenarios helped the plot detectors, and presumably their audience, to comprehend events that were, prima facie, unexpected, random, and unjust.

15. The fact that Euphiletus did not corroborate his version with the slave girl's testimony has raised suspicions about its merit: e.g., Scafuro 1997, 32 n. 5; and see Edwards 1999, 61, 77.

CHAPTER 2

Plotting and Other People's Possessions

Plots to appropriate possessions that rightfully belong to others are very commonly alleged in the speeches, although it is hard to say to what extent this reflects the ancient Athenians' frequent resorting to acquisitive plotting, the ingeniousness of our informants about these plots, or both. To be sure, however, accusations of conspiracy against proprietors or rival claimants to property tell us a great deal about the Athenian social relations, values, and perceptions that inform the depictions of plots and plotters.

PLOTTING AND CONTESTED INHERITANCES: ISAEUS

The extant speeches of the logographer Isaeus deal exclusively with disputed inheritances. Two of them in particular describe plots to take over estates or to defeat competing claims to them in illuminating detail.

On Euctemon's Estate reports a legal dispute over the estate of Euctemon of Cephisia between Chaerestratus, who claims it as Euctemon's adopted grandson, and two other Athenians, who claim it together with their guardian as Euctemon's sons. The speaker is Charestratus's supporting pleader, and he tries to undermine the opposition's case in various ways, including charges of plotting.[1] He informs the court that old

---

1. Is. 6. For the case, whose complexity cannot be reconstructed here, see Wyse 1904, 481–547; Rubinstein 1993, 120, no. 15; cf. Roisman 2005, 44–45.

Euctemon had forsaken his original family for a former slave and prostitute named Alce, who managed rental property for him. Using a variety of nefarious means, she had succeeded in persuading Euctemon to officially acknowledge the eldest of her sons by a former slave as his own. This led to a dispute between Euctemon and Philoctemon, his son by a different woman and Charestratus's adoptive father, which ended in an agreement that bequeathed most of the estate to the latter (Is. 6.19–26). Yet some time after Philoctemon's death, Chaerestratus's rivals moved to strip the estate of its assets. The speaker describes them contemptuously as "crouching before that woman," that is, acting as Alce's lackeys. Taking Euctemon's old age and feeble wits as license to launch their joint attack (*sunepitithentai*) on his property, they pressured him to cancel his will that would have favored Chaerestratus's claim and to convert assets into cash so that they could easily get hold of them (6.29). Their success in conspiring together (6.38, 55) apparently encouraged them to plot getting the rest of the property. Contriving what the speaker described as "the most horrible deed of all" (*kai pantōn deinotaton pragma kateskeuasan*), they registered Alce's sons as the sons of Euctemon's other dead sons and made themselves their guardians in the hope of collecting rents by leasing the estate's property. Fortunately, the plot was foiled in court by other relatives (6.35–37).

Notwithstanding the possible merit of these allegations, they display the classic marks of a conspiracy tale. These include collusions driven by a base motive, here greed, which target and bamboozle a vulnerable victim. The plotters are skilled in seizing the right opportunity, in employing legal and illegal devices, and are brazen and shameless (6.43, 45–46, 48, 50, 54). Finally, their resourcefulness and uninhibited lack of respect for basic values such as masculine honor and conformity to laws, customs, and kinship solidarity evoke both fear and the wish to punish them.

In a speech concerning a dispute over Ciron's estate (Is. 8), Isaeus makes extensive use of the motif of the "man behind the scene" in alleging a plot.[2] The contesting parties are Ciron's fraternal nephew, on the one hand, and his two grandsons by his daughter, one of whom is the speaker, on the other. The speaker dismisses his unnamed opponent as a hireling of Diocles', the brother of Ciron's second wife, who is not a party to the suit under discussion. Allegedly, Diocles procured (*paraskeusas*) the speaker's legal adversary for a small sum, and the purpose of their devising (*mēkhanōmenōn*) and fabricating (*kataskeuake*) a

---

2. For the case, see Wyse 1904, 585–624; Rubinstein 1993, esp. 102–3; 121 no. 19.

legal action is to deprive Ciron's grandsons of their rights to the property (8.3-4, 25, 27, 37, 43).

To add credibility to his accusations, as well as to account for Ciron's failure to make him and his brother his heirs, the speaker makes plotting Diocles' favorite modus operandi (cf. 8.40). He tells the jury that when old Ciron was alive, Diocles had plotted with his sister, getting her to tell her husband more than once that she was pregnant and then that she had miscarried, thus preventing him from adopting his grandsons (8.36).[3] Diocles also slandered the speaker's father by alleging that he had plotted against Ciron's estate, thus misleading the old man to allow Diocles to manage his property, which he now held (8.37). Diocles' unscrupulous avarice and conspiratorial ways had even dispossessed his own half-sisters of their inheritance, and when sued by one of their husbands, he had plotted (*epibouleusas*) to have him imprisoned and disenfranchised. He had the other husband killed by a slave, spirited the killer away, and threatened to frame his half-sister for the murder so that he could defraud her son, whose guardian he was, of his possessions (8.41). His success as predator had now emboldened him to go after our speaker (8.43).

Diocles' villainy may have been exceptional, but not so his plotting ways, which show an affinity to other conspiracies in the oratorical corpus. He hides behind proxies, who do his dirty work for him, be they his sister, a slave, or the speaker's adversary. He has victimized the weak, innocent, and honest, such as old Ciron, the grandsons, and his own relations. He is opportunistic and very clever, and the success rate of his many plots makes him almost omnipotent. He has deceived everybody, including his partner in the present trial. The speaker argues that Diocles promised his rival claimant only a fraction of Ciron's estate and did not tell him about money the old man had left (8.37). He is also greedy, brazen, shameless, devoid of any loyalty, and cuts an intimidating figure (8.1-2, 4, 40, 42). To cap it all, he is a notorious criminal and habitual adulterer (8.4, 44).

William Wyse, Isaeus's chief interpreter and surely his most skeptical reader, thinks that the attack on Diocles is a diversion designed to compensate for a weak case. The grandsons, he argues, cannot really disprove their opponent's contention that Ciron had no daughter and that they are the sons of an unrelated woman of non-Athenian decent. And even if they are related to the deceased, they have to persuade the court

---

3. Cf. Rubinstein 1993, 104. For suspicions of wives' loyalty to their natal houses: Roisman 2005, 36-38.

that as maternal grandsons, they have a greater right to the inheritance than collaterals.[4] It is indeed possible that the conspiracy tale aims to direct the jurors' ire against a man who is an inviting target for charges of plotting. Diocles appears to have been an unpopular man, with not a few enemies, and he had yet to answer a charge of hubris arising from his treatment of his brother-in-law (8.40–42, 45; cf. Is. frs. 7–8 [Forster]). We may ask, moreover, why the speaker's opponent, who had a legitimate and probably stronger claim to the estate, agreed to give it up for a pittance and to front for a man with significantly less right to it. Yet the conspiracy tales in the speech do not only serve to confound the jury. They delegitimize a rival claim as underhanded and sycophantic and malign the claimant by association. If on balance the legal case of the speaker's adversary seems stronger, the accusation of plotting tries to level the field in the name of equity. Moreover, if Diocles is indeed in possession of most of Ciron's estate (8.2, 37), the speaker's accusations are highly relevant to the case, because he is competing with another man for assets that Diocles holds.

These Isaean tales of conspiracy are not isolated cases. The motifs of opportunism, malevolent cunning, collusion to produce fraudulent claims or documents, and disguising self-serving aims behind fair-sounding, legal actions are likewise found in other, albeit less elaborate, charges of plotting in Isaeus's speeches. The latter also depict shameless conspirators disregarding family solidarity and unfairly using their power, experience, or skill against weaker parties. Finally, many of the conspiracy accusations claim to be exposing the plots in the name of truth and to protect the court from erroneous decisions.[5]

PLOTTING AND DEMOSTHENES' INHERITANCE

Some of the motifs discussed above appear in the orations of Isaeus's pupil Demosthenes, whose speeches against Onetor deal with Demosthenes' attempts to recover money and possessions from his guardians, whom Demosthenes had charged with misappropriating and mismanaging them (Dem. 30–31).[6] After successfully convicting the guardian

---

4. Is. 8.6–20, 30–34; Wyse 1904, 587, 613. For criticism of Wyse's tendency to disbelieve Isaeus and his clients, see Avramovic 1990, 41–55, esp. 41–42.
5. Is. 9.22–26; 11.14, 20–22, 32, 36; fr. 1 (Forster); cf. 1.6–8; 10.1, 7.
6. For the case against Onetor, see Davies 1971, 118–20; Kertsch 1971; Pearson 1981, 93–95; Cox 1998, 123–24; Usher 1999, 180–83. For the disputes with Aphobus, see the literature cited in Burke 1998, 45 n. 1.

Aphobus and being awarded ten talents in damages, and after defending his witness, Phanus, against a charge of false testimony made by Aphobus, Demosthenes proceeded to take a piece of land that was part of Aphobus's estate but that Onetor held and refused to hand over. Onetor claimed that he had obtained it from Aphobus as a security for a dowry Onetor had given him for marrying Onetor's sister, and that he was keeping it because Aphobus had not returned the dowry after divorcing his wife. In his ejection suit (*dikē exoulēs*) against Onetor, Demosthenes argues that these are lies aimed at concealing the collusion between Onetor and Aphobus. He asserts that no dowry had changed hands between the two, and that hence no security had been given. In fact, the divorce was a sham, because the couple had continued to live together after registering their divorce. The entire plot was designed to prevent Demosthenes from repossessing the aforementioned farm.

Fortunately, Demosthenes' account is detailed enough to allow us to check its validity. Scholars generally agree that he makes a sound case for a conspiracy against him, and it is fairly certain that the speaker sincerely believed that he was the target of a plot. However, we should note the highly circumstantial nature of his evidence. For if we subtract from Demosthenes' arguments those that are *ex silentio* or based on probability and expand our view of his rivals' actions beyond his self-centered explanation of them, we get the following attested facts.

1. Onetor's sister had been married first to Timocrates and then to Aphobus. After Timocrates divorced her, he held her dowry as a loan and paid the interest to Aphobus. Demosthenes argues that Timocrates' keeping the dowry shows that Aphobus had never received one, but Timocartes' payments of interest to Aphobus, and his and Onetor's claim that they had paid the dowry to Aphobus in installments, make it likely that over a period of time, Aphobus had received portions of the dowry in the form of interest payments from Timocrates.[7]

2. No one had witnessed the dowry transaction between Onetor and Aphobus. Demosthenes argues that, given the common practice of having people witness the giving of sizable dowries, especially to avoid future disputes over them, this shows that in actuality, no dowry had been handed over (30.19–21). Onetor

---

7. Dem. 30.9, 18–20. Cf. also Meyer-Laurin 1965, 27–28.

and Aphobus insist that a dowry did change hands. The assertions are equally plausible, and in the absence of witnesses, neither side can prove its claim.

3. Aphobus registered his divorce after Demosthenes had won his suit against him in court. Demosthenes claims that the timing shows that this was done to prevent him from getting the disputed land, under the pretext that it had been given to Onetor as security for the dowry (30.17). Like other people with conspiratorial mind-sets, the speaker uses the temporal proximity between two different events (i.e., his legal victory and the registration of the divorce) in order to relate them to each other causally. The link is probable, but no more than that, because only Aphobus knew for certain why he had registered the divorce at this particular time and whether the timing was indeed meaningful.

4. Aphobus and Onetor were friends both before and after the divorce. At Aphobus's trial, Onetor spoke on behalf of the defendant and even offered to stand surety for him. In the present trial against Onetor, the latter would call Aphobus and Timocrates as supporting witnesses (30.31–32, 38; cf. 29.28; 31.10–11). Demosthenes argues that this shows their collusion, that they are not involved in a dispute over the dowry, and that the divorce is a mere formality. Yet if Onetor had given a dowry to Aphobus and in return had received a piece of land as security, he had a clear interest in protecting his investment from Demosthenes' attempts to seize it. In addition, friends or not, Onetor had compelling reasons to produce Timocrates and Aphobus as witnesses in order to prove that Aphobus had received money from him (by way of Timocrates) and had mortgaged the disputed land as security for the dowry.

5. Aphobus farmed the land that he had surrendered to Onetor, and after he had lost the trial to Demosthenes, he had even carried off produce and other movables from it, without Onetor's protesting his actions. For Demosthenes, this is proof that the land had never really been handed over to Onetor (30.26–29). But if Aphobus rented the land from Onetor, he was within his rights both to work it and take its produce and other movables

that he owned. Besides, elsewhere in the speech, Demosthenes indicates that Aphobus gave back what he had taken from the land to Onetor.[8]

6. Demosthenes produces the testimony of one Pasiphon, who had treated Onetor's divorced sister when she was ill and had seen Aphobus sitting next to her (30.33–36; cf. 30. 25–26). The speaker presents this as a proof of their continuing cohabitation after the divorce right up to the year of the present trial, but his evidence is hardly compelling.[9] It is true that the segregation of elite women at home probably did not make it easy for Demosthenes to obtain information about this woman. But although he had had three years from the time of the divorce to the trial to collect evidence (30.33), the best that he could come up with was the testimony of someone who had seen them together on one occasion and under special circumstances. Demosthenes complains that Onetor had declined his challenge to torture a former slave of Aphobus's whom Demosthenes had obtained in lieu of unpaid restitution and three maids of Onetor's to get them to corroborate his assertion about Aphobus's divorce (30.27, 35–36). But given that challenges to torture slaves were rarely accepted in Athens, it is likely that Demosthenes challenged Onetor in the knowledge that he would refuse the demand and for the purpose of using his refusal as proof that Onetor's sister had lived with Aphobus.[10] Indeed, Pasiphon's testimony is not a conclusive proof that Onetor's sister continued to live with Aphobus. The testimony itself is now lost, but Demosthenes' report in another speech that Aphobus moved from Athens to Megara following his legal defeat (29.3) makes it likely that Pasiphon saw him and Onetor's sister, who now resided at her brother's house, during Aphobus's visit there. A man's show of concern for his former wife, then, did not mean that he had never left

---

8. Dem. 30.35. See Davies 1971, 119–20, and Kertsch 1971, 10–11, for Demosthenes' charging Onetor that he had removed the markers that showed that a house belonging to Aphobus served as a security for the dowry to the value of 2,000 drachmas.

9. Humphreys 1985, 327, thinks that doctors were considered reliable and impartial witnesses, but while this might have been true regarding the authenticity or gravity of injuries or sickness, that was not the case here.

10. For dare and torture, see chapter 1, n. 3. For the chronology of the events described in Dem. 30: Davies 1971, 119; Kertsch 1971, 3–7; MacDowell 1990, 2, 294.

her.[11] And even if Aphobus and Onetor's sister continued to occupy the same house after their divorce, it was no proof of their marital cohabitation. After all, Demosthenes' mother and Aphobus, who had promised Demosthenes' father to marry her, had lived prior to the present conflict in the same house for an unknown period of time without being married to each other.[12]

The purpose of this discussion is to direct attention to questions about Demosthenes' conspiracy thesis rather than argue that it is implausible. The fact that his evidence is circumstantial does not constitute proof that his allegations lack merit.[13] To this may be added the cumulative weight of his proofs, references in the sources to other kinds of collusions regarding contested property, and the fact that according to Demosthenes, Aphobus had liquidated, transferred, and even destroyed his assets following his legal defeat.[14] At the same time, all these points are insufficient to invalidate Onetor's denial that his sister had continued to live with Aphobus (30.29) or his assertions concerning the disputed land and that he had married off his sister with a dowry. Indeed, many of the pretrial dealings between Onetor and Ophebus concerning the land, which Demosthenes portrays as directed against him, may have had little to do with his claim to it, as shown above. Like other victims of real or imagined conspiracies, however, Demosthenes confidently depicts himself as the focus of their interactions and their raison d'être, interpreting every action his opponents took before and during the trial as a plot against him. He thus argues that they had joined together in robbing him (*sunaposterei*), that they had contrived their preparations and suborned witnesses for the trial, and that they had plotted (*epibouleusanta*) against him from the outset (30.3-4, 31; 31.14). He says that Onetor is fronting

---

11. See also MacDowell 2004, 77 n. 25. If this interpretation is correct, there is no need to assume that Onetor treated his sister's honor cavalierly by allowing her to live with her former husband: Pomeroy 1997: 177–78; cf. Cox 1998, 180. Cf. [Dem.] 59. 55–56 for a former wife taking care of her sick ex-husband. The manuscript of Dem. 30.35–36 is unclear and can be read as if Onetor's sister lived with him after her divorce, and that Demosthenes wished to torture the slaves in order to prove that she was *not* living with Aphobus. But such reading contradicts Demosthenes' efforts to prove the couple's cohabitation.

12. Dem. 27.13, 16, 32, 46; Cox 1998: 147.

13. Mirhady 2000, 195 thinks that Demosthenes' poor evidential proofs were the result of inadequate preparation. See, however, Plut. *Dem.* 7 for his practice of carefully preparing his public speeches. It is hard to imagine that he acted differently in a case regarding his own inheritance.

14. Dem. 29.3. Collusions regarding property: Osborne 1985a, 1–6; 1985b, 45; Cox 1998, 122–25.

(*proīstamenon*) for Aphobus in this trial and that the two had skillfully prearranged to protect themselves from harm (30.5–7). He highlights their friendship, because friends are expected to work in concert and support each other under most circumstances, even for the purpose of securing ill-gotten gains. Like other plotters, Onetor has acted brazenly and shamelessly (30.18; 31.2, 6). The entire affair is a fraud against, or shows contempt for, not only Demosthenes, but also the jurors and the laws (30.8, 18, 24, 26, 38; 31.1, 10, 12; cf. Dem. 45.67; 46.25). In this way, Demosthenes tries to impress upon the court that there is no explanation for his adversaries' behavior other than that they have colluded against him.

COLLUSIONS TO APPROPRIATE CONTESTED INHERITANCES

Some of the premises underlining Demosthenes' complaints or those of Isaeus's clients against their respective adversaries recur in two other speeches concerning disputed inheritances. One speech, wrongly attributed to Demosthenes' stylus, deals with Hagnias's estate and the efforts of the speaker, Sositheus, to show that, in accordance with Athenian rules of inheritance, his wife and son are more entitled to it than its present owner.[15] Within these efforts, Sositheus discusses a plot against his wife that had taken place in a previous trial and that had transferred the estate from her possession to that of Theopompus, the father of the present owner. Aiming to show that the earlier court's decision had been erroneous, Sositheus describes all of his wife's rival claimants at that legal procedure (*diadikasia*) as conspirators who had ganged up against her (43.1–10; and see Introduction above). He reinforces and reiterates this accusation later in the speech when he claims that those who had submitted the competing claims to the inheritance were actually Theopompus's partners (*tous koinōnous*), who supported his version because they were *sunagōnistai* (lit., fellow combatants or litigants) and did everything in common (*koinēi*) to disinherit her from the estate.[16] Yet before she was wronged by these plotters, she had won the estate, not by unjust conniving or conspiracy, but in a most honest way (*enikēsen oudemiai paraskeuēi adikōi oude sunōmosiai, all' ōs oion te dikaiotata*), proving that she had been Hagnias's nearest relation (43.32). At the trial in which

---

15. [Dem.] 43. For the dispute, see Thompson 1976; Cox 1998, 3–10.
16. [Dem.] 43.30. See Whitehead 2000, 286, for references to *sunagōnistai* as partners and supporters in a negative sense.

she lost the estate, however, these fellow conspirators had come fully prepared with many shameful means (*anaiskhunta pareskeuasanto*) to mislead the jury (43.38).

In spite of the speaker's extensive use of the Athenians' rich conspiratorial vocabulary, and his claim that the conspiracy was even recorded in a written agreement (43.7), he fails to prove the existence of such document. He also does not explain what moved the other claimants to help Theopompus win the case and so defeat their own claims to be Hagnias's heirs.[17] His version is made even more problematic by an Isaean speech written for Theopompus in a different legal contest whose account of the fateful trial names fewer contestants, among them a man whom our speaker fails (perhaps intentionally) to mention (Is. 11.8–10, 15–18). I am tempted to agree with William Wyse's somewhat too sweeping observation that "unsuccessful Athenian litigants are always victims of conspiracy."[18] Yet tales of plots serve as more than just a way to vent personal frustration. Both in the present trial and the former one, the speaker had to convince the court that his solitary version had greater merit than the one offered by a group of individuals who, notwithstanding their varied interests and claims, had all agreed that his claim was fraudulent. A charge of conspiracy helped him cope with this predicament. It also reduced the value of the earlier unfavorable legal decision as a moral and even legal precedent for the present jurors, preventing them from letting the opposition—endowed here with typical plotting attributes in the form of skilled planning and preparation, fearlessness, shamelessness, and craftiness (43.30, 39–40, 42)—get away with victimizing the woman, justice, the laws, and even themselves (cf. Dem. 44.37).

The Demosthenian speech *Against Olympiodorus* (Dem. 48) is highly unusual in pleading a case based on a pact that the speaker of the preceding speech would readily have identified as conspiratorial. Shortly after the wealthy Comon died, his relatives—the speaker, Callistratus, and his brother-in-law, Olympiodorus—had taken possession of his tangible assets. Each evidently being concerned about the other appropriating more than his fair share, as well as about other claimants to the inheritance, especially Callistratus's half-brother, Callippus, the two made

---

17. Thompson 1976, 66–67, however, believes in their cooperation. I am not arguing that such partnership was unlikely: see Dem. 48 (below). But in Dem. 48, the plotters were supposed to share the loot. Here the speaker says nothing about their expected gains, and, at most, alludes to their friendship: [Dem.] 43.7.

18. Wyse 1904, 673; cf. Thompson 1976, 68.

a pact to divide the estate evenly and to do everything regarding it in concert (*koinēi*). Callistratus repeatedly stresses that he and Olympiodorus had committed themselves to this distribution of the assets in a written document, which they confirmed by oaths and witnesses.[19] So after consulting together (*ebouleuometha . . . koinēi*) as to what would be the best and safest way to deal with rival claims (48.22), they decided that Olympiodorus would claim the entire estate, and Callistratus only half, given that his half-brother claimed only half too. But inasmuch as they were unready (*aparaskeuoi*) for so many claimants, they looked for an opportunity to postpone the legal session about the ownership of the estate in order to prepare (*paraskeuasasthai*) their case without pressure. It was lucky, then, that Olympiodorus had been called to military duty in Acarnania. Callistratus asked for postponement of the proceedings on this ground, but the other litigants persuaded the court that Olympiodorus was away because of the trial rather than because he had to perform military service. Olympiodorus's claim was rejected, and Callistratus said that he had given up on his claim "out of necessity," probably referring to his commitment to do everything together with his brother-in-law. The estate was then awarded to other claimants, including Callippus (48.23–26, 41; Libanius *Hypothesis to Dem.* 48.7).

When Olympiodorus returned home, the two discussed the matter. They decided to reclaim the estate, and that the safest way to achieve their goal was once again for each of them to claim the inheritance separately: Olympiodorus the entire estate, and Callistratus just half of it. According to their agreement and oaths, if either of them won, he would share the proceeds with the other (48.29–30, 42, 44). Olympiodorus pleaded his case first, and, according to Callistratus, made false statements about his status as an heir to, and proprietor of, the estate, and even produced witnesses to support his case. Callistratus, however, was sitting there all the while and did not interrupt or protest Olympiodorus's assertions.[20] "Given that the trial was arranged in this manner" (*touton de ton tropon kataskeuasthentos tou agōnos*), Olympiodorus won his case easily (48.31). He refused to honor the agreement and share the reward with Callistratus, however, and in particular money peculated by a slave of Comon's that Olympiodorus had managed to obtain. After

---

19. Dem. 48.9–10, 17–19, 28, 32. For a similar agreement, possibly conspiratorial as well, see Is. 11.24–25; Thompson 1976, 33–37.
20. Dem. 48.6, 31, 43–44. Here I follow Calhoun's (1918) interpretation of Callistratus's conduct.

making superhuman efforts to reach a compromise with his kinsman (esp. 48.1–4), Callistratus was compelled to sue him for damages.

More significant than the highly dubious merits of Callistratus's case is the question of how he thought he could persuade the court to decide in his favor and reward him for having helped a crook both to dispossess more rightful heirs to the estate and to deceive the former jury. It appears that Callistratus's strategy was born of necessity and a desire for revenge. He had no better grounds for suing Olympiodorus for damages than the pact between them, yet he presented the defendant as the chief villain in the story. If Callistratus won, he would make Olympiodorus pay for having gone back on the agreement. If he lost, he allegedly had nothing that he could be sued for (48.27), but his tale would induce the losing claimants to Comon's estate to renew their claims and sue Olympiodorus for misappropriating it.

Such a strategy accounts for Callistratus's straddling the worlds of legitimacy and conspiracy. On the one hand, the agreement between him and Olympiodorus broke no law.[21] Callistratus emphasizes that it had been duly confirmed in writing and by oaths taken in front of witnesses, and that their submission of separate claims to the estate had been done in a procedurally correct manner (48.29, 31). He also dresses their collaboration in nonconspiratorial attire. He repeatedly refers to their joint consultation or planning *(bouleuō)*—rather than to their conspiring *(epibouleuō)*—and characterizes their arrangement behind the scenes as the best and least risky way of dealing with the situation. In addition, it was not he, but Olympiodorus, who had lied about his relationship to the deceased and misled the jurors about his rights to the property. Callistratus had merely held his tongue.

On the other hand, the jurors would have had to be quite obtuse not to deduce that Olympiodorus had obtained the estate thanks to a conspiracy, because Callistratus took care to lead them to that conclusion, both implicitly and explicitly, by giving their collaboration all the marks of a plot: doing everything in concert, concealing their partnership; seizing an opportunity (i.e., Olympiodorus's military service), although with disappointing results; making long-term plans; showing up in court fully prepared; and making skillful or crafty use of legal procedures. When he focuses on Olympiodorus, Callistratus attributes to him conspiratorial

---

21. Gernet 1954, 2: 228–29; Christ 1998, 266, n.46. For the legal liabilities of contract, see note 28 below. It is noteworthy that Callistratus cannot verify his version of what the contract entailed, because Olympiodorus will not allow the contract to be produced in court: 48.46–51.

characteristics such as being deceptive, greedy, shameless, and taking unfair advantage of his adversary (48.1, 9, 36, 39, 40, 45–46, 51). He sums up his account of the trial won by Olympiodorus by saying that it was *kataskeuasthentos*, a word that I have translated above neutrally as "was arranged," although, in light of the frequent meaning of the verb *kataskeuazomai* in the oratorical corpus, it might equally be understood to mean "was contrived."[22] In short, without admitting to the conspiracy, Callistratus tells the jurors all that they need to know about it. Accusing his fellow plotter of having betrayed their agreement, he hopes that the jurors will favor him as the more worthy claimant to the estate and as the better of two shady characters.[23]

Callistratus's account is unique in at least two respects. First, the initial failure of these conspirators to get the estate shows that even successful plotters may encounter difficulties and disappointments on their way to attaining their goal. This runs counter to the many successful plotting schemes described in the orations as smoothly executed and unproblematic, probably because failures and hardships are incompatible with the image of plotters as exceedingly powerful and smart. The relentless pursuit of a target that these two conspirators exhibit, however, is quite common. Secondly, Callistratus's suit for damages is exceptional in that he presents himself as the victim, not of a conspiracy, but of a fellow plotter. Other damage suits are more conventional and tend to portray the speaker as the target of an evil plot.

PLOTTING, DESIRE, AND DAMAGE

According to the scholar of Athenian law Stephen Todd, the Athenian definition of damage that could be remedied through a legal action (*dikē blabēs*) was "broad, and seems to have covered any physical or material loss suffered by the plaintiff as a result of action or inaction on the part of the defendant" (Todd 1993, 366). The wide spectrum of this legal action was complemented by the broad application of the rhetoric of conspiracy to it, as evinced both by Callistratus's suit, discussed above, and by the very different case of fraud to be discussed presently. There was a strong incentive for the prosecution in both cases to use this rhetoric,

---

22. Even *bouleuō*, "to plan," can be ambivalent, because it is understood at times as "to plot": e.g., Harpocration s.v. *bouleusis* on Hyp. 3.18; Gagarin 1990, 84–85.
23. For his combining legal charges and slandering: Johnstone 1999, 63–65.

because plotting presupposed intentionality, and intentional damage was awarded double the amount of unintentional damage.[24]

Hyperides' *Against Athenogenes* (Hyp. 3) effectively uses the theme of plotters and their victims in a damage suit over a disputed business transaction. In essence, the speaker, Epicrates, argues that he had been deceived into believing that some slaves he had bought from Athenogenes, and who ran a perfumery shop, came with a small and solvable debt, while in fact their debt and the cost of their purchase amounted to the large sum of five talents. Faced with a major challenge in the form of a contract that he voluntarily signed when he purchased the slaves, he seeks to overturn it with a tale of a conspiracy against a naïve and besotted man. The extensive use of conspiratorial terms or vocabulary in this speech shows the centrality of this rhetoric to his argument.[25]

According to Epicrates, he had fallen in love with a young slave who worked with his father and brother in a perfume shop owned by the businessman Athenogenes. Epicrates offered to buy the boy, but Athenogenes refused, and the two might have quarreled on that account. A woman named Antigone offered to intercede on Epicrates' behalf and swore oaths in order to gain his trust, only to violate it later. Even though she had promised to be Epicrates' partner in his conflict (*sunagōnieisthai*) with Athenogenes, she had actually made Athenogenes her partner against him (*sunagōnistēn*) (3.1–3).[26] To prejudice the court against these two individuals, Epicrates places them outside the Athenian civic and moral community. He characterizes Antigone as a woman who had once been the most skilled courtesan of her time, a madam, the cause of one wealthy man's financial ruin, and currently Athenogenes' *hetaira*. He similarly maligns Athenogenes as an Egyptian and a man who makes his living in dubious and contemptible occupations.[27] With their mercenary record and experience in cheating and taking other people's

---

24. According to the author of the rhetorical handbook commonly known as *Rhetoric to Alexander,* in cases where the jurors had discretion over the penalty, it was useful to amplify defendants' offenses by showing that they were intentional and had involved much preparation ([Arist.] *Rhet. ad Alex.* 132 1426b34–27a3).

25. For Hyp. 3, see Meyer-Lauren 1965, 16–19; Engels 1993, 241–55; Scafuro 1997, 61–64; and esp. Whitehead 2000, 265–351. I have discussed the portrait of Epicrates in love in Roisman 2005, 168–70. My focus here is on the role of plotting in his assertions. Conspiratorial terms in the speech: Hyp. 3.7, 11, 12, 18, 21, 24, 26, 35; cf. 2–3.

26. As we shall see, the role of the chief plotter was easily transferable (here between Antigone and Athenogenes) to accommodate the wish to vilify more than one character.

27. Hyp. 3.3. To underline Athenogenes' villainy, the speaker reports later in the speech that he had deserted and betrayed Athens during its war with Philip and had treated the city of Troizen, Athens' historical benefactor, hubristically: 3.29–32. Of course, men in love can be plotters too. See Arist. *EN* 7 1149b14–20, which contrasts hot-tempered men who act in the open with lustful men who plot and beguile.

money, Athenogenes and Antigone constitute a formidable coalition, which explains his having fallen into their trap.

The trap was skillfully laid and well disguised. Antigone's prevailing upon Athenogenes to sell the boy to Epicrates was a sham. Athenogenes' suggestion prior to the signing of the deal that Epicrates should not buy the boy's father but use the boy free of charge had been insincere, and it would be produced in court in order to make Athenogenes seem a reasonable, moderate person (*metrios*). In fact, he had sent the youth to Epicrates to insist that he would not stay with him unless he freed his father and brother too (3.23–25). The subsequent reconciliation between Epicrates and Athenogenes allowed the latter to pretend to be Epicrates' well-wisher. He advised him that in order to retain control over the youth and his family and gain their gratitude, he should buy them outright, but concealed the true extent of their liability (3.5–6). Stripped of their conspiratorial attire, the actions of Epicrates' rival and his alleged partners appear both legal and harmless. Hence, the plotting scenario, in which no one but the victim is honest and no action or result is unintended. Conspiracy makes it inconceivable that Athenogenes, Antigone, or the boy had at any time shown goodwill or acted ingenuously, or that Athenogenes did not know how much the youth's father really owed (3.18). The speaker, we recall, is highly motivated to show that the damage is intentional.

Plotters are skillful in exploiting other people's vulnerability. Athenogenes accordingly relied for the success of his scheme on Epicrates' weaknesses, which included his yielding to desire (3.2) and his being a simple farmer who was ignorant of the art of business (3.26). Helpful too, for Athenogenes' purposes, was Epicrates' naïvely assuming that other people had his, and not their own, best interests at heart. Together, these weaknesses had made it easy for the plotter to predict the speaker's actions and reactions. They also accounted for Athenogenes' pulling out the contract the minute Epicrates agreed to the deal, for Epicrates' offhand signing of it out of eagerness to conclude the transaction in a hurry, and for the absence of friends to warn him of possible pitfalls (3.4, 8). As in other plots, he had been hit when he was most vulnerable.

Thus what was conceivably a lover's spendthrift expenditure and/or a bad investment became a plot to shake down an innocent man and get him pay other people's debts. This rhetorical strategy enables Hyperides to use Athenogenes' best evidence against him. Other litigants normally produce contracts to prove an adversary's claim wrong or to show that he has violated their legal agreement. Here, the speaker asks for the contract to be read as a proof that the agreement is morally wrong because it is a product of a scheme (3.12).[28] He also invokes the common remedy for plotting—upholding the rule of law—in order to persuade the court that it is up to Athenogenes, and not Epicrates, to pay the business debts. The law, he asserts, should decide this issue, because it had been established by the great democrat (and lawgiver) Solon and not by lovers or plotters (3.21). In fact, the speech uses the rhetoric of conspiracy to support a claim on legal and moral grounds.[29]

The law was also not supposed to help men who coveted other people's possessions. The speaker of Demosthenes' *Against Callicles* (Dem. 55) is a defendant in a damage suit, who charges his adversary with having conspired against him to get at his property. The bulk of the speech deals with the defendant's attempt to refute the charge that his father and he had been responsible for a flood that had damaged the land of his neighbor, Callicles. Such a line of defense, however, fails to explain Callicles' motives for suing him. He accordingly characterizes the lawsuit as a conspiracy to deprive him of his land and frames it in the context of similar attempts to dispossess him.[30] He thus commences his speech by asserting that Callicles is a greedy man, whose desire for the speaker's land has led him to mistreat the speaker "sycophantly," that is, through vexatious litigation. Callicles had first procured his cousin to lay claim to the speaker's land, but the attempt failed when the speaker overcame this intrigue (*skeuōria*). Callicles' other attempts were more successful. He was awarded a thousand-drachma fine in an arbitration process against the speaker, who had failed to show up. The defendant had lost again to Callicles' brother, whom Callicles had persuaded (*pistas*) to lay charges against him (Dem. 55.1–2). Toward the end of his speech, the speaker returns to the charge of plotting when he argues that Callicles' present accusation is a trick (*sophisma*), because it replicates the charge for which the speaker had already been fined, and that it is designed to induce him to give up his land. He also calls upon the jurors to condemn those who plot (*epibouleuontas*) and behave sycophantly in order to have an advantage over others (55.31–34).

28. Violating agreements: e.g., Dem. 35; 48; 56. For contracts, see Todd 1993, 58–60, 262–8; Christ 1998, 218–224; Whitehead 2000, 297. For equating breaking a contract with fraud and plotting: Dem. 35.27 and Dem. 48 above.
29. See, however, Meyer-Laurin 1965, 19, who insists that legal arguments prevail over arguments of equity in this speech.
30. For different interpretations of his allegation, see Carey 1997, 141; cf. Whitehead 1986, 77 n. 42. For the case, the unintentional damage, and the fixed fine (rather than double the amount) involved: Wolff 1943, with MacDowell 1978, 136–37, and Todd 1993, 280–81.

Although the conspiratorial portrait of Callicles is not fully developed in the speech, it is easily recognizable. He is motivated by an uninhibited passion for gain, hides behind agents who, as his kin, make likely co-conspirators, craftily abuses the legal system, and shows disrespect for the speaker and, by implication, the jurors. The unfair means used by this shady character have victimized and disadvantaged the speaker, who calls upon the jurors to help him.[31]

PLOTTING BORROWERS AND LENDERS

The notion of inflicting damage by means of conspiracy informs several speeches written by or attributed to Demosthenes that discuss debts and attempts to recover them. Although delivered in a legal procedure different from *dikē blabēs*, they resemble damage suits in their depictions of the adversary and in utilizing the rhetoric of conspiracy to compensate for a weak case.

Demosthenes 32, *Against Zenothemis*, was delivered by Demosthenes' uncle, Demon, in a *paragraphē* procedure that challenged Zenothemis's adversarial suit as illegal and thus enabled Demon to change roles from defendant to prosecutor.[32] Briefly, the speech concerns a convoluted case of maritime fraud, which originated in a loan given by Demon to Protus, a grain importer, to buy grain in Syracuse, with the grain serving as collateral. The speaker reports that among the men aboard the ship hired for the trip were Protus, the borrower; Hegestratus, the shipowner; and a passenger named Zenothemis. When the ship reached Syracuse, Hegestratus and Zenothemis each borrowed money on the security of the grain as if he owned it, with the other authenticating the false claim. They then sent the money they got to Massalia (Marseille), their hometown, and planned to sink the ship on its way to Athens. According to the norms of maritime trade, such a catastrophe relieved the borrower of having to repay the loan.

The ship left Syracuse, but, in a twist of events worthy of a novel, Hegestratus, the shipowner, was caught making a hole in its hull. Hotly pursued by the enraged passengers, he jumped overboard and disappeared into the sea. Zenothemis, who feigned ignorance, tried unsuc-

---

31. Cf. 55.34-35. For Callicles as a bad neighbor and friend: Millett 1991, 139-40; Christ 1998, 174-76.
32. For this procedure, see Wolff 1966; Isager in Isager and Hansen 1975, esp. 123-32; MacDowell 1990, 306-8, but also Carawan 2001. Zenothemis's original suit was regulated by the rules of maritime trade cases (*dikai emporikai*), and see Meyer-Laurin 1965, 8-11.

cessfully to persuade the crew to desert the damaged ship. After the ship limped to the western Greek island of Cephallenia, Zenothemis tried, in cooperation with some Massaliotes (apparently his creditors from Syracuse), to prevent it from continuing on to Athens, claiming that the borrowers, lenders, and the money involved in the grain transaction all came from Massalia. His claim was rejected, and the ship sailed to Athens, where Zenothemis took possession of the grain in compensation for the loan he claimed he had given Hegestratus to purchase it. His creditors supported his version, hoping to recover their losses from the cargo. Another character, named Aristophon, then surfaced. Even though Demon, the original financer of the transaction, had sent him to Cephallenia to support Protus's claim to the grain, Aristophon betrayed Demon, and, in collaboration with the villainous Zenothemis, persuaded Protus, the grain importer, to abandon his common cause with Demon and support Zenothemis's counterclaim. Protus's desertion was motivated by his wish not to lose money on the grain, which, in the meantime, had fallen in price.

Fortunately, Mogens Hansen's commentary on this speech spares me the need to show why Demon's charges were probably unfounded.[33] Suffice it to say here that Zenothemis might have had a valid claim to the grain if, as he asserted, he had indeed loaned Hegestratus the money to purchase it and had borrowed money from Massaliote lenders to that end (32.12). But more important than untangling this knotty tale is to show how the speechwriter utilizes the rhetoric of conspiracy to strengthen Demon's case.

Demon introduces his audience to the two major themes of his speech, the plot (*epiboulē*) to defraud him and Zenothemis's wickedness (*ponēria*), right at the outset of his speech (32.2). He goes on to develop both themes by way of an extensive use of conspiratorial terminology and associations. Zenothemis was Hegestratus's partner and accomplice (*ho koinōnos autou kai sunergos*), a contriver (*eskeuōrēmenon*), and an operator (*pepoiēkota*: 32.4, 7, 9). The two had jointly devised (*suneskeuasato*) the aforementioned scheme in Syracuse (32.4) and planned (*ebouleusanto*) to scuttle the ship on the way to Athens (32.5). While in Athens, Zenothemis had cooperated (*koinōsamenoi*) with Protus to effect the latter's disappearance to avoid paying his debt to Demon (32.30). Aristophon, who had allegedly deserted Demon for Zenothemis, was a member of a "workshop of

---

33. Hansen in Isager and Hansen 1975, 138–49. Appendix A provides a summary of his reconstruction and my points of difference with his interpretation. For doubts about the merits of Demon's case, see also Gernet 1954, 1: 113–15; cf. Wolff 1966, 35–47.

wicked men who contrived [mischief] together" (*ergastērion mokhthērōn anthrōpōn sunestēkotōn*), which was located in the Piraeus (notorious for its shady characters).[34] He was also the one who had contrived (*suntethēkotos*) the entire affair (32.24). All these individuals display attributes typical of plotters, such as brazenness and shamelessness (*tolma; anaideia*: 32.3, 9, 15); malicious cleverness and trickiness (*tekhnē*: 32.24–27); sycophancy (32.26); lying, or pretending ignorance (32.7); and general dishonesty (3.12, 26). By repeatedly harping on the theme of conspiracy, the speaker hopes to leave no doubt about its existence.

Demon also alternates the role and status of the plotters Zenothemis and Aristophon, seeking simultaneously to present them as the planners of the scheme but also derogatorily as hirelings of other plotters. Thus he introduces Zenothemis as Hegestratus's underling (*hupēretēs*: 32.4), promotes him later to being his partner (32.7), but in fact presents him as the chief villain in the story. He similarly argues that Aristophon hired himself to Zenothemis but was also the one who stood behind the entire attempt to defraud Demon of the grain in Athens (32.11). Aristophon was apparently involved in some well-known scandal (32.11) and thus made a convenient target for accusations of being the master schemer. The rest of the characters, regardless of their roles in the plot, resemble each other in their lack of loyalty and willingness to use an array of dishonest means.

We do not know how successful Demon was in persuading the court, but it is possible to see why he chose to rely on the rhetoric of conspiracy in this case. The only man who could have effectively corroborated his story and validated his claim to the cargo was Protus, but Protus, with whom he had quarreled, was nowhere in sight. Zenothemis's version, on the other hand, was supported by Aristophon and the Massaliote creditors. A plot could account for Demon's weak case by giving anyone whose assertions contradicted or weakened his claim a reason to unite against him. It also explained why Aristophon, who had been Demon's confidant and knew everything about his case, chose nevertheless to say that Zenotemis had the better claim. It even clarified why Protus would not testify for Demon and side with Zenothemis, even though Zenothemis told quite incriminating stories about Protus and sued him successfully in court. According to the speaker's convoluted explanation, Zenothemis, in spite of his alliance with Protus, had not dropped his suit against him for appearances' sake: he was concerned that forgoing the

---

34. Dem. 32.10. For *ergastērion* of sycophants and allusions to their professionalism: Christ 1998, 65–66.

suit would make his case against Demon look frivolous (32.27–28). As in the case of the claimants to Hagnias's estate, when a man faced a group of people of disparate backgrounds and interests and was forced to argue that they were all wrong but him, he might as well depict them as co-conspirators.[35]

Demosthenes' *Against Apaturius* (Dem. 33) also originated in a maritime loan, and the story it tells is only slightly less complicated.[36] It involves a maritime loan owed by the Byzantine shipowner Apaturius, which led, after some financial transactions and legal wrangling, to his suing the unnamed speaker of this oration to get money he (Apaturius) had been awarded in an arbitration process. Like Demon, the speaker used the *paragraphē* procedure to turn the tables on Apaturius and to become the prosecutor in the case. He mentions two plots in his speech. The minor one involved Apaturius's scheming (*epibouleuei*) to smuggle out a ship and slaves he owned, which he had given as a security for a loan (33.9, 24). The larger plot, however, serves to substantiate the speaker's contention that Apaturius's suit against him is sycophantic (33.2–3, 16).

As the speaker tells it, both he and another Byzantine merchant, Parmeno, had either helped to repay Apaturius's debt to his lenders or guaranteed its payment. After a series of suits and disputes involving this debt between Apaturius and the speaker, but especially between Apaturius and Parmeno, the two Byzantines resorted to private arbitration. They agreed on Phocritus as common arbitrator, with Apaturius choosing Aristocles, and Parmeno our speaker for the other slots on the arbitrating board. A unanimous or a majority decision was supposed to have been binding. As sureties for honoring the arbitration decision, Apaturius chose the arbitrator Aristocles, and Parmeno one Archippus, and the agreement was deposited with Aristocles (33.15–16). However, when Apaturius saw that two of the arbitrators, namely, the speaker and Phocritus, were in agreement, he tried to break the arbitration agreement together "with the one who held it" (Aristocles) and argued that only

---

35. Demon's conspiracy tale fails to utilize the topoi of the virtuous litigant and poor victim; see Rubinstein 2000, 174. In the original suit against Demon, it was the opposition that apparently tried to fight the plotting accusation by portraying Demon as the stronger party who brought in an oratorical big gun, his nephew Demosthenes, to help him (32.31). The speaker, however, denied getting any assistance from the orator. Cf. 32.3; Cohen 1992, 127; Rubinstein 2000, 128 with n. 20.

36. The speech is analyzed by Isager in Isager and Hansen 1975, 149–56, who does not discuss the plots mentioned in the speech. For the case, see also Cohen 1992, 154–58; Reed 2003, 102–3.

Aristocles was the arbitrator, while the other two were merely reconcilers (33.16–17). Parmeno demanded that Aristocles produce the agreement in order to refute this contention, but Aristocles claimed that his slave had lost it. The two parties failed to agree on a new arbitration, and Parmeno did not allow Aristocles to pronounce judgment. But after he had been forced to go home following an earthquake that had destroyed his house and killed his family, Aristocles ruled against him in his absence. Two years later, Apaturius sued the speaker as Parmeno's surety for the sum he had been awarded in the arbitration (33.19–27).

The speaker, however, denies his liability. He claims that Archippus is Parmeno's surety, not he. He goes on to disprove his accountability mostly on the basis of arguments from probability, arguing that if he had been Parmeno's guarantor, Apaturius would have sued him much earlier. He also stresses the disappearance of the agreement and concludes by asking why Apaturius did not sue Aristocles, the man who had the agreement and would not produce it, and why he used Aristocles as a witness, unless they had made common cause in their evil devices (*eiper mē koinēi meta toutou ekakotekhnei*: 33.38). Earlier in the speech, however, he blames another Athenian for the plot against him. He asserts that the person who had contrived (*kataskeuazōn*) the disappearance of the arbitration agreement and its outcome was Eryxias, a physician from the Piraeus and a close friend of Aristocles', who, having differences with our speaker, was responsible for the present action against him (33.3, 18).

The speaker's presentation of both himself and Parmeno as victims of a conspiracy is problematic. He builds much of his case on the disappearance of the arbitration agreement and implicates the arbitrator Aristocles in it. But Aristocles was an odd choice as a keeper of the agreement to begin with, given that he was Apaturius's nominee as arbitrator and the presence of Phocritus, said to have been a mutually agreed-upon arbitrator. The facts that it was Aristocles' slave who kept the agreement, that Parmeno forbade Aristocles to declare his judgment, and that Aristocles did so anyway give some merit to Apaturius's assertion that Aristocles was the only authorized arbitrator in the process. It is equally convenient for the speaker that the missing agreement is the only evidence that Archippus, rather than he, was Parmeno's surety.[37] In addition, the tactic of charging an arbitrator with collusion or bias to explain an un-

---

37. See Harrison 1971, 2: 66, 112–23. Harrison thinks that Apaturius suppressed the document, and adds that Archippus was not produced as a witness, and that the only evidence that the arbitration decision was by a majority vote was the lost document.

favorable decision is known from other litigations.[38] Lastly, the speaker's charges against the physician Eryxias (who possibly testified for Apaturius) are underdeveloped and look like an attempt to strengthen the plot scenario by incorporating into it the topos of the evil adviser (or plotter), who clandestinely masterminds the scheme and uses a sycophant to fight his battle for him.[39] In sum, the speaker seems to have taken advantage of Aristocles' losing the agreement to invalidate the arbitration decision against him by concocting a conspiracy story.

It appears that lenders involved in disputes over unpaid loans were fond of raising the specter of conspiracy. In another *paragraphē* procedure involving a maritime loan (Dem. 34), two speakers, Chrysippus and his brother and business partner (34.1, 38), report that they had loaned money to Phormio to finance shipping cargo from Athens to the Bosporus and returning with a different cargo. The agreement gave Phormio the option of repaying the loan with interest to the lenders in gold in case he failed to ship a cargo back to Athens. The man who would deliver the gold to the lenders was Lampis, possibly a shipowner, possibly a slave and the captain of a ship owned by Dion.[40] Phormio, however, was unable to sell the outgoing cargo in the Bosporus, and Lampis's ship, loaded with an unrelated cargo, sank on its way to Athens. The speakers report that Phormio argued first that he had loaded Lampis's ship with a return cargo and that the ship's loss relieved him from the debt, but later said that he had repaid the loan and given the gold to Lampis. Lampis had first denied getting money from Phormio, but when the dispute was referred to an arbitrator, he said that his former statement had been made when he had lost his mind, and that he had received the money from Phormio but was absolved from payment by the maritime disaster. The speaker argues that Phormio has "corrupted" Lampis by sharing the loan with him so that he would change his version and become his partner (*anekoinōsato*), that is, support him as a witness in this legal dispute. In short, Phormio and Lampis, his partner (*koinōnos*), had conspired (*sunistatai*) to defraud him.[41]

---

38. Is. 5.31–33; Dem. 52.30–31; Aes. 1.62–64; Isoc. 18.13; cf. Dem. 34.21. The two co-conspirators in the present case are, of course, shameless: 33.19, 22. For private arbitration in Athens: Hunter 1994, 55–62; Scafuro 1997, 119–27, 393–99.
39. Cf., e.g., Is. 5.7–8; Dem. 21.78; 32.11.
40. For Lampis's status, see Reed 2003, 105 n. 18.
41. Dem. 34.12, 18, 28, 34–35, 41, 48. For the division of the speech between the speakers: Libanius *Hypothesis to Dem. 34;* Rubinstein 2000, 32–33, 88–89; *contra:* MacDowell 2004, 114–15. For the different possibilities of Lampis's lying or telling the truth: Isager and Hansen 1975, 167–68.

As in the cases of Demon and Apaturius's prosecutions, the speaker had to discredit an alternative version of the affair that was well supported by a third party (Lampis), who presumably knew what happened. Lampis did not testify in this trial, but as suggested by the speaker, he confirmed Phormio's version. A conspiracy tale serves to overcome this difficulty, and to make the plot seem likely, the speaker attributed to his opponents two common incentives of schemers in the speeches: bribes and greed. Yet the best that he could come up with in support of his allegation was the assertion that both his opponent and Lampis had changed their versions about the issue in dispute. He poorly substantiated this claim, which in itself was insufficient to prove a conspiracy.

Demosthenes' *Against Pantaenetus* reports the rather unusual case of a debtor charging his creditor with a conspiracy (Dem. 37). The speech, delivered in a *paragraphē* procedure, describes a series of business and legal transactions and feuds involving the ownership and leasing of a factory specializing in crushing and processing silver ore. The prosecutor and speaker is Nicobulus, who, together with his partner, had loaned the defendant Pantaenetus money to lease the factory. The conspiracy allegation, however, is recorded in the text of Pantaenetus's indictment of Nicobulus for damages, which had preceded the present trial. This charged Nicobulus with plotting (*epibouleusas*) against him and his property. Pantaenetus alleges that Nicobolus had ordered his slave to take from Pantaenetus's slave silver he was bringing as payment to the state for the mining rights and so caused Pantaenetus to be registered as a state debtor for double the amount (37.22). Documents in the Attic orations are often suspected as later interpolations, inter alia, because they largely reuse information provided by the speeches in which they are cited. But if this indictment text is authentic—and its inclusion of otherwise unknown details indicates as much—it is a rare occurrence of a charge of plotting against another person's property in a formal legal suit, as opposed to its much more frequent use as a rhetorical means of persuasion.[42]

Nicobulus, however, characterizes the plotting charge against him as baseless, laughable, and sycophantic (37.23–24; cf. 37.8, 35, 49–50). Given the common association of sycophancy with plotting in the speeches, it looks as though he is trying to respond in kind to the con-

---

42. For the likely authenticity of this document, see Carey and Reid 1985, 134. They also note that deliberate damage, suggested by plotting, was punished by doubling the amount. For a conjectural reconstruction of this affair, see MacDowell 2004, 175.

spiracy charge against him. He reinforces his plotting charge by asserting that when he and his rival were about to enter the court, Pantaenetus came to him, surrounded by those about him, a gang of conspirators (*to ergastērion tōn sunestōtōn*, lit., a workshop of those who get together), and challenged him to decide the issue by torturing a slave (37.39). He also conventionally alleges collusion between his adversary and his witnesses when he characterizes the latter as co-conspirators (*sunestōsi*), who intend, together with the defendant, to deceive the court with their assertions and with appeals to pity (37.48). It was not difficult to portray friends who helped a litigant in a private suit by speaking on his behalf, or by supporting his version with testimony, as co-plotters. In the eyes of many, friends' solidarity could easily turn into harmful countersolidarity when challenged.[43] In addition to vilifying the opposition and undermining its credibility, this accusation portrays the speaker as the weaker side in the conflict and, along with the jury, the victim of a scheme.

Nicobulus, Pantaenetus, and all other plotters discussed in this chapter often come from the social and moral category to which Apollodorus, son of Pasion, refers in his speech against Stephanus. Having reached the point where he tries to incite the jurors against the defendant, whom he charges with false testimony, Apollodorus argues that as a wealthy man, Stephanus is unworthy of the court's indulgence. The difference between rich and poor wrongdoers, he argues, is that the latter are compelled by their circumstances to do wrong and so deserve compassion. The former, however, have no justifiable excuse, because they are moved by shameful greed, hubris, and the wish to make their plots (*sustaseis*) lord over the laws. It is in the jurors' interest to punish such men (Dem. 45.67). Apollodorus's statements demonstrate the appeal of the rhetoric of conspiracy in depriving litigants of judicial consideration and presenting them, even when they target private wealth, as threatening the polis's laws, security, and quality of life.[44] His words also show how easy it is for speakers to associate plotting accusations with popular prejudices against wealthy men, skillful pleaders, and powerful men in general, who are perceived as having the leisure and means to plan mischief. Indeed, regardless of whether the accuser is rich or powerful, his plotting allegations place him in the role of the poorer and weaker litigant, dimin-

---

43. For friends in court, see Humphreys 1985, 325, 336, 347–48; cf. Scafuro, 1994.
44. Cf. Lys. 22.15–17, 21; Dem. 44.3–4, 36; Aristotle *Pol.* 4 1295b33–4. For plotting out of (excusable) need: Isoc. 4.34; cf. Thuc. 1.2.4.

ishing the likelihood of his lodging a sycophantic suit, and he courts sympathy as such.[45] In addition, for jurors looking for the "truth of the matter" and faced with two conflicting accounts, plotting accusations discredit a rival version as well as the witnesses and the speakers who support it. Since both witnesses and supporting speakers in Athenian courts often signal, or purport to signal, to the jurors where the community and its subgroups stand on the issue, branding them as plotters undermines their claim to represent public opinion or the views of important individuals.[46]

Yet for this strategy to work, it was not enough to simply label individuals as conspirators. The plotting scenario had to appear more likely and have greater appeal than its denial or a nonconspiratorial counterversion. Speakers, then, offered their audience a hidden agenda, a universal motive such as greed, a complex plan that made sense of confusing events, and plotters who had the power and skills to execute the plan, with the implication that conspiracies abounded. Eli Sagan's linking of greed and its projection upon others, as well as general anxiety about plotters, to the paranoid position may suggest its presence in Athenian courts. Yet those who plot against others' possessions fail to show the violent aggression or the ambition to have sole control over others that Sagan ascribes to the paranoid position. At most, the conspiracies stories that are based on flimsy or nonexistent evidence indicate the Athenians' conspiracist mind-sets.

45. See also Isoc. 17.46; 21.15; Cf. Isoc.15.230; Lys. 19.2–3; Thuc. 3.37.2; Arist. *Pol.* 5 1313b20–21, 1314a14–18. For more references to plotting against other people's possessions, see, e.g., Lys. 24.19; Dem. 44.56, 45.13; Isoc. 7.24; 11.19; 15.24, 198; 17.8; cf. Lys. 31.17; [Aristotle] *Rhetoric to Alexander* 15 1424a23–24, 20 1424b10–13.

46. See Humphreys 1985. The problem was even more acute prior to the early fourth century, when oral testimonies, which allowed supporting speakers to appear as witnesses, had not yet been replaced by written depositions: Rubinstein 2000, 70–75.

CHAPTER 3

Legal Plots and Traps

Judging from the oratorical corpus, plots aiming to defeat a legal action or to ensnare a rival in a legal trap were almost as popular as conspiracies to deprive a man of his property.[1] One of the commonest charges of legal plotting involves the giving and taking of bribes in order to win a legal dispute. An Athenian law groups legal and political conspiracy and bribery together when it states that if anyone forms a conspiracy (*sunistētai*), bribes (in groups of ten: *sundekazēi*) Athenian courts and the Council, gives or takes money, forms a companionship (*hetaireia*) to overthrow the democracy, or takes money as a supporting speaker in private and public suits, he will be charged in a public action before the Thesmothetai.[2] Charges of bribery or of performing services for money in politics and the courts are far too numerous to be examined here. It is worth noting, however, that Apollodorus, who cites the above law in a speech against Stephanus for false testimony and phrases his accusations against the defendant in the language of this law, produces no evidence that Stephanus had been bribed. Instead, he attributes to Stephanus an

---

1. Adele Scafuro's insightful analysis of legal traps deals chiefly with New Comedy: Scafuro 1997, 329–79.
2. [Dem.] 46.26. For the authenticity of the law: Rubinstein 2000, 52 n. 75. I do not share Gernet's (1957, 2: 185) and MacDowell's (1983, 66) view that the references to political conspiracy in this law were interpolated into the text; cf. Hyp. 4.7–8, 30; Whitehead 2000, 188–89. Laws against bribery and interpretations of the above law: MacDowell 1983; Harvey 1985, 88–89. For more references, see Roisman 2005, 148 n. 51.

44

array of activities of a character explicitly or implicitly conspiratorial. He charges him with using evil tricks against him, lying as a witness for his adversary, stealing depositions, deceiving the jurors, and conspiring against justice (*sunistamenos d' epi tais dikais;* [Dem.] 46.25). To an extent, Apollodorus uses the law against bribery in support of his slandering the defendant as a conspirator.

PLOTS TO OBSTRUCT LITIGATION:
DEMOSTHENES AND THE CHALLENGE OF *ANTIDOSIS*

No less subversive than bribery were schemes to deter a man from pursuing a legal action. Demosthenes' personal experience illustrates such tactic. In the course of his feuding with his guardians over their handling of his late father's estate, he argues that they have restored to him only a fraction of what they owed him, and that they had conspired (*epibebouleukōs*) even in this respect.[3] In Athens, wealthy men were forced to perform costly public services (*leitourgiai*), but one could avoid this burden by challenging a wealthier Athenian to carry it out and daring him to exchange properties if he refused to take up the service. According to Demosthenes, the guardians had contrived (*pareskeuasan*) to use this procedure, called *antidosis*, to deter him from suing them. Their plan was to get someone to challenge him to exchange properties. If Demosthenes agreed to the exchange, he would forfeit the legal action against his guardian Aphobus that went with the estate. If he accepted the trierarchical *leiturgia* instead of exchanging possessions, he would be ruined financially. The one who offered the exchange was Thrasylochus, whom Demosthenes describes as his adversaries' aide (or servant; *hupēretēse*). After a failed attempt to overcome this ploy, Demosthenes decided, at a great cost to himself, to hold on to his estate, persist in his lawsuit, and pay for the *leitourgia* (Dem. 28.16–17).

About twenty years after his speech against Aphobus, Demosthenes mentions the above incident in a speech he has written against Thrasylochus's brother, Meidias, whom he charges with treating him hubristically. It appears that Demosthenes had initially agreed to the *antidosis* but had also tried to prevent Thrasylochus from entering his estate. In response, the brothers invaded Demosthenes' home, broke down the doors, and used obscene language in the presence of his young sister and mother. On top of this insulting and brutal behavior, they intended to drop the case against the guardians that belonged to the estate. It was

3. Dem. 28.16. The plot discussed here preceded the one discussed in chapter 2.

then that Demosthenes decided to decline the exchange and assume the costly public service (Dem. 21.78–80).

Generally, the orator's accounts of the affair in both speeches are fairly consistent with each other. In both speeches, he tries to leave no doubt in the jurors' minds that the *antidosis* proposal was designed to foil his suit against the guardians. In both, he points to the temporal proximity between the invasion of his house and the trial on his inheritance that was about to begin a few days later. These tactics and the use of terminology and telltale signs from the world of conspiracy, such as their skillful abuse of the judicial system and of an agent for the sake of ill-gotten gains, their collusion as a group against a lonely, vulnerable young man, and their shameless conduct, were all intended to impress upon the court in both trials that Demosthenes was the target of a sinister plot and of immoral, although legal, harassment.[4]

Yet there is a notable change of emphasis between the two speeches. It should come as no surprise that in his speech against Aphobus, Demosthenes highlights the guardians' wish to do him harm, while in his legal action against Meidias for hubris, he dwells on the latter's insolent behavior. Of interest, however, is the identity of the chief plotter in the two speeches, which changes with the contingencies of the case. In *Against Aphobus* (II), the main culprit and schemer is the defendant, with Thrasylochus functioning as his helper, and with Meidias absent from the story. In *Against Meidias,* Thrasylochus keeps his lowly role as a mere cover, but Aphobus disappears in favor of Meidias, who is described as the real author of these deeds (21.78). It has been argued that the differences arise from the fact that the speeches were written by two different logographers: Demosthenes composing Dem. 21, and another author (Isaeus?) writing, or helping Demosthenes to write, Dem. 28.[5] But judging by the story of the fraud in Syracuse that is the subject of Demosthenes' *Against Zenothemis* (see chapter 2 above), the role of the master schemer is interchangeable even within the same speech. The aim is simply to malign whoever happens to be in the speaker's sights. What counts is the charge of conspiracy rather than its details.

Moreover, Demosthenes' charge of collusion between the guardians and Thrasylochus is not well substantiated. In its favor stand the temporal proximity between the *antidosis* action and Demosthenes' suits

4. For the affair, see MacDowell 1990, 295–99, who largely accepts Demosthenes' version and suspects that Thrasýlochus was rewarded for his troubles on behalf of the guardians.
5. Badian 2000, 16–17.

against his guardians, as well as Thrasylochus's intention to drop the case against the latter. Stripped of its conspiratorial construction, however, the temporal relation between these procedures could have been coincidental or the result of a simpler causal link. Facing with the urgent need to pay for his (joint) trierarchy, Thrasylochus was primarily looking for another Athenian to take the burden from him. If indeed, as Demosthenes argued, he intended to drop the case against the guardians, it was not the hidden or ultimate goal of his action but its by-product, and was designed to accommodate his wishes rather than theirs. Thrasylocus might have been reluctant to enter a feud with the guardians, and in any case, his chances of winning were significantly smaller than those of Demosthenes, who had the motivation, the evidence, the moral ground, and overall, a much better case of personal damage than Thrasylochus. Yet, Demosthenes refused to acknowledge that actors might act for reasons unrelated to him, and he had no doubts that he was plotted against. We should not share his belief without reservations just because it made good conspiratorial sense.

THE CHOREGUS'S HOMICIDE TRIAL (ANT. 6)

Antiphon's speech *On the Chorus Boy* (Ant. 6) describes more sinister efforts to induce a man to drop his legal actions. The speaker is a choregus (chorus producer) who is charged with killing a boy in the chorus he sponsored. The boy had died after he had been given an apparently therapeutic drug, and the boy's brother, Philocrates, charged the choregus with planning (*bouleusanta*) the death unintentionally (in Athenian homicide law, the charge of planning to kill a person could include causing death without premeditation).[6] The choregus claims that he is innocent of the charge, saying that he had neither been present when the drug was administered nor instructed any person to give it to the boy. He also presents himself as the victim of legal plotting.

He says that when he was about to prosecute different individuals on two different occasions in an *eisangelia* (impeachment) process, the defendants in the two trials had colluded with the boy's brother and paid him money to press homicide charges so as to prevent the choregus from pursuing his prosecutions against them. Men accused of homicide were not allowed to appear in public places, including in court.

6. Ant. 6.16, 19; MacDowell 1963, 62–63; Gagarin 1990, 95–96; 1997, 223–24, and see also Carawan 1998, 251–81; Wilson 2000, 116–20.

The choregus's charges are not patently false or improbable. The Athenian practice of suing a litigator in order to force him to drop his suit has been well documented, and G. M. Calhoun has included this case among his prime examples of this tactic.[7] My aim here, however, is to show that the choregus's accusations are tenuous and based on two central tenets of the rhetoric of conspiracy, namely, the exposure of plotters who hide behind a paid agent and the ordering of actions and events in a causal sequence based on their temporal proximity.

The speaker prepares the ground for his tale of collusion in asserting that the prosecution is relying on "slander" and "deception" (*apatē*), the latter often associated with conspiracy (6.7; cf. Thuc. 4.86.6). He returns to the plotting theme shortly afterward, saying that the prosecution's charge is groundless, and that instead of sticking to the issue, as the law on homicide ordains, the boy's relatives are contriving (*suntithentes*) to malign his public activity (6.9). Continuing to expand at length on his innocence of the charge and to touch on Philocrates' dishonest reasons for accusing him of homicide (6.20–22), he turns to discuss the first plot against him in greater detail (6.33–38). Briefly, he argues that certain individuals, whom he had intended to prosecute for embezzlement in an *eisangelia* process, had "persuaded" his accuser (with money: 6.38, 48) to charge him with homicide in an effort to prevent him from appearing as a prosecutor in their trial. He provides the following proofs for his allegation: 1. Following the boy's death, Philocrates had done nothing for two days and had even talked with the speaker. But then, all of a sudden, he had announced in the court of the Thesmothetae on the day of the boy's funeral that the choregus had killed his brother. He had also registered his homicide charge with the Archon Basileus the day after the burial, even though the boy's funeral rites had not been completed. 2. The choregus had been about to prosecute one of four individuals he had accused of embezzlement on the very same day.[8] 3. The men he planned to prosecute had, in fact, used this trick (*emēkhanēsanto*), namely, of foiling litigation, before, against a different prosecutor (6.36).

The speaker's reconstruction of events has an attractive conspiratorial logic, like other plotting scenarios. His case rests on the alleged forg-

---

7. Calhoun 1913, 48–54, 104–5; and more recently: Rubinstein 2000, 187. Of the other cases Calhoun mentions, the most relevant to the present one is Dem. 21.104–22, and see also Xen. *Mem.* 2.9; Dem. 47.75; 58.22–23; 59.10; cf. Is. 4.30.
8. See Gagarin 1997, 239–40 for the possibility that he impeached only three men, and for this interpretation of 6.37 and the prosecutor's schedule.

ing of a relationship between his prosecutor and those he himself had been about to prosecute, on the basis of their having various reasons to be hostile to him, as well as on linkage between his charging the others and being charged with homicide himself on the basis of their proximity in time. This is insubstantial. Such linking neither is self-evident nor takes into account the possibility of coincidence or of other motives for the actors than serving the plot. Thus, there is nothing odd in Philocrates' taking two days to investigate his brother's death and decide on the choregus's guilt, proclaim it in public, and, then, promptly bring him to justice. His conduct does not necessarily suggest any urgent intent to accommodate others. According to the choregus, Philocrates' having talked to him prior to his registering the homicide charge implies that he did not regard him as his brother's killer. But since he does not volunteer the contents of their conversation, this information is meaningless. In addition, the fact that Philocrates sought to prevent the choregus from showing up in court by registering the homicide charge against him on the same day did not mean that he had done so to help others. Resentful of his brother's presumed killer, he might have wished to spoil his day of glory: the choregus reports that he was well prepared for the impeachment trial and presents himself as the chief prosecutor in the case (6.36). Finally, the choregus fails to prove that the men he aimed to prosecute had tried this scheme before, and even if they had, this did not prove that they were employing the same device in the present case. This allegation, however, presents their plotting as consistent with what they had done in the past, and hence likely. The choregus uses the same rhetorical technique against Philocrates later in the speech (see below).[9]

As it happened, the attempt to force the choregus out of court failed, because the Archon Basileus refused to accept Philocrates' homicide charge on the grounds that his term was too short to handle the trial (6.37, 41–43).[10] The speaker was thus able to follow up on his plan to prosecute the "schemers" (*tous tauta mēkhanōmenous*) and have them convicted. He claims that his victory moved the boy's relatives to seek reconciliation with him. This was duly arranged, and according to the

---

9. See Gagarin 2002, 145, 151 for establishing a criminal pattern for adversaries here and in Ant. 1, and Roisman 2005, 199–203, for the rhetoric of consistency. For the redeployment of the charge in Ant. 6.31, see Gagarin 1997, 240.
10. Philocrates argues that the archon colluded with the choregus not to take the trial during his term, and see Carlier 1984, 345–48, who argues for the likelihood of the charge.

choregus, he and the relatives met and spoke with one another on different occasions, including in their respective houses, and Philocrates even joined him on the podium in the Council, called him by name, and put his hand on his arm (6.38–40, 48). But then Philocrates decided to renew the charge of homicide. This too was due to a plot, which the choregus tries to prove along lines similar to the first charge of collusion. He argues that the prosecutor, or any one else in his situation, would have registered his charge of homicide as soon as the new Archon Basileus entered office. Yet Philocrates had chosen to wait some fifty days before doing so. Moreover, the victim's relatives would not have conversed with a man they suspected of having killed him. Their talking with the choregus on the one hand, and their charging him on the other, corresponded to their being paid or not respectively by certain officials (different from the ones he had prosecuted) against whom the choregus had begun legal proceedings (6.44–50).

It appears that the prosecutor, a man with an alleged sycophantic record (6.43), exhibited consistent, or rather unoriginal, conduct whenever he pressed charges against the choregus. Moved by the same mercenary motives and using the same charge, he was willing to prosecute the choregus whenever men who had committed crimes against the state plotted against our conscientious public watchdog. Yet all that the choregus has to show in support of his allegation of bribery is Philocrates' supposed fickleness and the temporal proximity between Philocrates' pressing charges and his own litigious industry. Indeed, as far as the choregus was concerned, Philocrates' timing was never right. He either registered his charge too soon (first attempt) or too late (second attempt).

Moreover, the choregus's linking his adversaries' change of heart to his judicial victory is his own conjecture. Also problematic is his depiction of a period of amicable relationship between him and the boy's relatives following their reconciliation and then their sudden metamorphosis. The phenomenon of reconciliations failing to resolve a conflict is hardly unique in Athens, although the present case is exceptional in attributing the failure to the bribing of one party to renew the dispute.[11] The reader would also have greater confidence in the choregus's explanation for the failed reconciliation if he reported the terms of their agree-

---

11. On private reconciliation and arbitration, see chapter 2 n. 38. Failed reconciliations not long after they were made: Is. 2.28–35, 38; Lys. 4.1–4; Dem. 41.1, 14; Hyp. 3.1–5; cf. Is. 1.35, 51; Isoc. 17.17–19. Relevant here is Demosthenes' allegation that Meidias tried to bribe relatives of a victim to falsely charge him with murder. Significantly, they refused: Dem. 21.104, 116.

ment and his own contribution to it. Athenian conflict resolutions normally entailed monetary settlements or mutual dropping of charges. Since the choregus mentions no countersuit against Philocrates that he could have forgone in return for Philocrates' dropping his, one wonders if his silence about the settlement's provisions and his sticking to them is innocent.[12] He also studiously avoids reporting the contents of his conversations with the boy's relatives, while his depiction of Philocrates' nonverbal behavior as friendly is clearly self-serving and relies on the susceptibility of gestures to partisan interpretation.[13] Can it be that his meetings with the boy's relatives were related to their unhappiness with the agreement or the choregus's failure to meet it?[14] The truth is that the speech does not allow one to tell with certainty when and why Philocrates changed his mind. The speaker's detecting bribery behind it, however, is both slanderous and conventional. In politics, for example, Demosthenes and Aeschines trade charges of bribery to account for each changing his conduct or position.[15] In this case, the charges of bribery and collusion strengthen the speaker's argument that the homicide charge is unwarranted. They also undermine the moral advantage enjoyed by a man whose motives as the avenger of his brother's death and protector of the city from pollution appear impeccable (cf. Ant. 5 in chapter 1 above). Indeed, there was no need for a plot to explain Philocrates' conduct and prosecution.

FRAMING IN CRIME: ANDOCIDES

Like the choregus, the politician Andocides alleges in his speech *On the Mysteries* (And. 1) that he is wrongly accused by men whose real aim is to force him to drop a rightful legal action. Unlike the choregus, however, he includes in the conspiracy against him an attempt to frame him for a crime.

---

12. Scafuro 1997, 135, 136 n. 55, however, postulates a mutual dropping of homicide and slander charges in our case. Carlier's (1984, 347–48) hypothesis that the basileus postponed the trial to effect reconciliation between the parties seems to judge motives from the results.

13. For what it's worth, the gesture he describes was not a handclasp that normally signified reconciliation and the end of aggression. For the latter, see Herman 1987, 49–53, and Boegehold 1999, 23–24, who notes the importance of context in understanding the gesture's meaning.

14. In addition to the above possibilities, different reasons for the renewal of the hostilities come to mind: regret about the reconciliation; Philocrates' preoccupation with more urgent tasks before re-registering his charge; and cf. Gagarin 1997, 222, 241; 2002, 144, for additional options.

15. E.g., Dem. 18.131–59; 19.16, 27–28; Aes. 3.64–68.

Much of Andocides' speech deals with one of the most celebrated scandals in Athenian history: the mutilation of the statues of Herms (*Hermai*) and the profanation of the Mysteries rites by members of the Athenian elite in 415. Andocides was among those charged with especially the first crime and avoided punishment by informing on others. He went into exile and returned to Athens after 403, following the grant of amnesty for most past wrongdoing. In 400 or 399, he was charged, however, with violating a decree prohibiting men guilty of impiety from entering Athenian temples and the agora, and with illegally placing a suppliant olive branch on the altar of the Eleusinion, two crimes that, according to the prosecutor, deserved the death penalty.[16]

Throughout the speech, Andocides labors to deny his involvement in any impious act, to contest the legality of the charges against him, and to show the villainy of his accusers. Integrated within these efforts is his assertion that he is the victim of a sinister plot orchestrated by the prominent Athenian Callias. He claims that Callias has conspired (*epebouleuthēn*) against him in order to remove him from a competition for the right to marry the sole heiress of a mutual kinsman, whom Callias wanted for his son, or, more accurately, for himself. Callias had paid off another suitor to renounce his stronger claim to the girl, but Andocides still refused to give up on her. Callias then suborned the Athenian Cephisius with 1,000 drachmas to indict Andocides for entering public temples illegally. He had hoped that the defendant would choose exile over standing trial, but Andocides did not budge (1.4, 117–21).

Callias's stamina in pursuing his plot was matched only by Andocides' resilience in fighting it. Seeing that Andocides stayed for the indictment proceedings, Callias tried to frame him for a crime by laying a suppliant branch on the altar and then charging him with this violation of the rules of the Mysteries festival. He even misled the Council, which was discussing this second indictment, telling them that the punishment for such an act was death, rather than a fine (1.110–16). In view of Andocides' refusal to give up, Callias tried to strike a bargain: if Andocides would withdraw his claim to the girl, Callias would effect the withdrawal of the legal proceedings against him and compensate him for his troubles. Andocides, defiant as ever and relying on the justice of his cause, told him to go ahead with his prosecution and with procuring (*paraskeuazein*) others (1.122–23).

Those "others" included his chief prosecutor, Cephisius, and sup-

---

16. For the speech and the charges see, conveniently, MacDowell 1962; Edwards 1995, 11–26, 163–89; Todd 2004; Carawan 2004.

porting speakers, thus enlarging the circle of those conspiring against him.[17] Together with Callias, they had plotted, or prepared (*sumparaskeuasasi*), the trial and spent money on it (1.132). Andocides provides each of the prosecutors with unworthy motives for prosecuting him or with a criminal, conspiratorial record. One is an embezzler, two others have oligarchic and sycophantic backgrounds, and a fourth man is a former tax collector who had conspired with others to make money at the city's expense and who wishes to destroy Andocides because the latter had outbid him at an auction for the right to collect taxes (1.92–99, 133–35; and see below). Towering over them in villainy, however, is Callias, who has shamelessly lived with a mother and her daughter and impoverished his wealthy household (1.124–31).

All of the above assertions demonstrate the moral turpitude of Andocides' accusers, even though they are not very relevant to the case or always corroborated by evidence. The proof of Andocides' main charge—that the source of the feud was the competition for the heiress, and that Callias was behind the legal attacks on him—may have, however, been included in testimony that has unfortunately not survived (1.122–23). Yet, judging by the testimony's immediate context, it likely dealt with Callias's offer of reconciliation, which assuredly did not include his admission of plotting. In truth, Andocides' highly tendentious account and the lack of additional sources for the plotting tale make contesting his version unrewarding. It is more profitable to discuss how he utilizes the rhetoric of conspiracy to delegitimize the prosecution's motives and methods.

That Andocides deems his conspiracy allegations important for the case is indicated by the fact that he commences his speech with them. "The plotting [or preparation; *paraskeuē*]," he tells the jury, "and keenness [*prothumia*] to do me harm in any way, whether justly or unjustly, ever since I first returned to Athens, are known to pretty well all of you."[18] From the outset, then, Andocides presents himself as facing incessant attacks by highly motivated men, who are able to use even fair, and hence more dangerous, means to entrap him. He reinforces his status as victim shortly afterward when he argues that as a defendant, he deserves more judicial goodwill than the prosecutors, who for a long time and at no risk to themselves have plotted (*epibouleusantes*) and contrived (together; *sunthentes*), while he is defending himself in fear, dan-

17. For other cases of "procuring" orators to help in trials, see, e.g., Is. 1.7; 8.37; Dem. 21.112; 44.3; 48.36; Lyc. 1.138.
18. And. 1.1; MacDowell's translation in Gagarin and MacDowell 1998, 101.

ger, and against a great prejudice (And. 1.6). Plotters in general unfairly use their power and other advantages to attack innocent men by surprise, and it is up to the Athenian jurors to level the playing field.[19]

Andocides' account of the plot against him is immediately followed by character assassinations of his prosecutors and Callias, which make their plotting likely (1.110–36). Callias is given the role of the master schemer, who uses others to front for him, enabling him to deceive both the court and public opinion about his malevolent intentions. Equally stereotypical is Callias's abuse of his expertise, both legal and religious, to subvert the legal system and to compel an adversary to drop his honest claim (cf. Ant. 6.7; Dem. 21.104–5; 59.10). He and his co-conspirators also exhibit characteristic brazenness (*tolma*) in charging Andocides with the crime of placing the olive branch on the altar of the Eleusinion, which they had contrived (*kataskeuasan*) after their plotting (*epebouleusan*) had failed (1.110). They are moved by base motives, such as lust and bribes, and will stop at nothing to achieve their goal. Indeed, Callias's offer of reconciliation shows that their charges lack any merit or public concern. The remedy Andocides offers against their conspiracies is conventional too: the jury's sense of justice will put an end to them (1.123).

Although there is nothing remarkable about Andocides' rhetoric of conspiracy, he uses it to skillfully convert the prosecution of serious offenses against Athens's religious beliefs and practices (cf. Lys. 6) into a scandalous attack on an individual in a private matter. He balances this slander of the opposition with his portrayal of himself as a lone man who, in spite of the odds, is manly enough to persevere in facing his formidable adversaries.[20] The jurors' acquittal of Andocides in this trial suggests his success in combining legal arguments with those of conspiracy, character and fairness.

FRAMING IN HOMICIDE

Mantitheus's speech against his half-brother Boeotus also includes the assertion that he has been falsely charged with a serious crime in order to neutralize him in an unrelated dispute. The two were contesting the exclusive right to bear the name Mantitheus, but the conflict also involved other issues, such as Boeotus's legitimate birth, which of the two had seniority in the family, and their respective conduct in their con-

---

19. See, e.g., Lys. 7.3; 19.1–3; Aes. 2.1; 3.1; Edwards 1995, 163.
20. For the manliness of Andocides, see Roisman 2005, 60–63. Andocides anticipates the theme of the cowardly opposition that hides behind other people's backs rather than face him in the open in an earlier speech: 2.4.

flict.[21] Mantitheus claims that his half-brother had conspired against him on several occasions. Together with one Menecles, who is described as the architect of the entire dispute, Boeotus had plotted (*epibouleusas*) the following scheme. After first provoking Mantitheus to a violent fight, Boeotus got a physician to inflict a cut on his own head. He then sued Mantitheus in the Areopagus for attempted homicide in an effort to have him exiled. Fortunately, the physician testified about the attempt to frame Mantitheus and the prosecution was defeated.[22] Later in the speech, Mantitheus explains that he is not living in a house that he claims as partially his, but that is occupied by his brother, because of his concern about the threat posed to the morals of his unwedded daughter by Boeotus's unruly companions and because Boeotus's contrivance of the homicide charge shows that he is completely unscrupulous and might poison him (40.56–57). Finally, he reinforces the portrait of Boeotus as a schemer (*epiboulos*) by asserting that the reason Boeotus has offered to have the dispute between them arbitrated is to void a decision against Boeotus in a previous arbitration, which stopped him from proceeding with his sycophantic suits (40.43).[23]

Mantitheus's charges of conspiracy are primarily intended to slander his opponent's character and actions by making him seem willing to stop at nothing to win a dispute. In addition, they turn Mantitheus's assault on his stepbrother and the latter's attempt to take legal advantage of it into a deliberate and premeditated entrapment by the victim of the assault. They also support Mantitheus's weak claim to a house that his brother possesses both de jure and de facto. Lastly, they challenge Boeotus's portrayal of himself as an unmeddlesome man who shuns litigation (40.32). Indeed, by characterizing his brother's arbitration proposal as shameful, Mantitheus, like Andocides in the case of Callias's attempt at compromise, turns an offer to resolve a dispute into a device to promote litigation, which in turn justifies his rejecting it. Together, these allegations seek to legitimize Mantitheus's suit against his half-brother on grounds that, as an aggressive adversary and conspirator, Boeotus has forfeited his right to sibling solidarity and to the settlement of their feud among family and friends rather than in the public sphere.

---

21. Dem. 39–40. For the dispute, see Roisman 2005, 42–44.
22. Dem. 40.32–34; cf. Lys. 4.9–10; Aes. 2.93; 3.212.
23. Mantitheus establishes a sycophantic record with strong conspiratorial attributes for Boeotus when he claims that Boeotus and Menecles were leaders of a sycophantic association that was behind a successful attempt to deceive Mantitheus's father into acknowledging Boeotus as his son: Dem. 39.2; 40.9–10; Christ 1998, 65, 247 nn. 86–87.

Apollodorus's speech *Against Neaera* (Dem. 59) reports another attempt to frame someone for homicide. The speaker is Theomnestus, Apollodorus's son-in-law, who, prior to surrendering the podium to Apollodorus to deliver the main speech against Neaera and her companion, Stephanus, presents a litany of grievances that he, and especially Apollodorus, have against Stephanus. One of these involves Stephanus's having falsely charged that when Apollodorus had gone to Aphidna in Attica in search of a fugitive slave, he had hit and killed a woman. Stephanus had suborned (*paraskeuasamenos*) witnesses, whom he had made out (*kataskeuasas*) to be men from Cyrene, but who were in fact his slaves, and publicly proclaimed that he would prosecute Apollodorus in the homicide court of the Palladium. His plan failed, however, when he was revealed as a false accuser and perjurer, and when it was shown that he had been paid by the Athenians Cephisophon and Apollophanes to bring about the exile and disenfranchisement of Apollodorus. The speaker sums up the affair by setting Stephanus's reputation for perjury and wickedness alongside the opposition's expenditure of 500 drachmas on the trial, netting only a few votes for conviction ([Dem.] 59.9–10).

Theomnestus's account is much too brief to allow us to ascertain its accuracy.[24] What is fairly clear, however, is the speaker's goal in bringing up these allegations. He intends to establish a record of enmity between himself, Apollodorus, and Stephanus that will show that the prosecutors have personal, rather than mercenary, reasons for proceeding against Neaera and her companion. This goal complements their wish to prepare the audience for subsequent tales of Stephanus's misdeeds and bad character that will equally show his lack of moral inhibitions and respect for the law, his sycophancy, and his machinations. Independently, the framing plot displays features that the Athenians were likely to recognize from other conspiracies, namely, falsely accusing an adversary of a serious crime in order to get rid of him or to paralyze his litigation, as well as paymasters who hired prosecutors and witnesses, and their exposure by the victim, who typically faced a coalition of schemers alone.

Isocrates' speech *Against Callimachus* (Isoc. 18) is more informative about an attempt to frame an Athenian for murder. The disputants in this case are the unnamed speaker and Callimachus, who claims that the speaker has been responsible for an unlawful confiscation of money that

---

24. Scholars tend to believe his account and place the trial in the context of political rivalry among the aforementioned Athenians: Carey 1992, 89–90; Trevett 1992, 148–49; Kapparis 1999, 182–89; Hamel 2003, 123–26. Stephanus might have prosecuted Apollodorus as the dead woman's master.

rightfully belongs to Callimachus. Among the incriminating tales the speaker tells about Callimachus, one concerns a dispute over a piece of land between Callimachus's brother-in-law and a man named Cratinus. Following a violent encounter between the two, Callimachus and his brother-in-law had hidden a maid, claimed that she had died from a wound inflicted by Cratinus, and sued him for murder in the Palladium. Cratinus had found out about their plots (*epiboulas*) but had kept the information to himself so not to give the opposition an opportunity to change its stratagem. At the trial, the brother-in-law acted as a prosecutor and Callimachus appeared as a witness, both asserting that the maid had died of her wounds. Cratinus, however, went to the maid's hideout, seized her by force, and brought her to court for all to see. Although fourteen witnesses had testified for the prosecution, the brother-in-law received not a single vote from among the 700 jurors. The text shows that the speaker produced witnesses in support of his account (18.52–54).[25]

The alleged attempt to frame Cratinus for homicide is not implausible, and judging by Stephanus's similar attempt to incriminate Apollodorus (see above), it was not unique either. Callimachus's role in it, however, should be put in perspective. The feud with Cratinus was not his, but his brother-in-law's, and the latter also played the central role in the affair as Cratinus's prosecutor. Although the speaker presents these affines as partners in crime, Callimachus's provable collaboration was limited to his being one of fourteen or so witnesses who testified for the prosecution. The reason why the speaker consistently names him, but leaves his brother-in-law nameless, is probably that he wishes to exaggerate Callimachus's role in the case.

Within the speech, the tale of the attempted frame-up is intended "to reveal the character of those [i.e., Callimachus] who do wrong" and to show that Callimachus deserves no consideration from the jury for the loss he has incurred (18.51–52, 55). Indeed, the incident is just one of several aimed at discrediting Callimachus as a shameless sycophant and plotter (see esp. 18.7). Earlier in the speech, the speaker reports that Callimachus was unsatisfied with an award he had received from the speaker following an arbitration and had conspired (*epibouleusas*) with one Xenotimus, described as a corrupter of laws, briber of courts, insulter of officeholders, and troublemaker, to sue the speaker for 10,000 drachmas (18.11). Even though nothing more is known about Xenotimus's career, it can be reasonably as-

---

25. Carawan 1991, 3–5; 1998, 144–47, discusses the legal aspects of this case. For the theatricality of producing the slave woman, see Hall 1995, 43, and more generally, Scafuro 1997, 329–79.

sumed that, like Diocles in Is. 8, Aristophon in Dem. 32, and Menecles in Dem. 39–40, he is included in the plot in the hope that some of his unpopularity and notoriety will rub off on his partner. The speaker returns to the theme of Callimachus's plotting shortly before his report on the attempted frame-up described above, when he depicts his opponent as a serial litigator who has plotted (*epibebouleuke*) against many men and been involved in all sorts of suits, conspiring (*sunesteke*) with some and falsely testifying against others (18.51). The unsuccessful murder charge is glossed as an example of Callimachus's amoral brazenness, untrustworthiness, and mendacity (18.55–57), which should all serve to make clear to the jurors that Callimachus's sycophantic claims against the speaker are in line with his conspiratorial record and character. They also constitute an effective response to Callimachus's charge, suggested at 18.57, 63, that it was the speaker who had lied and plotted to obtain other people's money.

But besides illustrating Callimachus's malice, the attempted frame-up also has didactic and even entertainment value. It shows how the cunning, preparations, and secretiveness of plotters can be prevailed against with greater cunning, patience, and secretiveness (cf. Thuc. 4.118.6). In addition, the audience were probably amused, perhaps even gratified, by Cratinus's victory.

LEGAL TRAPS: STEPHANUS AND EPAENETUS

Framing someone did not have to involve violent crime. Apollodorus, who charged Stephanus with having falsely accused him of murder, extended the latter's plotting into extortion as well. He informed the audience that Neaera had continued to work as a courtesan even after she had acquired her freedom and begun living with Stephanus as his household companion. They were both engaged in sycophancy, and when Stephanus caught a rich alien as her lover, he held him under house arrest as an adulterer and demanded large sums of money from him, which he used to support her lavish life style (59.41–42). This information both reuses and provides the necessary background for the following extortion attempt, described later in the speech.

Noting Stephanus's shameful greed and villainy, Apollodorus goes on to tell how Stephanus had targeted the alien Epaenetus of Andros, who was an old patron of Neaera's, had spent money on her, and stayed with her and Stephanus whenever he came to Athens. Stephanus had invited Epaenetus to the country, ostensibly for a sacrifice, caught him seducing Neaeara's daughter, Phano, and extorted 3,000 drachmas from him by intimidation for his adultery with her. He had agreed to let Epaenetus go to fetch the money after Epaenetus had named two Athenians as his sureties. Instead of paying, however, Epaenetus indicted Stephanus in court according to a law that established that a man wrongfully detained as an adulterer might indict the detainer before the Thesmothetai for wrongful imprisonment, and if he convicted him and was shown to have been plotted against unjustly (*adikōs epibebouleusthai*), he would suffer no penalty and his sureties would be free of liability. If he were judged to be an adulterer, he would be delivered to his legal adversary, who could do to him at court as he pleased, aside from using a knife.[26] Epaenetus admitted to having had relations with Phano but denied that he was an adulterer, claiming that she was not Stephanus's daughter but Neaera's, that he had used her with her mother's consent, and that he had spent money on both and on the upkeep of their household in the past. He cited legislation that forbade detaining a man as an adulterer for being with a woman who sat publicly in a workshop (*ergastērion*) or sold something in the agora, and argued that Stephanus's house was a workshop.[27] When Stephanus realized that he would be exposed as a brothel keeper and a sycophant, he submitted the dispute to the arbitration of Epaenetus's sureties, freeing them of liability provided Epaenetus withdrew his indictment. In the arbitration, Stephanus said nothing that was just but pleaded with Epaenetus to contribute to the dowry of Neaera's daughter, given her sad life story, his own poverty, and Epaenetus's moral obligation to reward her after having used her. The arbitrators persuaded Epaenetus to contribute 1,000 drachmas to her dowry ([Dem.] 59.64–70).

In support of his account, Apollodorus produces two documents. One is a deposition made by the arbitrators stating that they were Epaenetus's sureties when he was taken by Stephanus in adultery, that Epaenetus had later indicted Stephanus before the Thesmothetai for wrongful imprisonment, and that serving as conciliators, they had settled the matter as reported by Apollodorus. The second document includes the settlement terms, which established that the parties were not to refer to what had

---

26. [Dem.] 59.66. Kapparis thinks that Apollodorus cites the law mostly verbatim (1999, 308–9), but Scafuro (1997, 332–34) is of the opinion that he paraphrases it; cf. Johnstone 2000, 245 n. 40. It was encouraging to discover that some of the conclusions arrived at here independently resemble those of Hamel 2003, 95–97, 100.

27. [Dem.] 59.67. I follow Johnstone's (2000) reading of the text here. He convincingly shows that the manuscript's tradition should be preferred to its accepted emendation, which makes the text read as if the women were prostitutes and the workshop a brothel. See further below.

happened with regard to the imprisonment, that Epaenetus would contribute 1,000 drachmas toward Phano's dowry, since he had used her many times, and that Stephanus would hand Phano over to Epaenetus whenever he was in town and wanted her ([Dem.] 59.71).

Prima facie, Apollodorus's story of a legal entrapment is not implausible. It was possible in Athens to compensate the head of the family (*kurios*) for adulterous affairs in his household, and this practice might have tempted some Athenians to profit from it.[28] Still, there are several reasons to doubt the veracity of Apollodorus's account.[29] First, he reports this story for a reason: he wishes to demonstrate that Neaera is a noncitizen prostitute and that Phano is her daughter in order to counter Stephanus's plausible claim that Phano is his legitimate daughter by a different woman.[30] Second, if we let the actions of the characters speak for themselves rather than accepting the uncorroborated motives and statements that Apollodorus attaches to them, we get the following chain of events. A man had been invited to the country and was charged by his host with adultery. He had tried to beat the charge with a countercharge and, following a reconciliation process, had ended up paying his accuser a sum of money. Although it is possible, with Apollodorus, to see entrapment and an attempt to foil it here, I think that a likelier, and surely simpler, interpretation is to assume that Stephanus did not in fact entice Epaenetus or take advantage (whether by design or opportunistically) of his succumbing to Phano's charms in order to extort money from him, but that he actually caught Epaenetus in flagrante delicto with Phano.

Stephanus agreed to let Epaenetus go for a guaranteed sum of money. Apollodorus mentions 3,000 drachmas, but this seems too hefty a sum and is perhaps quoted to show that Stephanus, an alleged extortionist and sycophant, was willing later to stoop to a third of this amount. Once out of detention, Epaenetus tried to avoid payment by threatening Stephanus with a countersuit. He tailored it to fit the law that, as shown by Steven Johnstone, protected men from unlawful confinement as adulterers in cases where they had to do with women associated with workshops, probably as sellers. Johnstone may be right in arguing that the law's primary aim was to shield innocent customers from suspicious

---

28. Cohen 1991, 118; Kapparis 1999, 304.
29. Carey 1992, 121, thinks that the story is an invention owing to lack of adequately supporting testimonies, but see Kapparis 1999, 315, on this point. Kapparis 1999, 298–300, thinks that Stephanus and Neaera took advantage of Epaenetus's genuine love for Phano. See also Patteson 1978, 74; Cohen 1991, 108–9; Carey 1992, 108–9, 119–20.
30. Patterson 1994, 205–9; Scafuro 1997, 333–34; Kapparis 1999, 37–38, 300.

males related to women in the market.[31] It appears that in the present case, however, Epaenetus used it to depict Stephanus as a pimp, Phano and her mother as prostitutes, and himself as a regular customer of theirs who had been unlawfully arrested. In order to stop this campaign by both law and slander against him and the women, Stephanus agreed to a settlement.

Christopher Carey (1992, 120) has wondered why Stephanus let Epaenetus's sureties serve as conciliators and did not ask for a third party. There could have been several reasons. One was that the sureties might have been mutual friends of his and Epaenetus's. Releasing them from the pledge to guarantee Epaenetus's "debt" to Stephanus could also have earned him their goodwill. Lastly, Stephanus trusted that he had a strong case against Epaenetus. Indeed, the conciliators, far from absolving Epaenetus from any misconduct, instructed him to pay Stephanus 1,000 drachmas. The presentation of this payment as a contribution to Phano's future dowry looks like a face-saving solution for Epaenetus (and Stephanus), because it turns his fine for adultery into an act of benevolence, helping a poor girl find a husband. The claim that Stephanus begged Epaenetus for the money was invented either by Epaenetus or by Apollodorus after the fact.

What makes the above interpretation likely is Apollodorus's supporting documents. The first one confirms the trading of charges by the disputants and the fact that they had reconciled on the arbitrators' advice. Absent are the plot story, the allegations that Neaera and Phano were Epaenetus's former lovers, and Stephanus's request in court to Epaenetus that he help Phano. The second document, on the other hand, mentions the monetary settlement, but also unambiguously establishes Phano and Stephanus to be, respectively, a prostitute and a pimp. It is most unlikely that Stephanus would have agreed to such a resolution of the conflict. Indeed, the settlement record has rightly been rejected as a forgery.[32]

In sum, there are good reasons to suspect the charge of conspiracy against Stephanus. It is worth noting in this context that Athenian laws against false accusations, and even legal traps, were limited in range and appear not to have provided effective deterrence of such practices. For example, even the law cited above concerning false arrest of adulterers gave the latter freedom from prosecution but did not punish men for wrongfully accusing or arresting them. Such circumstances contributed

31. Johnstone 2000, 244–54, and see also 230 n. 4, 236–38, 246 n. 44.
32. See Kapparis 1999, 315–17, with references to views for and against its authenticity.

to the popularity of false accusations, not just by men like Stephanus but also by the likes of Epaenetus.[33]

PLOTS AND ENTRAPMENTS: APOLLODORUS AND NICOSTRATUS

To a large extent, Apollodorus's speech *Against Nicostratus* ([Dem.] 53) subsumes many of the plots discussed in this chapter. At issue is the status of two slaves, who, Apollodorus claims, belong to the state, but who, according to the defense, are private property. Yet much of the speech revolves around how Apollodorus was betrayed by his friend and neighbor Nicostratus, who conspired, or helped others to conspire, against him.[34]

Apollodorus makes considerable efforts in the first part of the speech to prove the purity of his motives in prosecuting Nicostratus, and that he had gone out of way to help him with loans and gifts when Nicostratus was in trouble ([Dem.] 53.1–13). In this way, he pits his own altruism and youthful naïveté against Nicostratus's selfish and dishonest refusal to repay loans he had taken from him. Apollodorus states that as soon as Nicostratus got the money, he began plotting (*epebouleue*) how not to repay it. Apollodorus was embroiled at that time in a dispute with his stepfather, Phormio, over the family estate, and Nicostratus conspired (*epibouleuei*) with Phormio and gave him his pledge—a characteristic conspiratorial act. He disclosed Apollodorus's arguments to Phormio, and followed this up by registering Apollodorus as a state debtor and having him fined, using Lycidas the miller to commence the legal procedure. Apollodorus argues that he had never been summoned to this hearing, but that Nicostratus had produced his brother Arethusius and another man as false witnesses to the effect that in fact he had been notified of it and had thus managed to get him fined. Nicostratus and his brother also contrived (*pareskeuazonto*) to denounce him as a state debtor and to have him imprisoned if he proceeded with the preliminary hearing of his suit against Phormio (53.13–15). So far, then, Nicostratus appears to be a conventional sycophant and plotter, who,

---

33. Legislation against false charges: e.g., Harvey 1990, 106–7; Christ 1998, 30–32. Cf. Harrison 1971, 2: 181–83, for the risk of losing 10 percent of the estate's value in claiming the right to an inheritance in a *diamaturia* process. Arresting a man, however, could provide grounds for a charge of hubris.

34. For the speech and its emphasis on friendship, see Roisman 2005, 54–55.

acting at times as an agent and at times hiding behind another man, has colluded with a number of men against a lone individual.[35]

After getting a judgment against Apollodorus on account of his debt, Nicostratus invaded his house and carried off the furniture. Apollodorus presented this lawful action as nothing short of robbery (53.15). He had retaliated by suing Nicostratus's brother Arethusius as a false witness, to which the latter responded by laying waste to Apollodorus's farm during the night. The next day, the brothers sent a young boy from the city to pick flowers in Apollodorus's rose garden, hoping to enrage him and get him to arrest or hit the boy, mistaking him for a slave, and thus expose himself to the charge of hubris. Apollodorus, however, did not swallow the bait.[36]

What made the brothers' scheme likely to succeed was the expectation that Apollodorus would vent his anger and use physical force as called for of a man protecting his own territory and possessions, and especially against a slave. The plot, like the ones allegedly hatched by Athenogenes against the passionate Epicrates (Hyp. 3) or Stephanos against Phano's lover ([Dem. 59.64–71), relied on the difficulties men had in controlling their emotions and desires. Fortunately, the culture of feuding and conspiracy had prepared Apollodorus for such ploys, and he had realized the need for caution and restraint. Apollodorus was wise to the tactic of causing harm through a third party both in this case and in the case of Lycidas, who had fronted for his adversaries in the debt hearing.

Adele Scafuro has suggested that the brothers hoped to force Apollodorus to drop his suit against Arethusius by threatening a hubris action (1997, 336). It is a likely interpretation, although one would expect Apollodorus to mention it in order to reinforce the portrayal of the brothers as sycophants. The fact, however, is that it is not easy to accept Apollodorus's account of the entrapment without some reservations. Although he calls for witnesses to support his report, he does it in a later part of the speech ([Dem.] 53.18), thus making it impossible to know whether they verified this or other misdeeds of his opponents. One also wonders how he (or his witnesses) knew who had damaged his farm at night, or that the boy acted on the brothers' orders, given, as the text

---

35. For the affair, see Lofberg 1917, 48–52; Harrison 1968–71, 1: 209–10; Trevett 1992, 9–10, 126–27; Christ 1998, 176–77. For doubts about the veracity of Apollodorus's account: Millett 1991, 267 n. 9. For retaining the manuscript's *epiboulēn* in 53.14: Gernet 1959, 3: 85 n. 2.

36. [Dem.] 53.15–16; Fisher 1992, 40, 56–57. Scafuro 1997, 334–36, 339, emphasizes the staginess of the plot.

implies, that he did not catch or arrest the boy (53.16). But whether Apollodorus was correct or not, his story made sense to the jurors, who expected schemes of this sort, especially from men of the elite versed in litigation.

Having impressed the jurors with the malevolent ingeniousness of his foes, Apollodorus continues to what he characterizes as their "greatest (or worst) plot against me" (*moi epibouleuousi tēn megistēn epiboulēn*: 53.16). A few days before he went to court to prosecute Arethusius for his false deposition, Arethusius had ambushed him late at night, punched him in the face, and tried to throw him into a nearby quarry. Fortunately, Apollodorus was saved by some people who had heard his cries for help (53.17).

Arethusius, it appears, was a habitual nocturnal prowler. Apollodorus describes the attack as a plot in order to remove any suspicion that it was an unpremeditated, spontaneous brawl, or that he had been the one who had started it. He did not sue Arethusius for attempted murder, but a few days later, he obtained a conviction against him in court for false testimony, and, showing commendable restraint, succeeded in persuading the jurors to hand down a lenient sentence rather than imposing the death penalty (53.18). Apollodorus thus made a virtue out of a disappointing result. His display of moderation fitted in well with his portrayal of himself as a man wrongly victimized by others, however, and contradicted his likely portrayal by his adversaries as the son of a former slave who had no qualms about harming native Athenians (ibid.). At the conclusion of his speech, appealing to the perception of plotters as undeserving of judicial pity, Apollodorus returns to the theme of his scheming adversaries, saying that they will attempt to influence the jurors by trickery and deceit and will procure (*kataskeuasantes*) orphans and heiresses or use other excuses to gain sympathy (53.29).

It will be recalled that Apollodorus's legal objective in this trial was to show that the two slaves in Nicostratus's possession were actually owned by Arethusius and hence should be surrendered to the state. The fact that many of his charges of plotting are not directly related to this issue shows his belief in the efficacy of the ideology of friendship and the rhetoric of conspiracy to improve his chances of winning the case. Hence, he depicts his legal action as a retaliatory response by a wronged friend and a victim of plots. And, like others discussed in this chapter, these plots involve the use of a front man, attempts to neutralize a legal adversary, legal entrapment, attempted homicide, and efforts to divert the jurors from doing justice by manipulating their emotions. The number and diversity of the plots may stretch a modern reader's credulity, but no less important than their factual basis is the audience's conspiratorial worldview, which lets the logographers make them such an important part of their cases.[37]

37. For more references to plotting in association with lying, fabricating claims, and accusations or procuring false witnesses: Lys. 3.26; 24.1; Dem. 21.115, 131; 22.1–2; 24.7; 38.3–6; 44.3, 36; Aes. 2.154–55; cf. Dem. 21.83–88, 106; 29.36; 45.5–6, 22, 41; 46.11, 18; Aes. 3.1; Xen. *Hell.* 1.7.18; and obstructing justice: Lys. 3.2; [Dem.] 43.32; cf. Is. 4.5.

CHAPTER 4

Political Conspiracies

Plots against the City and Its Regime

Athenians moved easily from the private to the public sphere without significantly changing their rhetoric of conspiracy, and depictions of political conspiracies and plots against the public interest closely resemble those of a nonpolitical nature. Generally, plotting in the public sphere targeted the city and its democratic government, and it was often attributed to the politically active and to public officials.

PLOTTING IN ARISTOPHANES AND THUCYDIDES

The earliest evidence for the rhetoric of political conspiracy in the period under discussion comes from Aristophanes' comedies. Given the genre of comedy, it has always been a challenge to identify what in his plays is a comic invention, pointed satire, or merely skews reality slightly (if at all). This is especially true of his characters' charges of plotting, which the poet renders cheap and absurd. Hence, I shall focus on the rhetorical attributes of conspiratorial allegations in Aristophanes' plays that later sources share. Thus, in the *Knights,* produced in 424, the playwright presents the politician Cleon (in the character of the Paphlagonian) as a man who resorts to charges of plotting almost as often as he makes a bid for ill-gotten gains. Cleon often links contacts with the enemy and military treason with bribe-taking and plots against the demos (usually *xunōmosia* and related words: *Knights* 235–39, 434–81).

He makes these charges for the sake of political power or survival, seeking to ally himself with the demos in the role of its watchdog (as the historical Cleon may have done), while it protects him from his domestic foes (*Knights* 255–57; cf. 451–52). As in the later oratorical corpus, Cleon's allegations of conspiracy are answered by countercharges, with each speaker displaying patriotic zeal and courage in exposing the plot and great confidence in his information (*Knights* 461–81; cf. Plato *Laws* 856b–c). Conspiracy charges thus serve to sustain a speaker's claims, and undermine competing ones, to the roles of lover, benefactor, and guardian of the people (*Knights* 847–66).

Thucydides' portrayal of Cleon suggests that Aristophanes' attribution to this politician of a fondness for conspiratorial rhetoric may not have been totally fantastic. According to the historian, Cleon appealed to the Athenians' fear of conspiracies in an attempt to persuade them to show no mercy to the Mytileneans, who had rebelled against them. Comparing the Athenian empire to a tyranny and the Mytileneans to conspirators, Cleon invokes concerns about constant inimical plotting that are typical of a tyrannical regime and calls upon Athens to treat those who endanger her safety and interests harshly. But he also presents the Athenians as undeserving victims of a Mytilenean plot, a status that morally justifies his recommendation to them to show the plotters no mercy.[1] It is true that there is no certainty that the words the historian puts in Cleon's mouth were actually spoken by him (cf. Thuc. 1.22.1), and possibly both he and Aristophanes aim to portray Cleon as a harmful demagogue. But if, as I think is likely, the two authors' presentations of Cleon as a plot detector and a manipulator of conspiratorial suspicions (Thucydides abroad and Aristophanes at home) were independent of each other, Cleon should be credited with popularizing this type of rhetoric in Athens.

In Aristophanes' *Wasps*, Cleon loses his role as a frequent resorter to charges of conspiracy to elderly jurors, described as his ardent followers and fans, as well as to ordinary Athenians. The play, produced in 422, both recycles and develops themes and characteristics found in the *Knights*. As in the earlier comedy, the charges of plotting revolve around

1. Thuc. 3.37.1–2, 39.1–2, 40.1, 5; cf. 6.37–40. Not without irony, Thucydides has the Mytileneans justify their morally ambiguous appeal to Sparta for aid in terms of fear of Athenian plots: 3.12.3. The Mytilenean debate took place in the summer of 427. Elsewhere the historian uses plotting vocabulary and notions chiefly to describe harmful plans, military designs, and conspiracies in action.

making contact with the enemy and alleged attempts to establish a tyranny in the city.[2] Among those making such charges are a fishmonger against a customer asking for a perch instead of sprats, another fishmonger against a customer requesting a free onion with his sardines, and a prostitute against a patron who asks her to ride him (*Wasps* 493–502). Aristophanes, needless to say, pokes fun at the ubiquity of suspicions of tyranny and conspiracy in Athens and at their abuse by ordinary citizens and politicians alike. At the same time, he shows how charges of plotting served as a form of self-defense against potential personal cost, or that they are made in an attempt to check and delegitimize conduct and views considered undesirable, unconventional, and critical of the system and individuals. The accused, in turn, plead both innocence and political quietism, thus making themselves seem like innocent victims (*Wasps* 340–45, 488–507). Finally, in both plays, the overthrow of the demos is perceived as possible only through secrecy and double-dealing, and as motivated by personal gain or advantage rather than by political ideology.[3]

Undoubtedly, Athens's state of war with Sparta, and concerns about young members of the Athenian elite who were perceived as lacking restraint in their political ambitions and over their appetites contributed to the popularity of charges of plotting in Athens.[4] What makes these charges noteworthy, however, is that they preceded real or perceived attempts at establishing an oligarchy or tyranny attested for the years 415, 411, and 404. This fact, and the recurrences of similar charges in the fourth century, when Athens enjoyed an extended period of political stability, point to the existence of a continuing concern about political conspiracies in the city, whose intensity probably varied according to triggering circumstances and speakers' success in appealing to it.[5]

---

2. *Wasps* 418, 463–65, 474–76, 480–83, 488–507; cf. Thuc. 6.11.7.

3. Democracy could be advantageous too. A speaker in a fragmentary self-defense speech written by Antiphon against a charge of treason in 411 insists that he is bound to incur private loss if the democracy is replaced by an oligarchy: Ant. fr. 1a (Thalheim).

4. Fears of young political aspirants: Ostwald 1986, 234; and of men addicted to pleasure: Davidson 1997, 267–70, 274–280, 297–301. Both scholars seemed to overprivilege these groups as the targets of plotting accusations, see, e.g., Aristophanes *Knights* 235–39, 451–52, 847–66; *Wasps* 340–45, 418.

5. For additional charges of tyrannical or oligarchic plots in Aristophanes' later plays, see *Birds* 1074 (produced in 414); *Lysistrata* 618–23, 630 (produced in 411); *Thesmophoriazusae* 331–37 (produced in 411); cf. *Plutus* 569–70 (produced in 388); MacDowell 1971, 180, 200. See Thuc. 6.11.7 for what looks like a feeble attempt by Nicias in 415 to join the ranks of the practitioners of the rhetoric of oligarchic conspiracy.

THE LEGACY OF OLIGARCHIC
CONSPIRACIES: ANDOCIDES AND *HETAIREIAI*

Athenians' sensitivity to political conspiracies must have been heightened by the mutilation of the Hermai and the Mysteries affair in 415 and the oligarchic regimes of 411 and 404, but in view of extensive discussion of these subjects elsewhere, I see no point in examining them here.[6] Instead, I wish to focus on the ways in which they are depicted in the speeches and on their rhetorical legacy.

The earliest plot affecting the public sphere that is recorded in the oratorical corpus took place on the eve of the Sicilian expedition in 415 and involved the mutilation of the images of Hermes that stood outside courtyards in Athens and on its roads and the profanation of the Mysteries. Andocides, who was charged with having taken part in the first crime, describes the events surrounding it about fifteen years later in the same speech in which he accuses Callias of having framed him for violating religious regulations concerning the Mysteries (see chapter 3 above). Briefly, he reports that one Euphiletus had approached him with the idea of mutilating the statues, and that he had vigorously opposed it. After he had been injured in a riding accident, however, Euphiletus took advantage of his being bedridden and lied to his companions, telling them that Andocides had agreed to participate in the crime. Following the mutilation of the Hermai, Euphiletus and his friend Meletus approached Andocides and demanded that he keep the secret, which he did (And. 1.61–67).

Because the ancient evidence, including Andocides' speech, for this incident is problematic, scholars have failed to reach a consensus on the aims of the perpetrators of this act or of the profanation of the Mysteries that was intimately linked to it. They have suggested reasons ranging from political subversion and an attempt to sabotage the Sicilian campaign to apolitical pranks.[7] But regardless of the mutilators' motives or, for that matter, the veracity of Andocides' account, it is noteworthy that he refrains from using the terminology of conspiracy in describing the crime or from ascribing any political meaning to it. In contrast, his contemporary Thucydides refers to the affairs more than once as a suspected conspiracy (*xunōmosia*) against the democracy, possibly with a view to establishing a tyranny or oligarchy, and so do later sources. The enemies

---

6. See the literature cited in the following notes.
7. See MacDowell 1962; Edwards 1995, 11–26, 163–89; Todd 2004; Carawan 2004, and, more controversially, Furley 1996.

of the prominent political leader Alcibiades, who sought to implicate him in the scandals, also linked them to an attempt to topple the democracy.[8] Andocides, however, variously refers to them as a plan (*boulē*), an affair (*pragma*), and a deed (*ergon*) and attributes the interpretation of the crime as aiming to overthrow the democracy to only two members of the board that investigated the scandal (And. 1.36, 61, 63–64). His need to defend himself from indictment for sacrilege may have moved him to focus on the impiety of the act.[9] Possibly, he strove in this way to minimize the antidemocratic significance of the affair and his share in it and to reserve the vocabulary of conspiracy for the judicial plots against him. He takes care to distance himself from the conspirators by denying that he had taken part in the mutilation and by showing how different he was from them. In contrast to his portrayal of himself as a model citizen and family man, his depiction of the perpetrators fits in well with the Athenians' image of conspirators as men who plan harm in secret and uninhibitedly pursue their goal. Andocides' involvement in the plot only went as far as keeping it secret, because being a man of one's word and loyal to friends was valued above reporting a crime to the state (1.64, 67).[10]

The Hermai and Mysteries affairs brought to the surface a fear of oligarchic conspiracy, which was greatly intensified by the attempt to establish an oligarchic regime in Athens in 411, and especially by the later extreme oligarchy of the Thirty in 404. The legacy of these experiences was exploited rhetorically chiefly in two ways. The more contemporary one around the time of the end of the Peloponnesian war involved accusing men of taking part in oligarchic plots to destroy the democracy (see below). The other and more perennial one was to describe an opponent as affiliated with an *hetaireia*.

The *hetaireiai*, or associations of companions (*hetairoi*), were relatively small groups of men of similar age and upper-class social background who met in private and helped one another in personal and public affairs, including litigation and politics. In 411 and 404, *hetaireiai* had been instrumental in oligarchic attempts to overthrow the democracy, but in the fourth century, they played no significant political role. Their

---

8. The scandals as political plots: Thuc. 6.27.3, 28.2, 60.1, 4; Diod. 13.2.3; Plut. *Alcibiades* 19. Alcibiades' enemies: Thuc. 6.28.2, 61.1; Isoc. 16.5–7; Ostwald 1986, 322–26; Gribble 1999, 192–93.
9. The only extant speech of his team of prosecutors has a similar focus: [Lys.] 6. Another bit of contemporary evidence also reflects the religious character of the crime: Tod no. 79 v. 111. Cf. MacDowell 1962, 192; Missiou 1992, 53.
10. See Roisman 2005, 62.

conspiratorial image persisted, however, and politicians and litigants looking to slander an opponent with the charge of unsavory partnership or keeping bad company called him a *hetairos* or associated him, explicitly and implicitly, with this institution.[11]

Thus Aeschines incorporated hetairic associations into his attack on the politician Timarchus, whom he charged with male prostitution in 346/5. He labels Timarchus's joining in an alleged embezzlement with other politicians, including his lover, as *philetairōs* (colluding friendship).[12] He attacks Demosthenes, who is Timarchus's supportive speaker, along similar lines. After describing the orator as a destructive parasite who had profited from a young man's love for him and eagerness to learn the art of politics from Demosthenes, Aeschines compares the latter to Socrates the sophist, who had been executed for tutoring Critias, a member of the ruthless oligarchy of the Thirty. He then accuses Demosthenes of protecting his *hetairoi*, of taking vengeance on average citizens and democratic men exercising their right to speak, and of bringing his pupils to court to do business and to show off his cleverness at the jurors' expense (Aes. 1.173). In this way, Aeschines combines the slandering of Demosthenes as a professional speaker in a world of amateurs, who abuses his skills to make money, manipulate people, and behave hubristically, with charges that he teaches his students political subversion and to become future tyrants. Friendship is portrayed as a conspiratorial association against the democracy in light of Demosthenes' and Timarchus's privileging of it over the state. In 343, Aeschines uses a similar collusion charge when he calls Demosthenes Philocrates' *hetairos* (Aes. 2.19). Philocrates was held responsible for a failed and unpopular peace with Macedonia, and because Demosthenes severely criticized the peace, Aeschines aims to portray him as a partner of and co-conspirator with the hated politician, as well as a hypocrite and opportunist.

Aeschines is hardly alone in seeking to discredit men in this way. In the legal arena, these labels often convert different forms of legal assistance practiced among friends into mercenary, clandestine, and conspiratorial acts that subvert legal or communal conventions and give unfair

---

11. On *hetaireiai*, see Calhoun 1913, 1–24, 126–23; Sartori 1957; Aurenche 1974; Ostwald 1986, 356–9; 469–71; Hansen 1987, 79–81, 164 n. 498. At times, however, *hetairos* could mean simply friend: And. 1.54; [Dem.] 52.14; MacDowell 1962, 98; Konstan 1997, 60–61; and see Aurenche 1974, 36–38, who argues for a distinction (too fine in my view), between a *hetaireia*, which did not have to be conspiratorial, and a conspiratorial *sunōmosia*.

12. Aes. 1.110; cf. And. 1.100. See Fisher 2001, 247–48, and cf. Davidson 1993, 65–66, for connotations of sexual and other misconduct that threatened the regime.

advantage and power over the individual to a group of comrades. The recommended response to such plots is for the people to close ranks against them.[13]

THE LEGACY OF OLIGARCHIC CONSPIRACIES: LYSIAS AND THE THIRTY

A more immediate legacy of the oligarchic regimes in Athens were attempts made by Athenians after the restoration of democracy to incriminate fellow citizens as supporters of these hateful governments in deed and word. Of these attempts the most pertinent to our subject is Lysias's speech *Against Agoratus* (Lys. 13).[14]

The speech was delivered between 400 and 398 by an anonymous prosecutor, who charged Agoratus with responsibility for the death of Dionysodorus, the speaker's cousin and brother-in-law, saying that Agoratus had willingly collaborated with the Thirty and that his denunciation of Dionysodorus as a plotter against the oligarchs had led to Dionysodorus's execution. Lysias's task was not an easy one. Agoratus may have been immune to prosecution under the amnesty of 403/2 and because of a statute of limitations on his alleged crime.[15] The speaker also had to convince the jurors that Agoratus was an accomplice of the oligarchs, even though he had impeccable democratic credentials. In 411, he had taken part in the murder of the oligarchic leader Phrynichus, and in 403, he had joined anti-oligarchic forces in their first significant actions against the Thirty (*IG* I³ 102.26–27; Lys. 13.77–79). In addition, Agoratus's insistence that he had been coerced to inform on fellow Athenians made him a victim of the oligarchs rather than their ally (see, e.g., 13.28, 52). Indeed, unlike informants in the earlier Mysteries affair (And. 1.11–12, 15, 27–28) or a fellow informer in the case under discussion (Lys. 13.55–56), Agoratus received no immunity for his testi-

---

13. Dem. 21.140. Legal hetairic collusions: Is. fr. 1 (Forster); Dem. 21.20, 139; 54.14–17, 31–40; cf. 29.22–23; 58.42; Aes. 3.255; [And.] 4.4. With or without these labels, the general idea is that friends or supporters of a rival do not help him but "are plotting" to help him: cf. Lys. 26.13.

14. For another attempt, in addition to Lys. 12 and 30 (discussed below), see Isoc. 20.10–13, who tries to link the defendant to antidemocratic activities in 411 and 404 on the basis of his alleged character. Isoc. 15.318 gives the perspective of those on the receiving end. See, generally, Strauss 1986, 89–120; Bearzot 1997, 1–92; Wolpert 2002b, 100–118

15. For the date of Lys. 13: Todd 1996, 118; Bearzot 1997, 74–76. For the legality of the suit and the procedure used: Hansen 1976, 101–2, 130–32; Bearzot 1997, 66–74, 79–86; Todd 2000, 138–39; Wolpert 2002b, 60–62.

mony but was actually put on trial in the Council following his arrest, although the speaker says that he was acquitted as the oligarchs' "benefactor" (13.38). Lastly, when Agoratus made his denunciation, he could not have known that the people he had named would be tried in a court dominated by the Thirty rather than in a popular court, in which the speaker himself opines that those denounced would have been acquitted (13.36). The speaker tries to overcome these difficulties by making Agoratus's informing a part of a well-planned oligarchic conspiracy that aimed to overthrow Athenian democracy. But he also seeks to gain his audience's favor by making the defendant and the Thirty exclusively responsible for an inglorious and tyrannical chapter in their history, or, as he puts it, have the people "see . . . in what way your democracy was overthrown and by whom" (13.4).

The speaker reports that after the Athenian defeat in the battle of Aegospotamoi (405), plotters had sought to institute oligarchy in Athens by taking advantage of the city's weakness, losses, and the presence of a Spartan fleet nearby (13.5–6). First, however, they had to get rid of the opposition, namely, the demos's leaders, the generals, and the taxiarchs. When the Spartans proposed peace, which included the demolition of portions of the Long Walls, the popular leader Cleophon opposed accepting their offer. In response, the politician Theramenes, who plotted against the people, volunteered to go and negotiate better terms with the Spartans. He stayed with the Spartans for a long time in order to make the people even more exhausted and desperate and thus willing to accept any terms (13.7–11). In the city, the conspirators brought Cleophon to trial, ostensibly for violation of military duty, but in reality because of his standing up for the people and his opposition to the destruction of the walls. The trial was rigged, and the oligarchs came to court and executed him (13.12). Theramenes then arrived with much harsher terms of surrender. The generals and the taxiarchs, including the prosecutor's cousin, Dionysodorus, opposed him, not because they did not want peace, but because they could see that the demolition of the walls and the surrender of the navy would mean the destruction of the democracy (13.13–16).

In order to slander these opponents and put them in harm's way, Theramenes and the conspirators got Agoratus to inform on the generals and the taxiarchs, saying that they were involved in a conspiracy. The speaker explains that the oligarchic plotters did not share their scheme with Agoratus, "a slave and a slave's son," who was neither their friend nor their confidant, but only used him as an informer. Their plan was to make Agoratus look like an unwilling informant and so render his denunciation credible. Accordingly, they sent one Theocritus, who was Agoratus's friend and *hetairos*, to the Council, which was corrupt and wished to destroy the democracy too. Theocritus informed the Council in a secret session of a conspiracy against the planned oligarchy but refused to name names, because he had taken an oath of secrecy with the plotters and because there were others who would name them. Then some councilmen went in search of Agoratus, found him in the agora, and agreed not to arrest him after certain Athenians had given their personal assurances that he would present himself to the Council. Agoratus and his sureties went to Artemis's shrine in Munychia in the Piraeus, where the sureties suggested that he leave Athens with them in boats they had ready, in order to avoid likely torture and having to inform under coercion. Agoratus, however, refused to go, which, according to the speaker, showed that he was part of the plot and knew that he would suffer no harm, and that he had only pretended to name names unwillingly (13.20–29). Thus, when men came from the Council to Munychia to fetch him, they did not, as Agoratus maintained, drag him from the altar; he had gone with them voluntarily. In the Council, without coercion, Agoratus had then denounced his sureties, the generals, the taxiarchs, and other citizens as plotters against the city. "This," says the speaker, "was the beginning of the whole trouble [or evil: 13.29]." Agoratus later repeated his denunciations in the Assembly, where it was moved that those denounced be tried by a court composed of 2,000 jurors.

When the aforementioned officials were arrested, the Spartan admiral Lysander entered the harbor, the ships were surrendered, the Long Walls demolished, and the Thirty were appointed. By now the people were impotent to help the prisoners, and the Thirty had them brought, not to the designated jury court, but to the Council. They attended the trial and arranged for an open ballot, instead of a secret one. No wonder, then, the speaker concludes, that everybody was convicted, except for Agoratus, who was let free as a "benefactor" (13.30–39, 48).

The speaker thus frames the tale of Agoratus's informing as a plot within a plot. The defendant had participated in a conspiracy to eliminate the opposition to a larger plot against Athenian democracy. In what follows, I shall discuss the problems with the prosecutor's account.

The speaker describes Athens under siege as embroiled in a struggle over the fate of its democracy. Yet other sources make the main issue of contention in the city less the safety of its democracy and more whether to accept Sparta's terms of surrender and peace, especially, the destruction of the Long Walls and the surrender of the Athenian fleet. In fact, they date the conflict over the nature of the government to the time following the surrender.[16] Thus, Xenophon and Plutarch state that Theramenes had met some opposition in the Assembly when he spoke about accepting the peace terms, and especially about the destruction of the walls (*Hell.* 2.2.22; Plut. *Lys.* 14). Even our speaker reports that Cleophon's opposition was to the destruction of the walls, although he presents it as done "on your [i.e., the people's] behalf" (Lys. 13.12). He also emphatically denies that those who opposed Theramenes had done so because they opposed peace; they had merely wished for better terms (13.15–16). It was true that some democratic leaders and their supporters equated Athens's surrender with the overthrow of the democracy, or tried to use the latter as a battle cry to rally the demos in opposition to the peace, but the burning issue at the time was not so much the survival of Athenian democracy as whether Athens should surrender and at what price to its survival or security.[17] Lysias's portrayal of the conflict as focused primarily on the fate of Athenian democracy, and of Cleophon, the opponent of peace, as a victim of its oligarchic enemies is anachronistic, then. Such depiction allows Lysias to present Cleophon's trial as a precursor of the generals' trial, however, in that both were based on preconcocted charges and abuse of the judicial process against the defenders of the demos. Agoratus's informing thus becomes part of an already established oligarchic modus operandi, which makes his role in the conspiracy likely.

For obvious reasons, the speaker depicts Agoratus as responsible for, or intimately associated with, the many evils that befell the de-

---

16. The only reported Spartan term that could have been construed as a threat to democracy was the request of the Athenians to adopt an "ancestral government" (*patrios politeia: Ath. Pol.* 34.3; Diod. 14.3.1). Some scholars have debated the authenticity of this clause, but even among those who accept it, doubts have been raised as to whether this vaguely phrased request meant a demand for a radical constitutional change. Ostwald (1986, 468–72) even thinks that Theramenes was responsible for including this term in order to protect Athens from oligarchy, and see Fuks 1953, 61, and the studies cited in Wolpert 2002b, 150 n. 46; cf. ibid. 14–15. Justin's testimony (5.8.5–8) that the terms included accepting thirty governors from Sparta is clearly anachronistic.

17. For Cleophon's opposition to the peace, see also Xen. *Hell.* 2.2.12–15; Aes. 2.76. He had opposed peace with Sparta on previous occasions as well: Renaud 1970, 471–72; Ostwald 1986, 207, 412–13; Munn 2000, 181–83. For equating surrender with overthrowing the demos: e.g., Lys. 28.11; Kerntz 1982, 42 n. 34. For identifying democracy with national security: Missiou 1992, 57–58.

feated city. At the same time, he stresses Agoratus's inferior status when he states that he was not one of the oligarchic conspirators, only their willing tool, and by attributing servile status to him (13.18, 64). Agoratus, it should be noted, was probably a citizen.[18] Presenting him as subordinate and servile is not only calculated to evoke contempt for and prejudice against the defendant but also accounts for the conspirators' success in prevailing upon him to agree to serve them, even though he would seem to neither to have had any incentive to join the plot nor any association with or sympathy for the conspirators before and after the plot. It also explains how the Council could have contemplated putting him to torture, from which citizens were normally exempt. Asserting that the plotters did not share their plan with Agoratus also helps the speaker to overcome the significant challenge of explaining how Agoratus could be a partner in an oligarchic plot about which he evidently knew nothing (13.18).[19] Lastly, and in the best tradition of conspiracism, Lysias transforms Agoratus's initial unwillingness to inform into a ploy designed to fool the people into believing that the information he would subsequently give was credible (13.19).

To strengthen these allegations, the speaker tells a rather convoluted story, which makes everyone either a conspirator or the victim of a plot. He argues for collusion between the oligarchs, Theocritus, the Council of the Five Hundred, and Agoratus. However, such a complicated, well-coordinated scheme, involving so many people, who, to make Agoratus's testimony appear trustworthy, all had to pretend that he was not the oligarchs' agent, seems highly unlikely. Indeed, the councilmen who allegedly took part in the plot had been elected before the Thirty assumed power and hence were likely to have been democratic and hostile to an oligarchic takeover. Aware of this problem, but needing to account for the Council's role in the affair, the speaker has to put quite an effort into depicting it as corrupt and pro-oligarchic (13.20).[20] Moreover, the proofs that he produces for this charade are of questionable value. They

---

18. Todd 2000, 135. Bearzot 1997, 273–75, however, opts for a resident alien status.
19. In contrast to his pleading Agoratus's ignorance of the plot in 13.18, the prosecutor states in 13.61 that the plotters had persuaded him to inform in return for a promise to share in their new government. This inconsistency reflects his difficulties in making the defendant both a servant and a partner of the Thirty.
20. Pace Bearzot 1997, 276. In *Against Nicomachus*, the speaker at least explained that the democratic Council that was involved in Cleophon's trial was dominated by two known oligarchs: Lys. 30.14. He produced no proof for this contention, however; see further below.

consist of asserting that many of the councilmen later served in the Council under the Thirty, labeling Theocritus an *hetairos* of Agoratus, and an *argumentum ex silentio,* which reads into what is *not* written in the Council's decree a deliberate refusal to force Theocritus to name his accomplices. Given that the Council's session was secret, it is unlikely that the speaker knew what moved it to allow Theocritus this privilege.

The prosecutor is equally ignorant of what moved Agoratus to stay in Athens after the Council ordered his arrest. His contention that Agoratus did not leave because he knew that the Council would not harm him was not a proof of Agoratus's guilt but an argument from hindsight. It also confidently, but unwarrantedly, assumes that had Agoratus been a truly reluctant informer, someone would have moved to torture him (13.25, 27, and see below). In sum, and as in other conspiracy scenarios, the speaker arranges events and actions in a tight logical and chronological sequence, deduces motives from results, and allows for no mishaps or for any action or event to be meritorious or coincidental.

Similar observations apply to the grander plot of converting the Athenian government into an oligarchy. As typical of conspirators, the Athenian oligarchs waited for the right opportunity to execute their plan and eliminated their enemies in underhanded ways, with the people too weak or ignorant to do much about it.[21] Here, too, aims are deduced from results and nothing happens unless it has been planned. For example, the speaker concludes from Theramenes' offer to negotiate peace with the Spartans and his later return with harsh terms that he had planned this all along.[22] Similarly, even though the fate of the generals and the taxiarchs was decided only after Theramenes had come back and the Thirty took power, the speaker implies that it was a foregone conclusion (13.7, 17, 34–35). He achieves this effect by conflating events separated by days and even months into a tightly linked series of conspiratorial actions, which creates a continuum from Cleophon's trial through the negotiation and the discussions of the peace with Sparta, Theramenes' mission, the surrender of Athens, the establishment of the

---

21. Bearzot 2000 argues that Lysias adopted a partisan vocabulary that legitimized democratic opposition as moral, legal, and open, and ascribed conspiracy to oligarchs, whose means were clandestine, immoral, illegal, and subversive, and who acted like enemies. As evinced by the present work, these means and attributes were not uniquely oligarchic: cf. Lys. 13.1, 48.

22. Xenophon, too, thought that Theramenes had delayed his return on purpose until the Athenians could stand no more, but like Lysias he could only guess what Theramenes' plan or intentions were: Xen. *Hell.* 2.2.16–17; Papyrus Michigan 5982. On this issue, see (with bibliography) Wolpert 2002b, 11–13; Stem 2003.

Thirty, and the trial of the democratic leaders in which Agoratus's denunciation is said to have played a key role.

The internal difficulties of Lysias's conspiratorial tale are compounded when one looks at other sources for the events he describes. The chronology of these events is the subject of scholarly debate, owing to the variant accounts of them. I side with the scholars who separate the city's surrender in April 404 from the Thirty's assumption of power in late summer, perhaps September 404, as opposed to those who (like Lysias) date both events to April 404.[23] Such reconstruction necessitates postulating two visits by Lysander to Athens: the first in April 404 to accept the city's surrender, and the second in late summer, and on his way from defeated Samos to Sparta, when he imposed the Thirty on the Athenians. It also means that although Lysias dates the oligarchic plot and the arrest of the military leaders to a time no later than April 404, it could be that the opposition to the oligarchs and the latter's elimination of it postdated the city's surrender.

I wish to argue, however, that there was no oligarchic conspiracy prior to the city's surrender and the appointment of the Thirty.[24] None of our other major informants, namely, Xenophon *Hellenica* 2.2.3–3.14; *Ath. Pol.* 34.2–35.1; Plut. *Lys.* 14–15; and Justin 5.8.1–11, say anything about such a plot. Diodorus is the only one who mentions what may be construed as an oligarchic preparation. He reports on a controversy over the city's constitution following its surrender and says that, while the political strife was going on, the oligarchs went to Lysander in Samos and gained his support. The Spartan admiral then came to Athens (apparently in late summer) and forced the Athenian Assembly to accept the Thirty as their rulers (Diod.14.3.1–5; cf. And. 3.11–12). Even if one insists that this trip to Samos deserves to be construed as a conspiratorial act, it was neither done in secret nor resembled anything reported by Lysias.

The reason for Lysias's uniqueness in reporting on a presurrender plot has less to do with the quality of his information, or lacunae in other sources, than with his finding such a plot rhetorically useful. In general, a tale about a pre-Thirty conspiracy was likely to have a significant appeal to a democratic audience, because it presented the Athenians as the helpless victims of a plot and so exonerated them of having assented to

---

23. Calhoun 1913, 106 n. 2, and Linttott 1982, 161, are among scholars who try to salvage Lysias's chronology, but see Green 1991; Munn 2000, app. D, 340–44; Wolpert 2002b, 126, 150 n. 48. On the following, cf. Renaud 1970, 474–76; Krentz 1982, 42–43.

24. The existence of such plot is commonly accepted: see, e.g., Calhoun 1913, 83–84, 105–6; Munn 2000, 211–17; Wolpert 2002b, 14–15, 125.

the oligarchs' rule without a struggle. In particular, such a plot helped Lysias to damn (and in one case to praise) people's actions prior to the oligarchic takeover. Thus, in *Against Agoratus,* an oligarchic plot accounts for Agoratus's involvement in Dionysodorus's death. In *Against Eratosthenes* (Lys. 12), Lysias makes the not altogether likely allegations that after the battle of Aegospotamoi, the *hetairoi* had assigned five ephores, including Critias and the defendant Eratosthenes, to be the conspirators' leaders and to oppose the democracy. They appointed cavalry commanders, controlled the assembly and the election, held power, and plotted against the people, knowing that the sufferings of the demos would make them ignore future evils (12.43–45). Lysias again brings up the oligarchic plot for the sake of the prosecutor of Nicomachus, who accuses the defendant and two known oligarchs of having taken part in a conspiracy to get rid of Cleophon (30.9–14). Conversely, he uses it for the benefit of a client, who claims that his father, Eucrates, had declined an offer to join an oligarchic conspiracy before the city's surrender (18.4–5). It appears, then, that the speechwriter uses a presurrender plot either to condemn a person (Agoratus, Theramenes, Eratosthenes, and Nicomachus) or to commend him (Eucrates). His multiple mentions of the plot are not an indication of its historicity but of its applicability.

Having detected the plot, Lysias depicts it with great skill, especially in *Against Eratosthenes* and *Against Agoratus.* In both of these speeches, he compresses events that occurred before and after the surrender in a way that incriminates the defendants as plotters. In both orations, the villainy of plotting from within, as opposed to the more legitimate plotting of enemies from without, adds outrage to their crimes. Finally, in both speeches, the speaker stresses the people's difficult circumstances, which both created the opportunity the oligarchic plotters were waiting for and account for the demos's acquiescence to their rule. Unlike *Against Agoratus,* however, *Against Eratosthenes* dwells at length on the evil Theramenes and makes him almost single-handedly responsible for putting the Thirty in power.[25] Lysias argues that Theramenes concealed his plan to establish oligarchy from the people and colluded with Lysander in the plot (to overthrow the democracy; 12.62–78), but he stresses the conspiratorial dimension of the oligarchic takeover less than in *Against Agoratus.* The differences in the presentations reflect Lysias's sensitivity to the specific needs of each speech. Since he cannot, as in Eratosthenes'

---

25. For Lysias's attack on Theramenes: Murphy 1989; Bearzot 1997; Chiron 2002; Stem 2003, 29; Carey 2005, 95–96.

case, associate Agoratus with Theramenes, he highlights the conspiratorial aspects of the oligarchic takeover, but diminishes Theramenes' role in it.

But if the evidence for an oligarchic plot prior to the Thirty's appointment is slander, how to account for the arrest of Dionysodorus and other democratic leaders? By all indications, their arrest was intended to crush their conspiracy. Theocritus suggested their plotting activity when he reported about their getting together and taking oaths. Agoratus too is said to have denounced them for "plotting against your people" (*epibouleuein tōi plēthei tōi humeterōi*).[26] Lysias portrays these plotters as fighting for the demos, but the language of Agoratus's denunciation implies that there were Athenians who saw them in a different light. The plotters, after all, opposed the terms of peace with Sparta and so could be viewed as prolonging the people's sufferings, if not as giving Sparta reasons to destroy the city.[27] Apparently realizing that their opposition was ineffective and perhaps not very popular, and fearing the fate of Cleophon, these men resorted to conspiracy.

It is most likely that Agoratus joined their plot. This would explain his knowledge of the plotters' identities and Theocritus's directing the Council toward him. The latter, a co-conspirator (13.21), might, then, have been more selective in his refusal to name plotters than the logographer would have us believe.

According to the speaker, Agoratus showed that he was in fact the oligarchs' willing tool when he declined to flee Athens (13.24–28). By denouncing his sureties, he also showed himself to be devoid of any moral scruples and gratitude (cf. 13.58). Yet these assertions are problematic for several reasons. First, as we have seen, they unjustly presuppose that Agoratus was about to be tortured by the Council and hence should have escaped. Second, they fail to account for the remarkable self-sacrifice of his sureties, who were willing to leave their families and households and lose the assurances they had given for the sake of helping Agoratus and the men he would name. No less likely than sheer altruism is the possibility that they were all involved in the democratic plot. Indeed, one of the guarantors, Aristophanes, was later

---

26. Lys. 13.21, 48; cf. 51, 84. I cannot share Munn's 2000, 211–17, speculations that the democratic plotters had fixed their hopes on Alcibiades, or that Theocritus was Lysander's agent.

27. After Athens's surrender, Thebes and Corinth demanded that Athens be destroyed: Munn 2000, 206, 408 n. 29. It was not a novel idea or exclusive to these two states.

arrested by the Council and executed, although unlike Agoratus, he refused to name names.[28] Third, the speaker states that he will produce witnesses and a Council decree to show that everything—namely, Agoratus's refusal to flee, his seeming reluctance to inform, his knowledge that he would not be harmed—was contrived (*pareskeuasthē*; lit., prepared).[29] The decree has not survived, but it is highly unlikely that it recorded Agoratus's betrayal of his sureties or his plotting with the oligarchs and the Council. Judging from the context, the decree must have given instructions to bring Agoratus to the Council.[30] Similarly, it is unknown who the prosecution's witnesses were and to what extent they corroborated its version. The only people who had certain knowledge of what happened at the altar in Munychia were Agoratus and his sureties, and the latter had been executed by the oligarchs (13.59). It is more likely that the witnesses for the prosecution were relatives or friends of those denounced by Agoratus, or men who claimed to have heard what transpired at the altar.

We can only speculate as to why Agoratus (and his sureties) did not escape, if, indeed, they contemplated this option. It has been suggested that Agoratus feared the Spartan blockade.[31] It is also possible that he thought that he could remain at the altar in Munychia until another informer was found, and perhaps he hoped to strike a deal with the Council, similar to the one made with Theocritus, which would allow him to name another source of information. Eventually, the Council sent men to Munychia to arrest the willing Agoratus (so the speaker) or to drag him from the altar (so Agoratus: 13.29). His denunciation of the generals, taxiarchs, and others in the Council and the Assembly led to their arrest (Lys. 13.31–33).

Agoratus might have been instrumental in the imprisonment of the democratic plotters, but their fate should be dissociated from their arrest. Lysias reports that even though the Assembly decreed that they be tried in a *dikastērion* of 2,000 jurors, the Thirty moved the trial to the Council. The logographer's remark that the prisoners would have been acquitted in the popular court and that the people were too weak to help them puts the best face on the collaboration of the demos with the ene-

---

28. Lys. 13.58–61. See Schweizer 1936, 48–49, but also Bearzot 1997, 280–81.
29. Lys. 13.28–29. The text notes that a decree follows, but Markland, based on 13.28, has reasonably added a testimony as well.
30. Lys. 13.29; Rhodes 1985, 165; Bearzot 1997, 285–88; cf. Naiden 2004, 79–80.
31. Krentz 1982, 43 n. 35. Yet dating the affair following the surrender would exclude this solution.

mies of democracy (13.36). But it also shows his predetermined perception of events and actions, which characterizes conspiratorial tales. Yet the fate of the democratic conspirators was not sealed by their arrest, and those involved in the investigation of the democratic plot, including Agoratus, did not plan or could not foresee that the plotters would eventually face trial in a Council supervised by the Thirty. In fact, even the allegedly pro-oligarchic Council could not be trusted to convict the defendants, as is shown by the Thirty's arranging for its members to cast their votes openly and under their watchful eyes. They had to resort to such means because the trial took place "immediately" after the Thirty took power (13.35). This left too little time to turn the democratic Council into an oligarchic tool, not to mention the fact that the Thirty had yet to display their ruthlessness. Apparently, the speechwriter hoped that his audience would confuse this Council with a later Council that was the Thirty's creation.[32]

Among those tried for their involvement in the plot was Agoratus, who was acquitted, probably in exchange for his information (13.38, 50). Yet one would expect a less risky and more tangible reward for his alleged service of the oligarchs. This was Agoratus's point, and in making it, he distinguished himself from another informer, Menestratus, whose information had led to many of the deaths Agoratus was charged with, but who, in contrast to Agoratus, was given immunity (13.55–56). Agoratus's trial makes his claim to have opposed the oligarchs and informed unwillingly deserving of more credit than the speaker's denial of it.[33]

In conclusion, the argument for the existence of a pre-Thirty oligarchic plot is uniquely Lysian and poorly supported by the evidence. The logographer reverses the role of plotters from democrats to oligarchs because following the trauma of the Thirty, it was easy to depict the latter as evil schemers and the former as their helpless victims.[34] In addition, although the Thirty could not have attained power without Spartan in-

---

32. The trial in the Council: Lys. 13.34–37; Hansen 1975, 86. The Council of the Thirty: Xen. *Hell.* 2.3.11; *Ath. Pol.* 35.1; Lys. 13.20; Rhode 1993, 437–38; 1985, 7, 29–30, 181. Renaud 1970, 473 n. 65 speculates that the Council leaned "to the left" of the Assembly. Xen. *Hell.* 2.3.28 has Critias asserting that Theramenes pushed the Thirty to treat the defendants harshly. The historian describes another, later abuse of the judicial process by the Thirty which also involved an open vote (Xen. *Hell.* 2.4.8–10).
33. Cf. Schweizer 1936, 63–64; Loening 1987, 75.
34. See also Wolpert 2002b, esp. 120–27; cf. 2002a, 120–21; Chiron 2002, esp. 44–51. Years later and unrelated to this case, Demosthenes justifies helping the Rhodians in spite of their joining Athens's enemies during the Social War by reminding his audience that they too had often been deceived by plotters but had refused to take responsibility for their actions (Dem. 15.15–16).

tervention (cf. And. 3.10–11), the narrative allows the Spartans and Lysander only a relatively minor role in the drama. Such presentation both augments the Thirty's culpability and answers the particular needs of *Against Agoratus,* since the defendant can be held responsible for the Thirty's actions, but not for those of Sparta.

Lysias uses many of the devices noted above in a speech written for the prosecutor of Nicomachus (Lys. 30) that was delivered close to the time of *Against Agoratus.*[35] One of the charges brought against the defendant concerns his involvement in a plot against Cleophon. The speaker's account of this affair both supplements and deviates from that of Agoratus's prosecutor.

The charge that Nicomachus was involved in Cleophon's death belongs to a duel in accusations of oligarchic affiliations between Nicomachus and his prosecutor, in which Nicomachus accused the latter of participating in the oligarchic rule of the Four Hundred in 411 (Lys. 30.8). In addition to denying the charge, the prosecutor promises the court that he will show that Nicomachus conspired against the "many," and that, as with Agoratus, his democratic façade conceals subversive acts against the people (30.10). He says that after the defeat at Aegospotamoi, a revolution was in the making, and Cleophon accused the Council of plotting and making decisions against the city's interests. In response, the councilman Satyrus persuaded the Council to arrest Cleophon and try him in a jury court. Since those who wished to destroy Cleophon were concerned that the court would not put him to death, they persuaded Nicomachus to produce a law that would incorporate the Council into the jury. Nicomachus openly showed that he was part of the plot when he produced the law on the day of the trial. The speaker concedes that Cleophon might have been guilty of many things but asserts that he was targeted for elimination by Satyrus and Chremon, who were members of the Thirty, and who wished to kill him in order to harm the people and overthrow the democracy. They were successful, thanks to Nicomachus, who, in order to please those who overthrew the democracy, allowed the Council to sit in judgment, a body where Satyrus and Chremon had the greatest power, and that executed the general Strombichides and other distinguished citizens (30.10–14).

As in Agoratus's case, the prosecutor has to overcome the challenge of turning a man with solid democratic credentials—Nicomachus went

---

35. For Lys. 30, see, Todd 1996, 101–31; Edwards 1999, 154–59; Munn 2000, 274–79; and for the following: Todd 1996, 117–19.

into exile when the Thirty were in power (30.15) and was twice commissioned by the democratic city to revise and inscribe its laws (30.2, 4)—into an oligarchic tool.[36] The speaker has also to find motives for the defendant to help the oligarchs, as well as to convince the jurors that the highly controversial and not universally liked Cleophon (30.12–13) deserves sympathy and retribution. He hoped that involving Nicomachus in an oligarchic conspiracy would solve these and other problems.

Inspired by Cleophon's rhetoric of conspiracy and treason against the Council, which significantly charged it with not doing what was best for the city rather than with oligarchic aspirations, the speaker focuses on a plot against democracy and Cleophon. He admits that Cleophon had many faults but stresses that his trial was harmful to public interest (30.12). To make the scheme against Cleophon seem likely, he gives it attributes common to other conspiracies, such as a two-step plan, here, the Council's resolution followed by the "fixed" trial; an opportune and well-coordinated strike, here, the pulling out of the law empowering the Council to judge on the day of trial; and taking unfair advantage of one's cleverness or expertise, here, Nicomachus's knowledge of the law. The rigging of Cleophon's trial largely resembles the judicial travesty that decided the fate of the military leaders in *Against Agoratus*. Yet in contrast to the wholesale condemnation of the Council as oligarchic in Lys. 13, this prosecutor identifies the chief culprits as two individuals who later became known as members or aides of the Thirty. By so doing, he can anachronistically date Nicomachus's collusion to a time "when the revolution was being effected" (30.14) and include Cleophon among the Thirty's victims.

The proofs produced for Nicomachus's involvement in the plot are as weak as those used against Agoratus. They consist of detecting an oligarchic revolution even before it occurred, the timing of Nicomachus's producing of the law, and the unproven contention that Satyrus and Chremdon were able to sway the votes both in the Council and the court.[37] Given such poor evidence, and Nicomachus's minor role in the affair, the speaker tries to compensate for his weak case by reiterating sev-

---

36. Like Agoratus, Nicomachus is demoted to servile origin and lowly status (30.2, 5–7, 26–30; with Todd 1996, 112–13, 119), although his prosecutor does not relate these attributes to Cleophon's trial. Nicomachus the democrat: Dow 1960, esp. 291, who goes, however, too far, in making him the champion of the demos, and see Todd 1996, 116–17.

37. It is hard to establish with certainty what Cleophon was charged with. Lys. 13.12 mentions a dereliction of military duty, but such a crime did not warrant a death penalty: Renaud 1970, 473 n. 64; Rhodes 1985, 183 n. 4. Ostwald postulates a treason charge: 1986, 457 n. 162. See also Hansen 1975, 116, no. 139 (*eisangelia*); Hamel 1998, 147, no. 31 (for the possibility that he was a general); Munn 2000, 409 n. 34.

eral times that Nicomachus was part of an oligarchic plot and that his action legitimized a miscarriage of justice (30.9, 11, 13, 14; cf. 16). He hopes that the Athenians will be partial to the charges, because, as in the case of Agoratus, blaming the defendant and the oligarchs exonerates the demos of having destroyed a man presented as their champion. The author of *Ath. Pol.* 28.3, however, offers a different perspective on Cleophon and the people's role in his fate. He depicts Cleophon's execution as an act of justice of sorts, through which "the many" showed their hatred of a leader who had deceived and corrupted them with public subsidies. Regardless of this author's hostile view of this democratic leader and his likely ignorance of his jurors' motives, he makes the people, rather than Lysias's oligarchs, directly responsible for his death.[38]

Judging by Lysias and other logographers, charges of conspiracy to overturn the democratic regime lost none of their appeal in years to come. Their targets tended to be politicians and officeholders, whose alleged plots ranged far and wide.

PLOTTING POLITICIANS AND PUBLIC OFFICIALS

Athenian politicians were expected to be useful to the city and both privately and publicly to respect the laws and moral conventions. But often, and much thanks to their rivals, they were viewed with suspicion as abusing their skills and public offices for self-enrichment and gratification of desires, or as aiming to wrest power and control away from the demos.[39] Such goals, as well as the politician's rhetorical proficiency and experience in politics and litigation, were frequently associated with plotting in the private and pubic spheres. Isocrates tried to combat these perceptions in his defense of his school of rhetoric and its students. He protested that skillful speech did not mean sycophancy and designs against other people's possessions and named Athenian politicians from Solon to Pericles as honest practitioners of the art (Isoc. 15.226–34; cf. 15.198). Clearly, he was swimming against the current. A Demosthenian preamble, for example, warned members of the Assembly of yielding to the persuasive efforts of men who were the oligarchs' hirelings and

---

38. Neither Lys. 19. 48, who says that Cleophon died a pauper, nor Xenophon *Hell.* 1.7.35, who situates his death in a context of a stasis, are helpful here.

39. See Roisman 2005, 130–62. Lys. 22 uniquely charges a nonpolitical association with conspiring against the city. He accuses grain retailers of trying to profit from the people's misery, i.e., when grain is scarce, of plotting against them like enemies, and of conspiring against the grain importers (Lys. 22.15, 17, 21).

so aiding those who plotted against them (Dem. *Pr.* 2.2; cf. 42.1–2). This not uncommon warning urged the Athenians to adopt an attitude of distrust toward their speakers and even their own judgment, because the work of antidemocratic plotters was facilitated by public gullibility.[40]

The inclination to bunch politicians together as a group of evildoers further enhanced their conspiratorial image. One speaker's interpretation of a clause in the Bouleutic oath that prohibited councilmen from arresting men who had provided sureties illustrates this perception. He argues that the purpose of this restriction is to prevent rhetores in the Council from colluding or getting together (*sunistamenoi*) to imprison citizens (Dem. 24.147; cf. 22.37; 58.61–65).

The plots that speakers ascribe to politicians frequently correspond to misdeeds cited in the Athenian law of impeachment (*nomos eisangeltikos*). The law includes a number of legal procedures against attempts to overthrow the democracy, acts of military treason, and against speakers (*rhetores*) who were bribed, who did not speak in the best interests of the people, or who failed to keep their promises to them.[41] Even though Athenian laws tended to group crimes by procedure rather than thematically, the sources indicate that all of these misdeeds were seen as related to each other and that they were often deemed conspiratorial. Thus Aristophanic Cleon tries to scare the opposition through charges that combine treason, bribery, and antidemocratic conspiracies (see above). In 390/89, a Lysian speaker uses a similar combination in his speech against the general Ergocles, who had joined an expedition that had mixed results, led by the general Thrasybulus.[42] To make the defendant appear hateful and a saboteur of democratic procedures, the speaker has him characterize as a hostile plot and sycophantic act a popular resolution demanding of Thrasybulus and other officials that they give an account of money they had received from Athens's allies. He then

---

40. For variants of this motif, see Dem. 15.30–33; Aes. 3.233–35; cf. Lys. 26.4, 15. For skillful speakers/politicians and plotting, see also Aes. 2.154–55; Dem. 57.8, Isoc. 18.51; and Dem. 23; 24 (chapter 5).

41. The most important sources for the law are Hyp. 4.7–8; *Lexicon Rhetoricum Cantabrigiense*, s.v. *eisangelia;* Pollux 8.52–53; [Dem.] 49.67. See Hansen 1975; Rhodes 1985, 162–64; Hansen 1991, 223; Whitehead 2000, esp. 82–84, 186–89; Rubinstein 2000, 111–22; Carey 2004, 115–16. The version of the law cited in Hyperides was probably updated in 411–401 (Hansen 1975, 17; Whitehead 2000, 188). The curse proclaimed at the beginning of the Assembly and the council sessions also combines these offenses: Rhodes 1985, 36–37; MacDowell 2000, 238. Men charged with treason and conspiracy to overthrow democracy could not be released on bail: Dem. 24.144; cf. Lyc. 1.25–26.

42. Lys. 28; cf. Lys. 29. For the trial, see Hansen 1975, 89, no. 73; Hamel 1998, 48, nos. 34–35.

depicts the defendant Ergocles and his like as plotting to bribe, commit treason, and institute an oligarchy in order to keep what they had dishonestly obtained on account of having held public office and to scare the people away from taking action against them (28.5–8, 11). In appealing to popular concern about plotting politicians, the speaker describes them as enemies of the city and its government, or at best, as competing with the people for control of the state and its resources.[43]

Andocides reports on a plot that aimed at abusing the system rather than changing it. In his trial for impiety in connection with the Mysteries festival, he describes one of his prosecutors, the democratic leader Agyrrhius, as a man who had plotted to deprive the city of revenues and who wished to avenge his having lost a bid for the office of customs collector to Andocides (And. 1.133–35). According to Andocides, two years before the trial, Agyrrhius had colluded with "all those who assembled with him under the poplar tree" to refrain from competing for the office of collecting the taxes so that he (Agyrrhius) could put in a low bid. They had all, in fact, shared in the bid and in the subsequent handsome profit of three talents. In view of the profitability of this arrangement, they then all got together (*sunestēsan*) once again, gave shares to other bidders, and submitted a low bid. Andocides had outbid them by raising the offer by six talents, however, which still allowed him to make "a small profit" for himself and his partners.

Thus, a plot by a politician and other men of dubious character to profit at the polis's expense and to subvert a mechanism for increasing its revenues was exposed by a conscientious citizen. Not fully trusting his audience's intelligence, Andocides uses the rhetorical device of putting words in his opponents' mouth (*hupophora*) to commend himself and his civic service. He has them say that Andocides does not take public money and guards against others who do so, and that he must be destroyed so that he will not take legal action against them. Their statements link their scheming against the polis to their judicial schemes in his trial.

To exclude themselves from the category of conspiring politicians, speakers portray themselves either as the objects of political plots or as the sole guardians of the public interest among a crowd of political plotters. Demosthenes exemplifies the first tactic in *On the Crown*, when he regales the court with an account of how the people had followed his ad-

---

43. Cf. [Lys.] 6.34; Aristophanes *Plutus* 569–70. Accusations of plotting against democracy and the state also centered on links between local plotters and foreign powers, for which see the discussion of Aristophanes and Thucydides earlier in this chapter, and of Philip II in chapters 6 and 7.

vice and trusted him with public responsibilities after Athens's defeat at Chaeronea by Philip, even though they could have been unkind to him in view of his strong advocacy of meeting the king in battle. In contrast, those who sought to do him harm had banded together (or conspired: *sustantōn*) and used a variety of legal means against him, including employing others to provide them with anonymity. He had persevered, however, thanks to the gods, "you," and other Athenians (Dem. 18.248–49; cf. 18.322). The speaker's aim is to create a divide between him and the people, on the one hand, and his rivals, on the other. But he also makes himself a victim of plots and the people his protectors from plotters, who, typically, attacked him when he was most vulnerable and with characteristic cowardice hid behind straw men.

Other speakers illustrate the tactic of setting themselves apart from the crowd of political plotters. Toward the end of his speech *On the Embassy*, Aeschines enumerates the virtues that entitle him to the court's mercy, among which is the fact that he has been the only one who has never conspired "against you" in his political contests (Aes. 2.181). The topos of a lone, worthy politician surrounded by political conspirators goes back at least to Aristophanes' Paphlagonian/Cleon (*Knights* 847–66) and recurs in a speech delivered in the late fourth century against the politician Aristogeiton, who faced a legal procedure (*endeixis*) on account of his debt to the state. Probably inspired by Aristophanes, Aristogeiton's prosecutor depicts him shouting in the Assembly: "I am your only well-wisher [*eunous*]. All the others are conspirators [*sunestasi*]. You are betrayed. I am the only man of goodwill left" (Dem. 25.64; cf. 25.40; Aes. 2.8). The speaker's sarcasm aside, the apparent commonness of this posture shows less its conventionality than its appeal. It disqualifies others from the position of the people's champion and offers the demos a chance to defeat the political cabal by supporting their "well-wisher."

One speech stands out among politicians' charges of collusion against the demos and ordinary citizens. The oration *Against Eubulides* (Dem. 57) portrays the speaker as an ordinary citizen facing a plotting politician, but the latter's cabal consists not of fellow politicians but of fellow members of the speaker's deme (township).

The context of the speech was the state's decision in 346/5 to scrutinize and revise the registers of Athenian citizens that were kept in the demes. The revision in the deme Halimus had resulted in striking the speaker, Euxitheus, from its register, and Euxitheus appealed the decision to an Athenian court in an effort to save his citizenship and possibly his liberty.[44] The speaker faced a double challenge: he had to convince the jurors that he was entitled to citizen status, and that the entire deme had been wrong about his civic status and he was right. Indeed, men in Euxitheus's position were at a disadvantage as far as their credibility was concerned. An Isaean litigant who confronts his deme in a trial involving property he had mortgaged to it observes that it is difficult to litigate against many, because their great number makes them appear to tell the truth (Is. fr. 6 [Forster]). Aeschines too asserts in reference to trials of men who, like Euxitheus, had lost their memberships in their demes that demesmen are supposed to know if an individual rightfully belongs to their deme, and that this assumption had led jurors to sustain the deme's verdict (Aes. 1.78).[45] Euxitheus accordingly calls upon his audience not to consider the deme's decision as a proof that he should not be a citizen and tries to refute what he describes as a strong argument against him in the form of the deme's vote (57.6, 62). But his main strategy for accounting for his ejection is to describe it as a product of a plot.[46]

Euxitheus puts the chief blame for the plot on Eubulides, the demarch of his deme, who was in charge of convening and running the deme's meetings. He argues that Eubulides wasted most of the session that resulted in Euxitheus's ejection on speeches and decrees, and not by accident. He schemed (*epibouleuōn*) to have the speaker's case heard as late as possible (57.9). Thus, when Euxitheus's turn came up for scrutiny, it was already dark, and the deme's elders had left for home. Only thirty or so members stayed, including those whom Eubulides had suborned (*pareskeuasmenoi*; 57.9–10). Eubulides, then, disputed Euxitheus's civic status but produced no witness to prove his charges. He also ignored Euxitheus's protests and request to postpone decision to the next day, which would have allowed him to bring supporting speakers and witnesses to authenticate his right to membership in the deme. Proceeding to the vote, Eubulides used the cover of dark to give two or three ballots

---

44. For the affair, see Osborne 1985a, 147–52; Whitehead 1986, esp. 291–301; Christ 1998, 179, 267 n. 63; Bers 2002; D. Cohen 2003, 82–90.

45. The speaker of Lys. 23, who argues that one Pancleon is not a citizen, uses as evidence the testimonies of members of the defendant's deme and men from his former town that they do not know him: 23.3, 5–8. This does not mean, of course, that such testimonies, or even the demes' registers, have been above suspicion: D. Cohen 2003, 82–83. See also E. Cohen 2000, 111, with Bers's (2002, 236–37) reservations.

46. An Isaean speaker in favor of a man who was also expelled from his deme makes a similar conspiratorial charge (Is. 12.12; Wyse 1904, 723) but without elaborating, perhaps because the theme is developed in another speech on behalf of the defendant or because the speech we have is fragmentary.

to each of those who joined in (*sunestōtes*) with him. The result was that even though there were no more than thirty men present, more than sixty ballots were counted (57.11–13, 16).

Thus, a meeting that could have lasted long because of a full agenda is presented as carefully designed to harm the speaker, because in a conspiracy scenario, there is no room for chance or for events to take place unless they are preconceived. By reducing the number of those attending the meeting to about thirty, and of the conspirators to even fewer than that, Euxitheus makes the collusion both plausible and feasible. He also hopes thus to overcome the problem of contradicting the many who presumably knew the truth about his status, as well as to change his conflict with the entire deme to one with a corrupt few. In addition, he makes sure to meet criteria that will firmly establish his status as a victim. He faced a powerful and clever planner; he was ignorant of the scheme and was caught by surprise (57.12; cf. 48); he stood alone against a cabal; and he was unable to defend himself owing to the unfair rules of contest and the plotters' underhanded tricks.

Yet the speaker's version is not above suspicion, chiefly because he provides no witnesses to prove that the vote was rigged. He tries to overcome this shortcoming by strengthening through reiteration the claim that he was unjustly set up,[47] but especially by maintaining that he cannot call on friends or other men to testify about the manipulation of the vote, because they had left the meeting owing to the lateness of the hour. Instead, he is forced to call as his witnesses those who have harmed him, and he has written depositions for them, which they will not be able to deny (57.14). In other words, none of those absent or present at the meeting can corroborate his story.[48] One would also have greater confidence in his allegation had he reported how many of the ballots counted were for and against him. Even if the ballot container was stuffed and there were only thirty voters left, they were not all Eubulides' accomplices, as he himself indicates (57.10, 13). He perhaps did not want to say that even those who had not been in the plot had voted against him. Lastly, other speakers use the trick of taking advantage of sparse attendance to account for unfavorable decisions, which suggests both the conventionality and popular appeal of this assertion.[49] His claim later in the speech that he and his father had passed earlier scrutinies in the deme be-

---

47. Dem. 57.2, 7, 17; cf. Bers 2002, 233. See above for a similar tactic in Lys. 30.
48. See also Osborne 1985a, 148–49; Whitehead 1986, 300, though cf. D. Cohen 2003, 87–88.
49. See Aes. 3.126 and chapter 7 n. 4.

cause no plot was involved (57.62) is similarly based on equating a favorable decision with honesty and an unfavorable one with conspiracy.

I do not wish categorically to discount the possibility that Euxitheus was trapped. Aeschines (although in an equally tendentious speech) describes an attempt to eject a deme member under false pretenses.[50] But Euxitheus does not prove his allegations, and his assurance to the court that if the whole deme had been present at the meeting, it would have supported him (57.16) is unprovable and no better than its opposite.

The tendentious logic of his conspiracy tale recurs in relation to his witnesses for his deme membership. After providing depositions regarding his and his father's legitimate status as Athenian citizens, Euxitheus says that if he had only one or two witnesses on his side, it would have been possible to claim that they had been suborned (*pareskeuasthai*). But all the kinship and non-kin groups that normally evince one's citizenship have confirmed his and his father's memberships in them, and it is impossible to say that all these people have been suborned (*kateskeuasthai*) to accept them. He also says that his father was not rich, which means that he could not have bribed so many relatives (57.24–25, cf. 53–54). Thus, a conspiracy of many is possible when it targets the speaker, but not in the case of those who have lent him support.[51]

The speaker returns to the conspiracy tale in other portions of his speech. He says that Eubulides is an old enemy who was just waiting for the review of the demes' registers and the general anger toward alien infiltrators in the polis to conspire (*epebouleusen*) against him and to play the sycophant (57.48–49). The assertion both highlights the opportunism of his adversary and supports the speaker's argument from probability that his membership in the deme would have been challenged earlier if he had been an alien. At another point, he uses the plot against him to flatter his audience when he commends jurors from other large demes for delaying review sessions and allowing people to prepare their cases, thus unmasking sycophants and those who conspire out of personal enmity (57.57). This comment leads him to contextualize his case in the villainous history of his deme, which makes the conspiracy to eject him

---

50. Aes. 1.114–15. See also the case of Agasicles, who was charged at a different time with bribing his way to citizenship and membership in Euxitheus's deme: Hyp. 4.3; Din. fr. 7 (Burtt); Whitehead 1986, 292–93; 2000, 179–80. Calhoun 1913, 113, 116 detects in our case the working of an Eubulides' club, and Whitehead 1986, 300, largely believes that the speaker fell victim to a plot; cf. Carey 1997, 231–32; Bers 2002, 235.

51. Humphreys 1985, 346, notes that it was in the interest of Eubulides' kinship group to demonstrate their solidarity with him because defeat "would leave his relatives in an embarrassing or perhaps even dangerous position."

hardly remarkable. He argues that in the past, the deme had denied and confirmed membership of different children of the same parents, or ejected poor fathers but kept their sons (57.58). Dramatically characterizing one incident as the most terrible thing that these plotters had done (although see 57.65), he reports that two aliens had been admitted to the deme upon paying each of the plotters (the remarkably cheap fee of) five drachmas.[52] That Eubulides "and those around him" had not expelled these alleged aliens in the scrutiny that occasioned his ejection shows that they have destroyed and saved many for money. To reinforce his portrayal of the corrupt deme and demarch, the speaker tells the court that when Eubulides' father, Antiphilus, was a demarch, he had contrived to get money by pretending to lose the register, thus appealing to the popular assumption that like father, like son. This forced the deme to conduct a review, in which Antiphilus had ten members ejected, although nine of them later won their appeals (57.60–61). This record of a miscarriage of justice delegitimizes the deme's decision against Euxitheus and should encourage the court to follow the precedents for revoking it.

Yet Euxitheus does not include his own case in the swindle operated by Eubulides and his associates, probably because even he is unable to claim that their motives have been mercenary in this instance.[53] He resolves this problem by saying that Eubulides dislikes him and his father (57.8, 48, 61). He has greater difficulties accounting for the motives of Eubulides' accomplices, however. So he informs the court that when he had administered the deme's affairs, he had made some people angry by exacting from them payments they owed the deme from renting sacred lands and from embezzlement of public funds. In response, these disgruntled individuals had conspired against him when they omitted from the oath the clause guaranteeing unbiased judgment (57.63).

Euxitheus is not entirely clear about the context of this oath, which could be the one taken during his scrutiny or, not less likely, and as surmised by David Whitehead, that taken when he had given an account of his term as demarch (*euthunai*).[54] Euxitheus is equally fuzzy about the

---

52. Dem. 57.59. See Whitehead 1986, 296 n. 16, who speculates that the sum was intended to show their low level of corruptibility, rather than that Euxitheus had too many enemies, which would have been counterproductive.
53. In 57.65, he says that the plotters had plundered his property as if he were already an exile, but he mentions this incident to show their contempt for the people and laws, and not in relation to their motives.
54. Whitehead 1986, 93 n. 29; 299 n. 29. See also ibid. 299–300, where the scholar observes in this passage an attempt to show how a good demarch should act, including his willingness to risk himself in the public interest.

identity of these delinquents and whether they included Eubulides' accomplices. Indeed, the issue of his collecting payments might have belonged to an altogether unrelated feud, as indicated by Euxitheus's asking for the court's indulgence in digressing to his demarchy (57.63). The confusion appears to have been intentional and designed to lead the court to conclude that those who conspired against him in his membership review wanted to get even with him for his debt collection.

He also charges the debtors with another evil plot (*sunōmnuon autoi*) against him. They had sacrilegiously stolen arms he had dedicated to Athene and erased a decree that the deme had inscribed in his honor. Then, in a (typically conspiratorial) display of brazenness (*anaideia*), they had spread a rumor that it was he who had committed these acts to bolster his defense. Euxethius points out that he is not so insane as to erase an inscription that honored him and to risk death penalty (for stealing from the temple), even in order to get such important evidence for his case (57.64). The speaker's reasons for not perpetrating these acts make good sense. Less clear, however, is how his enemies presented the stealing of the armor and, especially, erasing the honorary decree as helpful to his appeal. Apparently, they argued that he had done this so as to appear to be the victim of a frame-up. Given the centrality of the theme of victimization by tricks in his speech, their allegation should not be dismissed out of hand.[55] But regardless of what happened in the temple of Athene, it is noteworthy that the speaker prudently leaves others the option of calling witnesses to prove his contention (57.65). True or false, his rendition of his enemies' ingenious mischief demonstrates the Athenians' receptiveness to such conspiracy tales.

Euxitheus's multiple plotting accusations were born of his need to contend with a problem faced by other litigants discussed in this book (see, e.g., Dem. 32; 43): how to convince an Athenian court that an individual had a better claim to justice and truth than a group of adversaries who seemingly lacked a common agenda, who were more likely to know the facts, and who, in this case, expressed through their vote a communal wish that deserved consideration. By expanding the topos of the plotting politician to the entire group, the speaker strove to weaken the moral and legal advantage that this association had over the indi-

---

55. The affair is murky, but the following speculation can serve as an alternative explanation. It is possible that the debtors stole the arms and erased the inscription to avenge Euxitheus's tax collecting. These actions had nothing to do with his scrutiny. Later, however, when his appeal came out, they argued that he had done it for the sake of seeming the victim of a plot, while he used the incident to suggest that they wanted to eliminate evidence useful to his appeal.

vidual, to impugn its motives and actions, and to undermine its credibility and the democratic process it used to pass decisions.

Overall, the stereotype of evil politicians greedy for power and profit is employed in the speeches to give credence and rationale to tales of political conspiracies. At times, political plotters appear all-powerful and able to orchestrate events at will. Yet such depictions show less a paranoid fear of omnipotent conspirators than a wish to explain events that called for explanation because they had a significant unfavorable impact on the individual or the public. Moreover, in the cases both of the oligarchic takeover of 404 and of Euxitheus's loss of citizenship, faulting political conspirators relieved the demos or the deme from responsibility for them. It appears that the Athenian conspiratorial worldview served to sustain civic and political ideology rather than to question it.

CHAPTER 5

Plotting Legislation and Political Measures

Since political activists in Athens were often busy proposing laws or decrees for the people's approval, it is no wonder that their opponents discovered conspiracies behind this too. After all, one effective way of demonstrating public virtue was to catch political conspirators in the act. In the speeches, several prosecutors of citizens for making illegal proposals claim such credit for themselves, showing off their vigilance as protectors of the people and the laws. Since the laws were perceived as safeguards of democracy from revolution (Hyp. 1.12; cf. Aes. 1.5), it was possible to describe an alleged attempt to modify or change a law as a plot against democracy (Dem. 24.206; cf. 153–54).

In the period under discussion, the Athenians had two legal means of dealing with illegal legislation. One was the *graphē paranomōn*, a public action against the mover of a decree (*psēphisma*) in the Council or the Assembly on the charge that it contradicted the existing laws and/or that it had been passed in a procedurally improper manner. The other was the *graphē nomon mē epitēdeion theinai*, which charged a mover on the grounds that the law (*nomos*) he had proposed was unsuitable or harmful. Demosthenes' *Against Aristocrates* and *Against Timocrates* use both legal procedures to attack two different decrees respectively, which they described as the products of plots.[1]

1. See Hansen 1974, esp. 28–65; 1991, 161–77, 212, for more information about the differences between decrees and the more permanent laws, legislation procedures, and safeguarding the laws.

DEMOSTHENES' *AGAINST ARISTOCRATES* (DEM. 23)

Demosthenes wrote the speech *Against Aristocrates* for Euthycles, who in 352 prosecuted the defendant for making an illegal proposal (*graphē paranomōn*).[2] Aristocrates had moved a decree (*probouleuma*) in the Council ordaining that anyone who killed the naturalized Athenian citizen Charidemus of Oreus, a mercenary general in the service of the Thracian king Cersebleptes, should be apprehended and handed over, presumably to Athens, and that giving the killer shelter would result in exclusion from a treaty with Athens.[3] It probably also commended both Cersebleptes and Charidemus as friends and benefactors of Athens (see below). But before the decree reached the Assembly, Euthycles challenged it as illegal and effectively suspended it. In the ensuing trial, Euthycles focused his prosecution speech on showing that Aristocrates' proposal was illegal and contrary to Athenian interests, and that Charidemus did not deserve the protection and honor offered to him. Yet even before addressing these points, he presented the decree as conspiratorial.

The speaker informs the court that when the Thracian king Cotys died, his kingdom had been divided among three rival rulers, Cersebeleptes, Amadocus, and Berisades, each of whom had sought Athenian support, a situation that was in Athens's favor (23.8). Certain (unnamed) individuals, however, wanted to put an end to this state of affairs, to overthrow Amadocus and Berisades, and to make Cersebleptes ruler of the unified kingdom. To that end, they had effected (*diaprattontai*) this decree (*probouleuma*), whose words obscured its real aim (23.9). Following Berisades' death, Cersebleptes had waged war upon his heirs and on Amadocus. It was obvious that his rivals would be assisted by their respective commanders and chief aides, who were Athenians citizens by birth or naturalization (23.10). So they (the aforementioned individuals) wondered how they could make these Athenian commanders take no action, leaving their rulers helpless, so that Charidemus, who hoped to get the Thracian kingdom for Cersebleptes, could take over. They planned to have the Athenians vote, first, that anyone who killed Charidemos be

---

2. Euthycles as the speaker: Libanius, *Hypothesis to Dem. 23*. See Badian 2000, 44 n. 42 against Sealey's (1993, 131) conjecture that the speaker might have been Demosthenes. For the legal action: Hansen 1974, 33, no. 14. For the date, see Appendix B. Papillon 1998 provides a useful rhetorical analysis of the speech.

3. For this interpretation of the decree, see the previous note as well as Koch 1989, esp. 547 n. 6, 554–55; Sealey 1993, 131.

seized and surrendered, and, second, to elect him an Athenian general (23.11). They reasoned that the Athenian commanders in the service of the other Thracian kings would not dare confront an Athenian general in battle or answer for the legal consequences if Charidemus died (23.12). Thus, at the outset of their war, the Athenian Aristomachus had arrived in Athens as their envoy. In his speech to the Assembly, Aristomachus said that Charidemus and Cersebleptes wished the Athenians well and had no intention of incurring Athens's enmity by capturing the Chersonese. He suggested that the people elect Charidemus general, saying that he was the only man who could win Amphipolis for Athens. The plotters had a decree ready for the Assembly's approval if the people were persuaded by Aristomachus, but the speaker stepped in and prevented the confirmation of this harmful decree by the deluded demos (23.13–18, 110).

The speaker's description of the affair relies heavily on the conventions and vocabulary of the rhetoric of conspiracy. He thus claims that he was stirred to action when he saw people contriving (*kataskeuazontas*) against the polis (23.5; cf. 190). He asserts that the facts speak against their device (*kataskeuasma;* 23.13) and asks in what more crafty (*tekhnikōteron*) or harmful (*kakourgoteron*) manner these persons could have contrived together (*sumpareskeuasan*) to get Cersebleptes' rivals banished, make Cersebleptes ruler of all of Thrace, and free of fear the man (Charidemus) who had contrived (*kataskeuazonti*) to make Cersebleptes the sole ruler (23.15). The conspiracy itself is typically based on an indirect approach and precise planning. Chronologically, first comes the preparation in advance (*hetoimasto . . . prodiōikēto*) of the decree (23.14). As soon as the war in Thrace began, Aristomachus arrived in Athens to seduce the demos with false hopes. With perfect timing, his speech is followed by moving the decree in the Council. The temporal sequence that the speaker creates among these events is also his best proof that there was a conspiracy.[4] As in other cases of illegal legislative initiatives discussed below, the plotters assume that the demos is ignorant and can easily be manipulated. Typically, the plotters disguise their private agenda with promises of public benefit and concern for the interests of the polis. Typically, as well, the plan leaves little room for mishaps and its execution is smooth till our speaker, the watchful patriot, intervenes to uncover its true purpose and

---

4. Dem. 23.13. Cf. Papillon 1998, 26–27, who argues that the narrative of 23.8–17 is germane to the deliberative proof of the speech.

spoil it. Later in the speech, the logographer renews his conspiratorial search for hidden meaning in his discussion of the illegality of the decree, where he often focuses on what the decree neglects to specify or say, rather than on what it actually states (23.22–99). He uses this technique again to similarly interpret another illegal proposal made by Timocrates in a different speech (see below).

Another feature of this alleged plot is the speaker's failure clearly to identify the plotters. He obliquely refers to "those who wished" (*boulomenoi tines*) to change the status quo in Thrace (23.9) and leaves them anonymous throughout 24.8–18. An obvious candidate is the defendant Aristocrates (24.3, 93). Yet the prosecutor reports on more than one plotter, while elsewhere in the speech, he discusses Aristocrates mostly in the context of the decree's violation of established laws and institutions, rather than in reference to his plotting it. He also names the Athenian Aristomachus and reports his Assembly speech, but he presents him more as instrumental to the plot than its initiator (23.9, 110). This leaves Cersebleptes and especially Charidemus, who sometimes appear as the men behind the plot (24.12–14) and sometimes as benefiting from its contrivance by others (24.9, 11, 15). Later in the speech, however, Euthycles identifies Charidemus as the master plotter. He says that he decided to oppose Charidemus in court seeing that he had contrived (*proskataskeuazomenon*) to get men to deceive the people and thus make Athens's friends (i.e., Cersebleptes' opponents in Thrace) impotent to deter him. He adds that Charidemus had contrived (*kateskeuazeto*) a great deed unprofitable to the polis (23.189–90). It should be noted, however, that these comments are made in the context of a vicious attack on Charidemus's character, designed not to unmask the plotters but to show why he does not deserve present or previous public thanks and benefactions. The speaker also fails to explain adequately what moved Aristocrates to help Cersebleptes and Charidemus.[5]

How to account for Demosthenes' reluctance clearly to identify the plotters? It has been claimed that his reticence amounted to an unnamed attack on Eubulus's policy, but we do not really know what Eubulus's policy on the Chersonese was at the time of the decree or the trial. We are equally ignorant about the possibility that the speaker and his fellow prosecutors divided up the tasks of challenging the decree (Euthycles)

---

5. Later in the speech, he alludes to the conventional incentive of bribery, though not in the context of affecting an easy war in Thrace but in that of honoring these unworthy individuals: 23.146–47, 184–86, 201. Cf. Tod no. 86 for a charge of bribery behind an honorary decree dated to 409.

and attacking the plotters more vigorously (presumably the other accusers).[6] The speaker's ambiguity is probably owing to a combination of factors. He could have been concerned that dwelling on the plot and its authors would divert attention from his main efforts of discrediting the decree itself and Charidemus.[7] His ambiguity also gave him the flexibility of sharing the blame among as many persons as he wished, including Athenian rhetors in general, but with a reduced risk of retaliation from those he failed to name (23.146–47, 184–86, 201, 208–10). Lastly, the lack of clarity evoked an image of a plot hatched by faceless individuals, whose anonymity increased their power and gave them the ability to scheme.

But was the decree a plot designed to help Charidemus and Cersebleptes overcome their neighbors? In Appendix B, I discuss the historical and chronological setting of the decree, agreeing with Robin Lane Fox's 1997 dating of it to 356 as opposed to the prevailing view of 353/2. I date Aristocrates' trial to the less controversial year of 352. But even the traditional dating of the decree does not resolve the problem with Demosthenes' conspiracy scenario. The speaker discusses at great length how beneficial the decree is to Charidemus and Cersebleptes and how harmful it can be to Athens. For obvious reasons, he puts little effort, however, into explaining how the decree was justified to the Athenian audience. Athens normally honored, crowned, or gave protection to outsiders and citizens in return for services rendered by the honorands or their ancestors, or for services expected.[8] Indeed, the speech suggests that Charidemus (or Cersebleptes) was presented to the Athenians as their *euergetēs* (benefactor), to whom they owed gratitude.[9] Our tendentious

---

6. Unnamed attack on Eubulus: Usher 1999, 205, inspired by Jaeger 1938, 102–4. For Eubulus and Demosthenes, see Papillon 1998, 105–11. Team of prosecutors in this case: Rubinstein 2000, 238, no. 23, (who does not discuss the above hypothetical division of labor).

7. For Demosthenes' greater interest in condemning the decree and Charidemus than the proposer: Pearson 1981, 73; Badian 2000, 24–25; cf. Papillon 1998, 51–54. Yet in other *graphē paranomōn* prosecutions speeches, such as Dem. 22 or 24, the logographer successfully combined these two interests.

8. E.g., Tod nos. 97, 109, 110, 116, 131 (Mytilene and individuals); 133, 135, 139 (with 2: 118); 143, 167; 170; 175 (the city of Tenedos); 178; 181; Dem. 23.185, 188; Kelly 1990, 106 with n. 25. Koch (1989, 549–51) collected sixteen additional examples of foreigners, mostly *proxenoi*, who were given protection similar to that granted to Charidemus, and cf. Henry 1983, 168–71. One decree (Tod no. 173 = R&O no. 70) gave the Epirote Arybbas and his children protection from assassination in a way that should have made our speaker less upset about its legality.

9. Dem. 23.6–7, 19, 89, 184; cf. 23.13, 145. One could be honored also for being *anēr agathos* to the city, e.g., Tod no. 117 = R&O no. 2; Henry 1983, passim. Charidemus, however, was not just a "good man," but an *euergetēs*. Kelly 1990, 106, thinks that

speaker and the meager extra-Demosthenian evidence recommend caution in filling up the gap in the history of Charidemus's relationship with Athens, but I wish to argue that to earn the honorific title of benefactor, he, together with or apart from Cersebleptes, had to have done the city some unrecorded favors, which Aristocrates mentioned in promoting his decree.[10]

But honors given to individuals were also expected to yield future benefits (Libanius *Hypothesis to Dem.* 23). Aristomachus recommended electing Charidemus as a general because he was the only one capable of winning Amphipolis for them (23.14). Ideally, this meant that he would do so on his own, but, more realistically, that if the Athenians contemplated a military expedition to regain the city from Philip, they could expect this mercenary general, and most probably Cersebleptes too, to contribute troops or money to the project. The assistance could have also come in the form of diplomacy, because some Athenians believed that Philip had promised to restore Amphipolis to them.[11] According to the historian Theopompus (*FGrHist* 115 F 30), one Charidemus participated in negotiations with Philip over Amphipolis sometime after the latter had captured the city in 357. If Raphael Sealey's identification of this individual with our Charidemus (Sealey 1993, 109–10), representing Cersebleptes in the talks, is correct, Aristomachus's recommendation that Charidemus be sent to deal with Philip over Amphipolis would have been doubly appealing. In addition, Aristomachus's claim that Cersebleptes had no intention or incentive to take the Chersonese (23.110) probably meant, as noted in Appendix B, that the Thracian would not take advantage of Athens's engagement in the Social War to harm her interests in the region.[12] In short, the proposals to elect Charidemus general and to protect him from assassination might have been, and were

---

Demosthenes calls him "benefactor" sarcastically, but the sarcasm is about Charidemus's being unworthy of the title. Mitchell's (1997, 146–47) discussion of the Thracians' lack of reciprocity in their relationship with Athens focuses only on Athenian grants of citizenship to Thracians and overrates the latter's power in the relationship.

10. The favor(s) surely included more than the forced and untruthful statements of friendship to Athens that the speaker attributed to him: 23.184. Kelly 1990, 103, does not support his 357 dating of Cersebleptes' giving up on the Chersonese to Athens.

11. Cf. Papillon 1998, 12. Philip's promise: Ste Croix 1963, 36–38.

12. The apprehension about Cersebleptes' policy in the Chersonese continued to occupy the Athenians even after the war: Isoc. 8.22. In 23.103, the speaker mentions (Athenian) "citizens living in the Chersonese," who will benefit from making Cersebleptes a weak ruler. If this is a reference to Athenian cleruchs sent there in 352 (*IG* II² 1613.297), Demosthenes must have added it later to his speech: Lane Fox 1997, 186.

surely presented as, beneficial to Athens. If so, there was no need for a conspiracy to get them passed.

Indeed, even if the decree could help Cersebleptes prevail against his local rivals, it is uncertain whether all Athenians shared the speaker's bleak view of the likely effect of this on their interests in the Chersonese. Euthycles argues that it is to Athens's advantage that there not be a single strong ruler in Thrace but a balance of power among three weak kingdoms, preferably hostile to one another (23.102–3; cf. 114–17, 144–83). His position is sensible and has rhetorical appeal, but having a strong friend in the region might be no less useful. In fact, the speaker himself regards the idea of Charidemus establishing a single king over Thrace positively, provided that he does it in cooperation with Athens, when he criticizes Charidemus's failure in 360/59 to take this tack (Dem. 24.164). A balance of power in the case of a weak Cersebleptes would also have been in the interest of the other Thracian kings, and one wonders if the speaker, who had participated in an earlier expedition to the region (23.5, 165–67), did not perhaps favor Cersebleptes' rivals and their Athenian commanders.[13] This does not mean that the prosecutor's analysis and advice are hopelessly partisan, only that his detecting a corrupt politician and a hidden agenda behind Aristocrates' proposal is an attempt to malign an alternative policy and motion that might have promoted a good deal for Athens in both the Chersonese and Amphipolis.

But what did Cersebleptes expect to gain from the Athenians? For all we know, he wished, as the speaker argues, to exploit the friendship between himself, Charidemus, and Athens in his fight against his Thracian rivals. It is no less likely, however, that he hoped in this way to curb Athens's predatory policy in Thrace and the Chersonese (see esp. Isoc. 8.24) and to seek protection from the aggression of the other Thracian kings. For if we free ourselves from the grip of Demosthenes' biased and Athenocentric discussion of Cersebleptes and his conflicts, and part company with the scholarly literature that has followed it, it can be seen that this king and his general were often busy defending themselves and their interests from Athenian incursions into Thrace and the Chersonese, as

---

13. For Demosthenes' personal enmity toward Charidemus: Sealey, 1993, 100, 254. Although the speaker states that he will not recommend issuing a decree the like of Aristocrates' to protect the other Athenian commanders in Thrace (23.123), he also describes the latter as those "who care for you," or as "friends who wish to do you good" (23.12, 189). Lane Fox 1997, 181–87, and Papilon 1998, 92–93, discuss Demosthenes' advocacy of balance of power policy in speeches 16 and 23.

well as from coalitions led or joined by their Thracian rivals (Dem. 23.163–78).[14]

There is a similar advantage to distinguishing between what the decree actually states and the aims attributed to it by the speaker. To recall, the decree proposed that anyone who killed Charidemus be apprehended and removed from the territory of Athens's allies, and that giving the killer shelter would result in an exclusion from the treaty with Athens.[15] A nonconspiratorial reading of the resolution's language suggests that it was intended to protect Charidemus, not from Athenian commanders on the battlefield, but from plots against his life by Athens's allies in Thrace. Such protection had special appeal to both Charidemus and his Thracian employer in view of the assassination around 360/59 of Cersebleptes' father, Cotys. Cotys's killers appear to have found employment under Milocythes, who had been a rebel against the Thracian throne, and who was, for a while, a friend of Athens.[16] For the Athenians, the grant of protection to Charidemus meant warning their allies in the region not to kill a man who could help Athens regain Amphipolis, even if his death were in the allies' best interests.

Moreover, the speaker's interpretation of the decree as aiming at preventing the Thracian kings' senior aides from checking Cersebleptes' expansionist designs is misguided at best. It optimistically presumes that these Athenians by birth or naturalization will not dare violate Athenian popular decrees. It also Athenocentrically supposes that, even though these commanders' power is locally based and they are all tied to their Thracian rulers by marriage, their affections and loyalties to Athens, or their fear of standing trial there, will be stronger than any other consideration (23.12, 103, 180). Apparently, the Thracian kings and their generals would never have dreamed of imitating Iphicrates, whom the

---

14. Proving the above assertion in detail is a subject for another publication. The following example illustrates Demosthenes' impact on modern historians. Even though no source names Cersebleptes as the leader of a Thracian attack on Crenides in 356, which led to this city's appeal to Philip for help, he has been presented as the aggressor since the publication of Collart 1937, 152–54, followed by, e.g., Ellis 1976, 68; Griffith in Hammond and Griffith 1979, 2: 248; and more recently, Mitchell 1997, 145; cf. R&O, 257. Contra: Badian 1983, 55–56; Harris 1995, 190–91 n. 10. Cf. also Badian's remarks on Athens's relationship with Cotys's heirs: Badian 1983, 55 n. 13.

15. Esp. 23.16, 27, 50, 60, 75, 84, 91, 143 where selective phrases of the decree, and often the same single phrase, are actually cited. Elsewhere the decree is subjected to the speaker's interpretation. See also Koch 1989, and cf. West 1995 for Demosthenes' citation of decrees in his speeches.

16. Cf. Kelly 1990, 105. Milocythes, Cotys, and Athens: Theopompus *FGrH* 115 F 30; Dem. 23.119; Badian 1983, 54 with n. 10, who thinks that Milocythes plotted Cotys' death; Heskel 1997, 142–46.

speaker himself cites as an exemplary Athenian citizen, who had fought Athenian generals in the service of the Thracian king Cotys.[17] It is also in the interest of asserting that the decree would have a harmful impact that the speaker presents the Thracian kings as utterly dependent on their aides and the latter as irreplaceable (23.11; cf. 189).

In sum, Euthycles justly links Aristomachus's proposal to make Charidemus general to Aristocrates' decree, but the linkage is not necessarily conspiratorial. Rather than hiding wicked designs, the decree was moved with an eye to enhancing Athens's interests in Amphipolis and the Chersonese. Our speaker thinks otherwise and resolutely attacks the motion as harmful to the city. He may have been equally sincere in believing that it was the product of a plot, and, like other conspiracy-minded people, in order to reconstruct its background and identify its ends, he asks the basic, and at times simplistic, question "Cui bono?" Having done so, he places the conspiracy at the beginning of his speech to prepare his audience for his later discrediting of the proposal and its authors on legal, political, and ethical grounds. It should be noted, however, that in comparison to Demosthenes' later charges of collusion between foreigners and local politicians, this one is underdeveloped. Yet Demosthenes, who was known for his studiousness and aversion to rhetorical mishaps (Plut. *Dem.* 6–8, 10), was a good and eager student of public speaking. As we shall see, he improved his rhetoric of conspiracy in his later speeches that dealt with Philip and Athenian public figures, left fewer gaping holes in his arguments, and at the same time, increased the range of plots to include international politics and military conflicts.

DEMOSTHENES' *AGAINST TIMOCRATES* (DEM. 24)

Demosthenes also uses the formula of an ostensibly beneficial and straightforward decree that hides a harmful plot and selfish agenda in *Against Timocrates*. In 353, Timocrates proposed a law to relieve certain kinds of state debtors, who provided sureties, from imprisonment till the ninth prytany, or toward the end of the Athenian calendar year.[18] The politician Diodorus, the speaker of Dem. 24, challenged the law as unsuitable and alleged that it was the product of a plot between Timocrates

---

17. Dem. 23.130; cf. 12.9; Mitchell 1997, 147. All the three Thracian rulers are likely to have been Athenian citizens too: Mitchell 1997, 144.
18. The chronology of the speech and of the events described in it cannot be safely secured. I follow Sealey's chronology (1993, 106, 119). Rubinstein 2000, 135 n. 36, 237–38, opts for 354/3.

and three former envoys, Melanopus, Glaucestas, and Androtion, who had hired him to help them avoid paying a debt to the polis and the penalties associated with it.[19] The debt had originated in a diplomatic mission to Caria at least a year before Timocrates' trial. The three envoys, and the trierarchs of the ship they sailed on, named Archebius and Lysitheides, had captured a ship sailing from Naucratis in Egypt, and the cargo they seized and kept was later proclaimed state property (see esp. 24.11–16).

Did Timocrates conspire with the three envoys to move his law, for a fee or out of friendship, in order to spare them payment and imprisonment? Sealey has suggested that the law could have aimed at general reform. He draws attention to Timocrates' legislation a few years earlier of a similar nature, which limited the period of arrest of people indicted in the legal procedure of *eisangelia*.[20] It is tempting, indeed, to speculate that Timocrates wished to correct an unintended consequence of his previous law, which imprisoned those convicted and fined in *eisangelia* till they paid their fines. But Sealey also concedes that Timocrates' legislation concerning state debtors benefited the envoys, one of whom, Androtion, was an old friend and political ally of his. Together with other scholars, Sealey places the trial in the context of long-standing political or personal feuds between Demosthenes, the speechwriter, and Timocrates, as well between Diodorus (the speaker) and the politician Euctemon, on the one hand, and Androtion, on the other.[21]

I don't think that we shall ever be able confidently to ascertain Timocrates' motives and goals. What is possible to show, however, is that Diodorus's depiction of Timocrates' law as the outcome of collusion is flawed and cannot be accepted without serious reservations or doubts.

Before discussing the problems with Diodorus's account, it will be useful to summarize it. The speaker reports on the origins of Timocrates' law first in the context of his efforts to impress upon the court that he has personal reasons to bring Androtion to justice. He informs the jurors about his, and Euctemon's, past legal feuds with Androtion, and says

---

19. Dem. 24.3, 14; cf. 65–67, 112, 120, 122, 137, 166, 200–203. See Hansen, 1974, esp. 44; 1991, 212, for the view that the procedure used here was *graphē nomon mē epitēdeion theinai*. Badian 2000, 41–42 n. 40, however, goes back to the view that Dem. 24 was a case of *graphē paranomōn*.

20. Dem. 24.63–64; Sealey 1993, 119–20, 127–28. The fourth-century (C.E.) scholar Libanius thought that Timocrates' later law was humane (*First Hypoth. to Dem. 24*).

21. Sealey 1965, 172–76; 1993, 98; and, e.g., Davies 1971, 514, no. 13772; Badian 2000, 22–24; Rowe 2000, 282–33; 2002, 149–51; though see also Harding 1976, esp. 188–89.

Plotting Legislation and Political Measures 105

that he has found out that Androtion had cheated the city out of money when he collected taxes, had manufactured processional utensils, and had refused to give up money that belonged to the state, to Athene, and to the heroes (24.7–8). The last accusation refers most probably to the profit made from the aforementioned captured ship (cf. 24.9, 11). He and Euctemon, then, decided to take action against Androtion. The Council, we are told, decided against Androtion, the Assembly debated the issue all day, and a court of 1,001 jurors rendered its sentence. When there were no tricks left to prevent giving up the money, Timocrates proposed his law (24.8–9). In response, Diodorus and Euctemon decided to challenge the law in court (24.10).

So far, the speaker's account focuses on Androtion's political and legal tribulations but is not terribly clear or generous with details about Timocrates' law. Probably sensing that it is time to address the main issue of the speech, Diodorus expresses the wish to make it easy for the jurors to understand what had happened from start to finish (24.10). He reports that the (veteran politician) Aristophon had moved in the Assembly that a board of officials (*zētētai*) be set up to enquire about individuals who privately held public or sacred money and urged people to give information about them. Following the endorsement of Aristophon's proposal, Euctemon named two trierarchs, Archebius and Lysitheides, as holding goods captured from a ship from Naucratis worth the hefty sum of nine talents and 3,000 drachmas. He went to the Council, which advised the Assembly to hear Euctemon out and decide if it wished to continue the investigation (24.11).[22] Euctemon then told the Assembly that the ship had been captured in the course of the envoys' diplomatic mission to Caria and added that when the original owners of the cargo had come to Athens and petitioned for it as suppliants, the Assembly had refused their request, treating the cargo as "unfriendly," which probably meant enemy property.[23] He asserted that legally this made the ship's contents state property (24.12). The former envoys, we are told, created

---

22. The nature of the *prokheirotonia* procedure used for the investigation is controversial due to our deficient evidence. Here I follow Rhodes' interpretation of it: 1993, 529–31; Rhodes and Lewis 1997, 13, 15–16; but see also Hansen 1983, 1: 123–30; 1989, 2: 66–71.
23. As Badian 2000, 41 n. 38 notes, Demosthenes' use of these words regarding the cargo—*mē philia einai tote* (unfriendly: 24.12)—is odd. The incident occurred during the Social War, and the phrase appears to say that the cargo was deemed as belonging, or helpful, to Athens's enemies. Cf. Wyate [1882] 1979, xxxvi, 94. Harding 1994, 21, discusses the nature of the mission to Caria, and see Harding 1976, 195–96; Sealey 1993, 106, and Badian 2000, 23, for interpretations of this incident in terms of Athenian foreign policy.

a commotion but also released the trierarchs from their liability and admitted to having the money. Following their speeches, Euctemon put forward a proposal, which the speaker describes as "most fair" (ōs dunaton dikaiotatēn), that instructed the state to collect the payment from the trierarchs, but also suggested that the trierarchs might turn to the envoys for the money or resort to legal procedure in case of a dispute, with the loser assuming the debt to the state (24.13).[24] The envoys in response challenged the proposal as illegal in court but lost their case. At this juncture, Timocrates offered the three envoys his services for money (24.14–15).

The speaker adds that the envoys lost their *graphē paranomōn* case against Euctemon in the month of Scirophorion (May-June, probably of 353). They then hired Timocrates, and spread a rumor that they were willing to pay the amount in question, but not a fine, which could double it. Diodorus opines that they had never intended to pay any money and characterizes their offer as deceptive and insulting (*enedra meta khleuasias*; lit., a trap combined with mockery), and as a fabrication (*kataskeuasmos*) intended to distract attention from Timocrates' law, which, as stated above, was supposed to free the envoys from any payment. His proof: they had paid not one drachma to the state all that time (24.15–16).

From information provided later in the speech, the court was able to learn that Timocrates had colluded with a certain councilman to move his law on the 12th of Hecatombaeon (June-July) in a special session of *nomothetai* called to discuss the Panathenaean Festival. The jurors also heard that the three envoys had surrendered the money to the state after all, although belatedly, unwillingly, and only after they had been convicted by three juries (24.187, 196; cf. 137, 145, 175).

The speaker's account raises several questions. It is unclear what the chronological or causal link is between Diodorus's and Euctemon's conflicts with Androtion and the events surrounding the challenges of the legality of Euctemon's proposal and of Timocrates' law. It is equally unclear why Euctemon moved to demand money from the trierarchs after the envoys had confessed to holding it. Lastly, how exactly did Timocrates' law benefit the envoys?

It will be helpful first to examine what the law ordains. According to the speaker, it establishes that a state debtor who had been fined or or-

---

24. For the recommended procedure of *diadikasia*: see, e.g., Harrison 1971, 2: 32, 34, 88, 235; Rhodes 1985, 158; Todd 1993, 119–20, 228–29.

dered to restore stolen or misappropriated public property, and who had been punished with the additional penalty of imprisonment, can be released from prison if he produces sureties for the amount he owes. The sureties have to be approved by the Assembly, and his release from prison can be achieved only if he or his sureties pay the debt no later than the ninth prytany.[25] In his extensive discourse on the law, the speaker argues that it prohibits the jurors from imposing imprisonment on state debtors, and especially, that it has so many loopholes that the envoys, or any other state debtors, can avoid paying their debt, as well as the fine on it, or serving any term of imprisonment imposed on them (esp. Dem. 24.71–90; cf. 22.5–20). His interpretation is not unlikely, but it is also highly tendentious and, especially, based on what the law does *not* say rather than on what it actually states. In spite of the speaker's contentions, the law nowhere grants debtors unconditional immunity from payment of debts, or from fines, or even from serving time in prison if they fail to pay their debts, and it certainly does not prevent anyone from bringing them to justice if they abuse the law in the ways he suggests people can. We may question, then, whether obtaining for the envoys, not a relief from restitution, but merely a delay of imprisonment and payment till the ninth prytany justifies the elaborate conspiracy the speaker attributes to Timocrates' law.[26]

There is also the question of the envoys' conviction that led to their payment of a debt to the state (24.196). The speaker fails to provide details of this verdict or to fit it into his chronological reconstruction of the events surrounding Timocrates' law. Well over a century ago, scholars such as Arnold Schäfer, Friedrich Blass, and William Wyate had already noticed that the first part of the speech treats the envoys as criminals who have escaped justice, while the later part, especially 24.187–218, acknowledges their payment of the money, and they argued therefore that Demosthenes or Diodorus had edited the speech from a draft written before the envoys paid the money into a version that incorporated this later

---

25. Dem. 24.39–40 cites the text of the law, which is corroborated by the narrative of the speech, and see 24.60–65. For this interpretation of the law, see Rhodes 1985, 148–51. For the term "additional penalty of imprisonment" (*desmou prostimaō*), see Hunter 1997, 304 n. 23. I focus only on the portions of the law that are relevant to the issue at hand.
26. Many payments to the states were made in the ninth prytany: And. 1.73; *Ath. Pol.* 47.3–4. In a best-case scenario for the envoys, they could have gained one-year delay of payment or conditional relief from imprisonment from the time of Timocrates' proposal on the 12th of Hecatombaeon (June-July). Charges of *graphē nomon mē epitēdeion theinai* against the proposer of the law could be brought no later than a year from the passing of the law, and see MacDowell 1978, 50, for this lag of time in Dem. 24.

development.[27] This attractive suggestion, however, only sharpens the question about Timocrates' alleged goal or usefulness for the envoys, because the envoys appear to have suffered no fine or imprisonment even before his proposal came into effect and in accordance with the established laws, so vigorously defended by the speaker.[28]

No less puzzling is Euctemon's proposal, which demanded restitution from the trierarchs in spite of the envoys' insistence that they held the property. Euctemon was a declared enemy of Androtion's.[29] Why would he, then, put the onus of returning the money on the trierarchs and not on Androtion and his colleagues? Diodorus's account is problematic or faulty and short on details when silence and obfuscation serve his purpose. In the absence of any other evidence, the following reconstruction of the events includes some speculation but may also clarify the speaker's account.

Diodorus links his attack on Timocrates' law to a series of political and legal feuds between himself, Euctemon, and Androtion. The conflict under discussion, however, commenced with Aristophon's call to investigate public and sacred money held by private individuals.[30] It is tempting to see the helping hands of Diodorus and Euctemon behind Aristophon's initiative, but I shall resist detecting conspiracies in every corner.[31] In any case, at some later point, Euctemon followed Aristophon's proposal by denouncing the two trierarchs for holding the Egyptian cargo.

The affair of the Egyptian ship deserves close attention. It appears from the speaker's account that nothing had been done or decided about the cargo till its original owners petitioned to have it back. This left the cargo or its monetary equivalent in the hands of those who had seized it. Given that the property, or the profits of its sale, was ultimately held by the envoys, I suspect that, some time between the ship's capture and Eu-

---

27. Schaefer 1856–58, 3.2: 65; Blass 1887, 3.1: 244–49; Wyate [1882] 1979, xli–xlv, 235–36; cf. Dover 1968, 162–63.
28. It is reasonable to assume that had they been fined, Demosthenes would have triumphantly produced this penalty to demonstrate the demos's hatred of, and anger at, Androtion and his colleagues.
29. Dem. 22.1; 24.7; cf. 24.117; Harding 1994, 20, 22.
30. In our speech, Diodorus's search for incriminating information about Androtion and his taking action against him together with Euctemon is reported before we are informed of Aristophon's proposal, but this does not mean that it preceded it chronologically. The information about his going against Androtion aims to establish his personal enmity to the politician, while this about Aristophon comes at the beginning of the part that purports to help the court follow the events from their outset (*ex arkhēs*: 24.10).
31. Rowe 2000, 287, 291, 300, and esp. 297 with n. 63, has renewed earlier conjectures about a political alliance between Demosthenes and Aristophon.

ctemon's decree ordering its surrender to the state, the trierarchs and the envoys struck a deal that transferred it to the envoys' possession. It made sense for the trierarchs to do so, because holding on to the cargo could have exposed them to charges of illegally using a state vessel for personal profit. After all, as the trireme's captains, they shared greater responsibility for, and had probably played a greater role in, overtaking the merchant ship, than the envoys who were their passengers.[32]

The question of the cargo's status became a public concern only after its original owners arrived and petitioned the Athenian Assembly for it. The Assembly (following the trierarchs' and the envoys' recommendation?) defined their encounter with the Athenian ship as an act of war, however, and rejected their petition. The speaker provides no details about the status of the cargo following this decision. I can think of only two possibilities. One is that the Assembly left the issue of the ownership of the cargo unresolved and the cargo itself effectively in the hands of its holders. The other is that the Assembly confiscated the property and, as could be expected in such cases, instructed the Council and the *Pōlētai* to sell it. I wish to argue in favor of the first possibility. Libanius, the author in late antiquity of the first Hypothesis concerning Demosthenes 24, seems to have similarly understood the speech, saying that after the Assembly had rejected the merchants' petition, the trierarchs took the money (*eiseprattonto ta khrēmata*). But even if Libanius's testimony has no independent value, the speaker's statements provide indirect support for this interpretation. He says that Euctemon reminded the Assembly at a later stage of laws that established circumstances under which the property in question belonged to the polis (24.12). Such a reminder or effort at persuasion would have been superfluous had the property already been declared state property.[33]

After denouncing the trierarchs, Euctemon went to the Council, which referred the matter to the Assembly (24.11). It is probably this Council decision that Diodorus describes as directed against Andotion, and that he mentions earlier in the speech when he discusses his finding

---

32. Cf. Wyate [1882] 1979, xxxvii. For illegal private use of a warship, cf. Gabrielsen 1994, 100.

33. The *Second Hypothesis to Demosthenes 24* asserts that the property had been confiscated, but, as noted above, this would obviate Euctemon's later attempt to convince the people that the property belongs to them. This hypothesis also includes too many errors: Wyate [1882] 1979, 79–84. For the procedure of confiscated property in Athens, mostly following litigation: *Ath. Pol.* 43.4, 47.2–3; 52.1; Harrison 1971, 2: 178–81, 212–17. Pritchett 1971–91, 1: 85; 5: 383–84, maintains that booty became state property upon arrival at Athens.

out about Androtion's crimes.[34] Euctemon returned to the Assembly in order to convince it that the ship had been taken in the course of an official state mission, and, hence, that its cargo should be defined as state property, now in private hands (24.12). One can easily imagine the level of interest in his speech rising dramatically if he used the words "nine talents and thirty minae." In good years or bad, Athens could always find use for the money. The speaker argues that although the envoys had raised a clamor, they had exonerated the trierarchs of responsibility for the money, conceding that they themselves had it and indicating that the search for it should involve them, rather than the trierachs. This may seem a noble gesture or a graceful admission of the facts (so Wyate [1882] 1979, xxxvii), but it also looks like courting trouble and rather odd behavior on the part of men said to have conspired with Timocrates shortly afterward to help them avoid paying the money and the fine, as well as serving time in prison. There is something amiss in the speaker's account, and I suggest that the envoys admitted to holding the property but also argued that their doing so was perfectly legal, because hitherto no decision had been made that converted it into state property. This is indicated by Euctemon's need to make a legal case for defining the cargo as common property. It is also implied by the speaker's statement that "you" (i.e., the Assembly) thought that all that Euctemon had said was right (*dikaia legein*; 24.12–13), showing an attempt to convince the court that Euctemon's position was above dispute. Apparently, not every one thought so, especially not the envoys.

Euctemon's subsequent proposal (*psēphisma*) officially made the status of the property public when it called on the people to demand it from the trierarchs. This was in accordance with the information he had lodged against them earlier and their perceived greater responsibility for capturing the ship. Yet, in a city where it was illegal to hold property that had been confiscated by the state from another proprietor, it should not have been difficult for Euctemon to make the envoys the prime target of his edict, especially after they admitted to having the money.[35] His reluctance to name the envoys in his proposal is even more remarkable in view of the intimate link between the prosecution of Timocrates and the speaker's and Euctemon's vendetta against Androtion, their avowed enemy (24.7–10). It appears that the speaker's

---

34. Dem. 24.9; Rhodes 1985, 158 n. 1; Hansen 1989, 2: 278. See note 22 above for the council's decision and the subsequent legislative procedure.

35. Actions against people who said to hold other people's confiscated property: Lys. 29; fr. 2 (Thalheim); cf. [Dem.] 53; and cases no. A (i); B (i) in Osborne 1985b, 54.

depiction of Euctemon's proposal as "most fair" was misplaced. Galen Rowe has shown that Androtion, the envoy, and Lysitheides, the trierarch, had all studied at Isocrates' school and has suggested that Isocrates' prominent pupils often cooperated among themselves in politics or in litigation.[36] I propose that Euctemon focused on the trierarchs because of their greater accountability for the ship's capture and the possibility that the Assembly allowed them de facto to have the money, but especially because he wished to sow discord between them and the envoys. The prospect of having these individuals engaged in a legal conflict in which one side would inevitably lose must have warmed his inimical heart.

As potentially illegal holders of state money or property, the envoys could be fined, lose part of their civic rights, and possibly imprisoned. They also became inviting targets: the legal procedures of *phasis* or *apographē* against misappropriation of state property were open to every citizen and, if successful, resulted in a financial reward for the prosecutor.[37] So the envoys hastened to court in an attempt to block Euctemon's proposal as illegal, but they lost their case (24.14). This was probably the conviction of Androtion by a court of 1,001 jurors to which Diodorus refers earlier in his speech (24.9).[38] The loss must have raised the envoys' level of anxiety considerably. It put them, rather than the trierarchs, on the spot, and it was an indication that public opinion was hostile, which could affect a subsequent suit against them. Their defeat could have also been used as a "proof" of their guilt. So they announced their readiness for a compromise. They would pay back the debt, but not the fine, which could have been added to the amount by the court, or could double the amount in the event that the debt was not paid by the end of the year ([Dem.] 59.7). The speaker, however, characterizes their offer as a ruse: a rumor contrived to distract people's attention from Timocrates' law,

---

36. Rowe 2000, esp. 283. Harding 1994, 17–19, has his doubts about Androtion's having studied under Isocrates, but they are not strong enough to negate the sources about it. I am less convinced by Rowe's claim that Isocrates' students were inspired by his doctrines in their political, legal, and business operations. The evidence he produces for Timocrates' Isocratean education is tenuous.

37. State debtors: Rhodes 1985, 148–51; cf. Todd 1993, 143–44. State debtors and imprisonment: Hunter 1997, 304-7. Rewarding the prosecutor: [Dem.] 53.2, with Osborne 1985b, 45, for amending the text from three-quarters to one-third of the denounced property as the reward.

38. So Hansen 1974, 32–33, no. 13. See Rubinstein 2000, 238, no. 20, for MacDowell's 1990, 327–28, objection to Androtion's participation in this legal action. Rubinstein 2000, 238, no. 21 raises the intriguing possibility that 24.9 refers not to this failed *graphē paranomōn* but to an unidentified public action brought by Diodorus against Androtion.

which "gave any one who wishes immunity to plunder public money" (24.9, 15–16). But if we strip the envoys' offer of its conspiratorial wrappings, it appears to be an attempt to impress upon the Athenians, and especially potential jurors in a future trial, that they were able to pay the debt, but not the fine . . . . *dipla d' ou dunēsontai*). The rumor also suggested that they actually expected to be accountable for the money, rather than trying to avoid paying it. As it happened, sometime between the events just described and the trial of Timocrates, the envoys paid the money to the state.

If the interpretation offered above is reasonable, the depiction of Timocrates' law as a product of conspiratorial machination loses much of its appeal. The law in fact appears to have been beneficial to, and considerate of, people who owed the state money rather than those who paid their debts (cf. 24.125, 190, 192). Indeed, one of Timocrates' strongest arguments against the speaker's conspiracy theory must have been that the envoys actually returned the money to the state (cf. 24.187; Libanius's *First Hypothesis to Dem.* 24). Diodorus, accordingly, resorts to quite desperate means when he discusses their payment. He says that Timocrates' law is faulty because he admitted that he had proposed it in favor of the envoys (which he apparently never did; cf. Dem. 24.67) or because he could not prove that the law was good and universal, and besides, their paying the money was irrelevant to the issue of the trial (24.187–89).

A law could also be challenged on procedural grounds, and the speaker extends his conspiracy tale to include Timocrates' violation of legislative procedure (24.26–32). He surveys the Athenian legislative regulations in order to show that they make the process deliberately slow and transparent so as to allow people to review and oppose harmful proposals. He claims that Timocrates had violated every one of these rules. He had never displayed his law for public review before its deliberation. He had introduced his law past the date assigned for appointing speakers to defend earlier laws that could be abolished because of his proposal. He had also conspired with a certain Council member (named Epicrates? 24.27) in the following scheme. The councilman moved to set up a meeting of *nomothetai* to deal with the Panathenaean Festival, and made a proposal, illegal in itself, to call them to an emergency session the next day about ensuring sufficient funds for the festival. His real intention, however, was to allow Timocrates to introduce his law without opposition, advance notice, or debate. The proof of this collusion is that in this session, no business was conducted regarding the festival, but Timocrates produced his law, even though it was legally unrelated to the festival and was not moved on the date assigned to debating new laws.[39] The speaker stresses the conspiratorial features of the procedural violations. He says that Timocrates had effected the setting up of the *nomothetai* with those who plotted (*epibouleuontōn*) against "you," that the whole thing had been the work of conspirators (*suntaxamenoi*), and that nothing had happened by chance or been done spontaneously (*ouden apo tautomatou*: 24.26–7). He reiterates these charges elsewhere in the speech when he depicts proper legislative procedure as designed to prevent plotting (24.38) and argues that everything about Timocrates' law had been contrived (*epibouleusas*), and that there was nothing unintentional or unpremeditated about it (24.110).

The speaker's assertions reflect a typical conspiratorial mind-set that refuses to recognize in human conduct or past events coincidences, good intentions, and a noncausal link among actions. The plotters' modus operandi is equally reminiscent of other conspiracy tales in which skilled operators take advantage of other people's lack of knowledge or attention to effect their scheme.

Yet the story raises some questions. To all appearances, Timocrates was able to pass his motion with ease and with no cries of foul play at the session. Are we to believe that when he spoke on issues unrelated to the festival, not one of the presumably 1,001 *nomothetai* present (24.27), who were called specifically to this irregular session, protested at the time? Furthermore, if the councilman's proposal to call a *nomothetai* session was illegal, why was he not charged with violating the law?[40] I do not wish categorically to deny the possibility of cooperation between Timocrates and the councilman.[41] But if we assume that the convenor of the meeting on the festival acted legally and in good faith when he called it, that no measure was proposed concerning the funding of the festival, because it was shown that there was sufficient funding (cf. 24.28), and that Timocrates decided to take advantage of a session that was left without business in order to move his proposal, then these and other questions can be put to rest.

All this does not mean that Timocrates was not an opportunist or averse to the possibility that his law might help the envoys (cf. 24.196–97), and

---

39. For the above legislative procedure, see Sinclair 1988, 83–84; Hansen 1991, 168–69.
40. For another puzzlement concerning the link between the Council and the *nomothetai* in this case, see Rhodes 1985, 51.
41. Cf. Aes. 3.3; Hansen 1987, 163 n. 490; 1991, 281.

that every one of Demosthenes' complaints against his proposal is unjustified. *Pace* Demosthenes, however, such reservations do not constitute proof that Timocrates moved his law in order to rescue the envoys from their predicament and that the potential evil consequences of his law were premeditated. Since the law appears to have been considerate of all public debtors, and was surely presented as such (cf. 24.196, 201), one effective way of maligning it and its author was to present the latter as a conspirator and the law as intended to benefit private citizens at public expense. Hence the plots discussed above; hence, the description of Timocrates' supportive speakers as a conspiratorial group who came to his rescue in order to cover up their own mischief (24.157–59); hence also, the speaker's insistence here and elsewhere that Timocrates' conduct, methods, and motives are thoroughly conspiratorial and premeditated, and that there was nothing in them that evinces spontaneity or chance (24.26–27, 47–49, 67, 157, 206). Throughout the speech, he ascribes stereotypical attributes of plotters such as greed, brazen shamelessness, and underhandedness to Timocrates.[42] He adds that a conspiratorial act, unlike an error of judgment, is undeserving of judicial mercy (24.48, 110), a fact that partially accounts for the use of the rhetoric of conspiracy here and in other speeches. But there may have been an added reason for Demosthenes' conspiratorial allegations here. Slightly more than a decade before the present trial, he had charged Timocrates with collusion with Demosthenes' guardians to prevent him from collecting his legal reward from them. Apparently, once a plotter, always a plotter.[43]

PLOTTING MOTIONS AND HONORS

Needless to say, Demosthenes had no monopoly on rhetoric depicting legislative initiatives and decrees as conspiratorial. Aeschines similarly alleges conspiracy in a *graphē paranomōn* prosecution speech against Ctesiphon for proposing (for a fee, of course) a decree to honor his old enemy Demosthenes with a crown for his public service (Aes. 3.242). Generally speaking, and judging by his three extant speeches, Aeschines was not as fond of, or proficient in, employing the rhetoric of conspiracy as his famous rival. In the case of Ctesiphon's proposal, however, he aims to show Demosthenes' unworthiness of the honor by, inter alia, as-

---

42. Dem. 24.65, 111,138, 155, 159, 170, 174, 195. For Timocrates' greed, see Roisman 2005, 175.
43. Dem. 29.28; 30.9; cf. Rowe 2000, 297.

sociating him with conspiratorial activity of the kind that had allegedly facilitated the passing of Timocrates' law.

At the beginning of his speech, Aeschines obliquely refers to men who readily make illegal proposals, which are put to vote by others, who in turn have become presidents of the Assembly not by lot but by intrigue (*ek paraskeuēs*; 3.3). He does not reveal more details of the nature of this collusion and trickery, but later on, he makes similar allegations in relation to Demosthenes' political activity. Wishing to taint his rival with collaboration with the hated politician Philocrates, who had been held responsible for an unpopular peace with Philip, he tells how Philocrates' motion to allow Philip's envoys to come and discuss the peace had been blocked as illegal. In the ensuing trial, Philocrates was acquitted after defending himself with the help of Demosthenes, his supporting speaker. Then came the year 347/6. In order to help Philocrates, Demosthenes, like the aforementioned president of the Assembly, became a councilman, not by proper procedure, but by purchasing his seat through intrigue (*ek paraskeuēs priamenos*). Philocrates then made a second proposal to send envoys, including Demosthenes, to Philip. The motion passed, and when Demosthenes came back from Macedonia, he moved, in agreement with Philocrates, to allow Philip's envoys to come to Athens (3.62–63).

Regardless of the veracity of Aeschines' report, it includes the familiar features of skilled plotters duping the people and subverting basic democratic mechanisms; describing disparate events that spanned in this case over two years, namely, Philocrates' first motion, Demosthenes' election to the Council, his mission to Macedonia, and Philocrates' and Demosthenes' subsequent motion, as fully integrated parts of a single plan; and explaining political positions and alliances in terms of collusion.

Shortly afterward, Aeschines recycles the above charges in relation to another alleged cooperation between these two politicians. He says that when the Athenians were discussing who among the Greeks should be allowed to join the peace, Demosthenes and Philocrates cooperated in betraying the Thracian ruler Cersebleptes to Philip. Philocrates clandestinely inserted into a decree a clause that practically excluded Cersebleptes from an alliance with Philip, and Demosthenes, who presided over the Assembly after he had gain admittance to the Council *ek paraskeuēs* (by intrigue), was the one who put it to the vote.[44] Aeschines' accusations resemble each other for a reason. They establish a pattern of

---

44. Aes. 3.73–74; cf. 2.82–90; *contra*: Dem. 19.174,179–81.

conspiratorial activity, which, in turn, makes his allegations credible. At the same time, he presents himself stereotypically as a civic-minded plaintiff facing a cabal of rhetors and generals in the form of a well-prepared defense team.[45]

According to the Athenian Epichares, the politician Theocrinus of the deme Hubadai used similar rhetoric successfully in a *graphē paranomōn* action against Epichares' father (Dem. 58.30–32). In a speech alleging that Theocrinus is a state debtor, Epichares uses his father's conviction to illustrate Theocrinus's villainy but especially to display the purity of his own motives in bringing Theocrinus to justice as his father's avenger, rather than as a mere sycophant. He says that when Theocrinus entered politics, he had sued Epichares' father for moving a decree that had honored the son of the general Ischomachus with the right to free meals in the *prytaneion* building. Theocrinus contended that the decree constituted a plot against the boy. After the general's death, another Athenian, most likely the boy's maternal grandfather, had adopted him as his son, and Theocrinus claimed that the decree aimed at the boy's return to his natal household. Such a move invalidated the adoption and prevented the boy from inheriting his adoptive estate, because one was not allowed to be the heir of both one's natal and adoptive households. The man responsible for the plot was Polyeuctus, who was married to the boy's mother, apparently the heiress of the boy's adoptive estate, who was after the inheritance. The speaker maintains that the jury were swayed by Theocrinus's ostensible defense of the boy's interests, found Epichares' father guilty, and fined him heavily.[46]

The speaker's tendentious account of the incident and his portrait of Theocrinus as a vile career sycophant hardly make him a reliable source for the defendant's actions or motives. Yet Theocrinus's rhetoric of conspiracy rings authentic, or likely, because it includes the stock motifs of a scheme driven by desire for other people's possessions, of a hidden planner and beneficiary, of an indirect approach strategy (first the decree, then appropriating the boy's property), and of interpreting apparent good intentions (i.e., honoring the boy) as a guise for evil designs. Theocrinus also presents himself typically as caring for the demos and as

---

45. Aes. 3.1, 7, 193; cf. 2.1; Dem. 58.40–41; Din. 1.112.
46. The above reconstruction of the case is based on the (at times varied) interpretations of Davies 1971, 6–7; Hansen 1974, 35, no. 23; Osborne 1985b, 48–49 (postulating a political motive for Theocrinus's action); Rubinstein 1993, 60; 2000, 96 n. 53; 109 n. 81; 239, no. 28 (arguing for the limited responsibility of Epichares' father for the decree); Cox 1998, 90.

a volunteer guardian against threats to overthrow democracy in the form of illegal proposals or plots (58.30, 34).

He even depicts Epichares' suit against him as a plot. Epichares complains that Theocrinus will try to divert attention from his debt to the state and to impugn Epichares' motives by arguing that he (Theocrinus) is a victim of a conspiracy (*katastasiazetai*) because of his past prosecutions of men in *graphē paranamōn* actions.[47] It may be that Epichares is trying to discredit Theocrinus as a frequent abuser of the rhetoric of conspiracy. But it is not less likely that these two adversaries are dueling with accusations of plotting and claims of victimhood. While Theocrinus defines the legal action against him as a conspiracy against democracy and its defender, Epichares denies the charge and claims that he is much more entitled to the status of a victim because he is inexperienced in litigation and has been betrayed by a *hetaireia* of men (including Demosthenes) who had pretended to be Theocrinus's enemies and promised to testify against him, but then settled their differences with him (58.1, 4, 40–43).

Overall, litigants who depict legislative proposals and decrees as schemes share with other practitioners and consumers of the rhetoric of conspiracy a fundamental refusal to take manifest goals at face value unless they are selfish, to interpret conduct and actions as anything but deliberate, and, generally, to put their trust in others. The operating principle of distrust enables people to seek and find plots even behind an established record of good deeds. In an effort to persuade the court that criminals should stay in prison even when they post bail, Timocrates' prosecutor goes back in Athenian history and argues that in the good old days, the demos did not take into consideration a man's past good record and reputation when they punished him for recent misdeeds. Rather, they regarded his past honesty as a ploy (*epibouleuōn;* lit., by plot) to gain their trust.[48] The speaker, of course, is attributing to the wise ancestors a suspicious attitude that he wishes his audience to adopt. Yet his assertion reflects an Athenian conspiratorial worldview that effortlessly detects malevolent agendas even behind actual displays of benevolence and reputable public service.

47. Dem. 58.22–23; cf. [Arist.] *Rhet. ad Alex.* 75 1437a10–14.
48. Dem. 24.131–33; cf. Lys. 19.60; Dem. 19.277.

CHAPTER 6

Foreign and Domestic Plotters

The accusation of being an agent of a foreign power seems to have been commonplace among Athenian politicians. Demosthenes deconstructs this charge to its basic ingredients in his prosecution of Aeschines for misconduct as an envoy to Philip in 346. Encouraging his audience to distrust their military and political leaders, and even producing an oracle to this effect, Demosthenes argues that acquitting Aeschines after listening to his supporters will delight Philip, Athens's enemy, and go against the gods' injunction to punish the enemy's servant. He then puts it plainly: "Outside are the plotters; inside, the collaborators [*exōthen oi epibouleuontes, endothen oi sumprattontes;* lit., co-workers]. It is the plotters who give and the collaborators who take or rescue those who have taken" (Dem. 19.297–99). Ironically, Hyperides would use a variant of this simplistic formula against its author in 324/3, when Demosthenes was put on trial for bribe-taking after accepting money from Alexander's runaway treasurer, Harpalus. Hyperides mocks Demosthenes for his posture as an incorruptible politician and says that those who conspire against the Greeks overcome small city-states by force of arms and large ones by buying men of influence in them, Philip being an example of this (Hyp. 5.14–15).

Allegations about Philip's plotting and bribing of local politicians fill the speeches of Demosthenes and, to a lesser degree, other speakers.[1]

---

1. The subject of bribery in Athens has been extensively discussed: see, e.g., MacDowell 1983; Harvey 1985, 88–89; and further references cited in Roisman 2005, 148 n.

Public speakers were fond of allegations of collusion with foreign potentates, both because of their slanderous effect and because exposing plots earned them points in public opinion. These incentives and the borderline conventionality of these charges argue against enumerating or verifying them all. I shall focus instead on those allegations of plots that are most revealing of speakers' use of the rhetoric of conspiracy, especially in relation to Philip's designs to control Greece, and to men who colluded with him. It is true that the speakers' use of conspiratorial vocabulary (especially *epibouleuein* and its derivatives) to describe foreign plots denotes primarily harmful or hostile designs, but since these plans are presumed to be concealed, or to include intrigues, it is justifiable to regard them as plots.

Before Philip became the foremost of the orators' foreign plotters, it was the Persians or their king who were perceived as harboring designs on Greece. Already around 380, Isocrates argues that the Persians are plotting harm and plan to take over Greece, and he repeats this message in later writings. By attribution of such aims to the Persians, Isocrates seeks to justify acts of panhellenic aggression against a presumably hostile and imperialistic power.[2] A rumor around 354/3 that the Persian king had assembled a large navy against Greece led some Athenian politicians to make a similar attempt to rally an anti-Persian Greek coalition, although of a more defensive nature. Demosthenes, who used the occasion to deliver his first Assembly speech, advised caution and restraint, however, until Athens was adequately prepared for such a confrontation and the other Greek states were willing to join it (Dem. 14).[3] He questioned whether the Persian king indeed had such designs but also presented the latter as a skillful plotter who would offer bribes or statements of friendship to other Greek states that would appeal to their selfish separatist policies and draw them away from Athens (Dem. 14.4–5, 36–37). He also mocked the advocates of war for naïvely thinking that warning other Greeks against the king's plots would move them to join Athens against him. The Greek states were well aware of the Persian threat, but they ranked their fear of Persia below their quarrels with Athens or other Greeks (Dem. 14.12–13).

---

51. Philip and bribery: Ryder 1994, esp. 228–32, 254; Cawkwell 1996, 101–4; Mitchell 1997, 181–86.

2. Isoc. 4.155, 183; 5.76; cf. 4.67, 136; 12.102, 159, 163; 5.103. Sparta and even Athens are also said to have harmful designs against the Greeks: Isoc. 8.97; 12.114; Dem. 15.2–3.

3. For Dem.14, see Sealey 1993, 128–29; Badian 2000, 28–30.

Demosthenes' observations illustrate the limited exhortative power of a rhetoric that seeks to exploit the fear of harmful designs (cf. Dem. 8.35). By simultaneously raising doubts about these designs and arguing that the man behind them is too good a plotter, and that his victims are preoccupied with other threats, Demosthenes hopes to undermine a military adventure and preventive action based on fear of menacing plots.[4]

In his later speeches, Demosthenes substitutes Philip of Macedon for the Persian king as plotting to take over Greece. Since there was and is no knowing what Philip had in mind, the best we can do is analyze the speakers' aims in warning against him, and the rhetoric by which they imputed such a plan to the Macedonian king, rather than speculating as to whether or not he actually intended to conquer Greece and when exactly he had conceived the ambition.[5]

To judge from the extant speeches, it was not Demosthenes but Aeschines who, in an Assembly speech delivered in 348/7, first warned against Philip's plan to take over Greece.[6] Athens was negotiating peace with Philip at that time, but the Macedonian king's capture of Olynthus made them apprehensive of his intentions. Aeschines, who opposed a settlement with Philip and advocated joint action against him, described the king as a master strategist, who employed bribed agents against his unsuspecting victims. He argued that Philip had hostile designs against Greece, that he had corrupted Arcadian leaders, and that he had built a powerful coalition in Greece while Athens slept. Infusing his speech with the patriotic themes of defending the fatherland and memories of the Persian war, Aeschines evoked the specter of an imminent barbarian invasion, which could be checked, however, if the Greeks followed their ancestors' example of uniting their forces and punishing local collaborators. The speech caused so much alarm that the prominent politician Eubulus moved to send envoys to different Greek states with an invitation to a conference in Athens on a war against Philip. Aeschines himself went to Arcadia, where he tried to convince the locals of the great harm that men bribed by Philip were doing to their respective states and

---

4. The theme of the Persian king's bribing Greeks in order to rule over Greece or defeat Athens recurs in Dem. 9.36–39; 15.23–24.
5. The following discussion focuses on warnings against Philip's hegemonic ambition prior to Chaeronea, and ignores its hindsight attributions to him as in Dem. 18.156; Diod. 16.84.1; Just. 8.1.3; 9.1.1.
6. Demosthenes, who is the source for Aeschines' speech, discusses it in order to demonstrate Aeschines' later transformation from Philip's foe to his friend, allegedly for a bribe. But his information is considered to be generally reliable: Dem. 19.9–12, 302–6, and cf. Aes. 2.79; Harris 1995, 50–51; MacDowell 2000, 208–11, 337–40.

to the whole of Greece. Nothing came out of this effort, however, largely for reasons similar to the ones that Demosthenes had given the Greeks in 354/3 for not joining Athens in a war against Persia (i.e., Philip's craftiness and their greater apprehension of Athens).

Yet Aeschines' failure had no impact on the appeal of the rhetoric that alerted Athenians and other Greeks to Philip's far-reaching aims. The reason had to do with the challenge faced by speakers who regarded Philip as a menace to Greece and their cities, but who were addressing an audience skeptical of the danger, especially inasmuch as the king appeared to be friendly and was far away. By attributing a plot to take over Greece to Philip, speakers argued that, although he was busy elsewhere, sooner or later, he would imperil the homeland, and that the people had better do something about it, whether on their own or in conjunction with other potential targets. In other words, a Macedonian plan to conquer Greece was first and foremost a threat to one's home.

Indeed, Isocrates' criticism of those who charged Philip in 346 with having designs to rule Greece shows both that Aeschines did not lack imitators and that warning of a danger to Greece as a whole had a specific local meaning. In his address to Philip, the logographer discusses anonymous "word makers" who assert that the king has augmented his power, not on behalf of, but against Greece, saying, "You [Philip] have plotted [*epibouleueis*] against us all for a long time already." Philip may have declared it to be his intention to help Messene, the wordsmiths say, but in fact he aimed to incorporate the whole of the Peloponnese into his realm. Sketching the course of his expansion, they have him first settle the affairs of Phocis and then, joined by Thessaly, Argos, Messene, Megalopolis, and others, descend on Sparta to destroy her. This accomplished, he will easily become the lord of all the Greeks.[7] With heavy-handed sarcasm, Isocrates shows how misguided these doomsayers are. Yet their rhetoric belongs squarely to the school of conspiracy theory in its purported detection of a hidden agenda, hunger for power, and long-term planning. It also claims a characteristically full knowledge of what the plotter wants and how he is going to accomplish it, and a reluctance to concede the possibility of his failure. In line with the view that Philip's threat to the Greek world is actually a local threat, these speakers center his plan on his intention to march on Sparta.

Judging by the extant speeches, Demosthenes, who describes Athens

---

7. Isoc. 5.73–74. Cf. Perlman 1973, 312–15; Griffith in Hammond and Griffith 1979, 2: 456–58. On the term "word-makers," see Too 1995, 118–19.

as the chief obstacle to Philip's advance in northern Greece in his early speeches, waited until 344 to warn her in his *Second Philippic* against the Macedonian king's all-embracing plots and to describe her as standing in the way of his taking over Greece.[8] Demosthenes complains about the Athenians' inaction despite Philip's violation of the peace of Philocrates and his plotting against the whole of Greece, but also explains that the king courts Thebes and not Athens, because he knows that honorable and selfless Athens will not let him to pursue his desire to have more (*pleonexia*) and his wish to control everything.[9] The speaker's Athenocentric slant, which portrays Philip's aims as directed primarily against Athens wherever he is active and whatever he allegedly covets, recurs in other speeches.[10]

Intimately linked with the attribution to Philip of plans to take over Greece, or even more modest goals, are speakers' allegations of his collusion with, and bribing of, local agents. One such charge revolves around schemes to rescue the king from his predicament. In both *On the False Embassy* and *On the Crown*, Demosthenes argues that Philip wanted to have peace with Athens, not only in order to deal with pirates harassing his land, but also to dissuade her from blocking his way at the strategic pass of Thermopylae, which would prevent him from destroying Phocis. To attain both goals, he used Athenian public figures, prominent among them his accomplice (*sunergos kai sunagōnistēs*; lit., his fellow worker and co-combatant; 18.41) Aeschines, to mislead the Athenians into taking no action and to trusting the king's false promises[11] Demosthenes returns to the theme of Philip's employing conspirators when he lumps Aeschines together with other Greeks who have deceived, corrupted, enslaved, and betrayed their communities to Philip in order to satisfy their greed and other desires. In contrast, Demosthenes asserts, his own policy has freed Athens from shameful and notorious conspiracy (*sustasis*), wickedness, and the betrayal of Greek freedom.[12]

Aeschines, conversely, turns the refusal to assist Philip into a plot. In his speech *On the Embassy,* he describes Demosthenes and others who opposed joining Philip in his campaign against Phocis in 346, and so pre-

---

8. See below, as well as Usher 1993, 8; cf. Ryder 2000, 45.
9. Dem. 6.2, 6–8; cf. 6.13, 16–19, 26–29, 35; 9.27–28; 10.2, 12–13.
10. Dem. 8.34–37, 46; 9.17, 25–62, 69–72; 10.11, 15–16, 49–50, 60–61; cf. 18.66.
11. Esp. Dem. 18.31–41; 19.230, 315–25. For Demosthenes' reuse of these terms, including in relation to places outside Athens, see 18.25, 61, 163; cf. 6.12; 19.144.
12. Dem. 18.294–98; cf. 8.13, 20. For criticism of Demosthenes' slandering here of men who might have been Greek patriots, see Polybius 18.14, followed by Cawkwell 1996, 100, 104, 115.

sumably failed to influence his settlement of the Third Sacred War and especially to mitigate his punishment of Phocis, as co-conspirators against the common good (Aes. 2.138). He uses a similar accusation, with the usual allegation of bribery, when he charges Demosthenes with conspiring with Philocrates against Athenian interests (Aes. 2.54; 3.58).

As the above assertions suggest, plotting charges belonged to the arsenal of feuding politicians, who traded them in the form of unspecific accusations or in relation to the same issue or event. Thus, joining Philip's war against Phocis was as much a conspiracy as staying out of it. Similarly, Demosthenes maintains that Aeschines was corrupt and had sold himself to Philip when the two were members of the first Athenian embassy that went to Macedonia to negotiate peace in 346 (Dem. 19.13). Aeschines, who rightly understands this as allegation of conspiracy (Aes. 2.123), retaliates with charges of duplicity and lack of collegiality toward his fellow envoys on Demosthenes' part, which he terms plotting (Aes. 2.22, 43, 54, 97). In anticipation of the last charge, Demosthenes claims to have been victimized by the envoys' plots throughout the journey and says that he had the choice of either joining them in their wrongdoing or becoming their prosecutor (Dem. 19.188). It should be noted that Demosthenes' description of the embassy earlier in his speech mentions no plot against him but only disagreements among its members. His conspiracy charge is as well founded as most of the accusations hitherto mentioned and is designed in this particular case to legitimize his opposition to the peace and his breach of solidarity with men with whom he had shared a table, duty, and probably even policy (cf. Dem. 19.202).

Elsewhere in the speech, Demosthenes uses charges of conspiracy to depict Aeschines as an enemy of the polis and its government (Dem. 19.110, 175, 294–95).[13] His and Aeschines' varied use of plotting accusations, the ease with which they throw them at each other, and the conventionality of these charges, diminishes their credibility in modern eyes. Already in the fifth century, Aristophanes could mock charges of political conspiracy and treason, suggesting a similar skepticism on the part

---

13. Aeschines mocks another of Demosthenes' plotting charges against him, namely, that he had sneaked out of his tent one night, rowed to Philip's quarters, and helped the king to write a letter to the Athenians that persuaded them to support the peace (Aes. 2.124–25). Demosthenes' extant speech, however, fails to mention Aeschines' rowing and gives a different time and place for Aeschines' nocturnal visit to Philip (Dem. 19.36, 175). For attempts to reconcile the differences in this collusion tale, see Harris 1995, 178 n. 6; Paulsen 1999, 433–34.

of at least some Athenians (see chapter 4 above). Yet it would be safe to assume that both Demosthenes and Aeschines were aware of this risk. That they nevertheless used these charges frequently implies that they feared losing their audience's trust less than they hoped to appeal to an Athenian conspiratorial worldview that would render their allegations plausible.

All these charges and countercharges appear in forensic speeches that tend to focus more on Philip's local collaborators than on the plots and culpability of their alleged employer. Demosthenes has the former even exceeding the king's expectations of cooperation or independently initiating deception and acts of collusion (Dem. 19.68–69, 122–25, 136). Such presentations are largely owing to the constraints of arguing a case in court, not against Philip, but against his alleged partners. In addition, speakers have to take into account the distinction the Athenians make between an outsider, who is semi-entitled to conspire and bribe to further his cause, and insiders who deserve nothing but indignation and harsh punishment for helping him (see Introduction). In contrast, some of Demosthenes' deliberative speeches fail to show equal interest, if any, in the king's local collaborators.

An examination of this orator's extant deliberative speeches shows, in fact, that it took him time to develop the theme of Philip's collusions with Athenian agents.[14] The closest he comes to it in the *First Philippic* (Dem. 4), delivered in 352/1, which is his first surviving speech dealing with the king, is an aside about those who make it their business to inform Philip about Athenian affairs and a warning that the Athenians will have to fight the king in Attica if they fail to fight him in northern Greece (4.18, 50). Demosthenes' next speech, the *First Olynthiac* (Dem. 1), delivered in 349, focuses on the need to send aid to Olynthus lest Philip descend on Attica, but mentions no conspiracy. The *Second Olynthiac,* (Dem. 2), delivered in the same year, has much to say about Philip's egoistical search for fame, his wickedness, and his growing in power through deceit and false promises, but nothing about his plotting against Athens or about Athenian traitors. Demosthenes' subsequent *Third Olynthiac* (Dem. 3), also delivered in 349, refers to Athenian politicians busy enriching themselves and wresting power from the people (Dem. 3.30–32), but not to any plot.

---

14. In the following, I adopt Sealey's chronology of Demosthenes' public speeches, which is based on Dionysius of Halicarnassus's dates (*Ad Ammaeum* 1.4, 10): Sealey 1955; 1993.

It is in his next extant speech, *On the Peace* (Dem. 5), delivered in 346, that the orator alludes for the first time to a local collaborator with the Macedonian king. He reminds the Athenians how he, alone of all the Athenians, had identified the actor Neoptolemus, who had supported talking peace with the king, as Philip's man (5.6–9). It should be noted, however, that he makes this point not so much to deplore the actor's or the king's machinations as to highlight his own powers of observation and to show that he was right and the people were wrong about Neoptolemus. He strengthens his claim to possess superior acumen when he maintains that he, unlike some other speakers, does not make optimistic statements about good prospects for Athens in Boeotia, Euboia, and Amphipolis following the peace with Philip, and that those who make these deceptive promises are talking nonsense. He attributes his exceptional wisdom in politics to good fortune and to the fact that that his political speeches and actions are disinterested and not influenced by hope of gain (Dem. 5.9–12; cf. 9.5). The last fleeting remark about bribes must have had a minimal impact in a speech that revolves mostly around the speaker's qualified support of the peace.

Demosthenes' oblique reference to corrupt politicians becomes clearer and more assertive in his *Second Philippic,* delivered in 344, where he accuses anonymous politicians of taking bribes from Philip to mislead the people with promises of benefits to Athens following the peace (Dem. 6.29–34). In his prosecution speech against Aeschines the following year, Demosthenes goes further and identifies these politicians as Philocrates and especially Aeschines, greatly expanding on the latter's collusion with Philip to deceive the people with empty promises for money (Dem. 19, esp. 19–28, 41–46). The difference in presentation is partly owing to Demosthenes' generally refraining in his deliberative speeches from abusing or maligning resident Athenians by name or in great detail.[15] But, and as indicated above, it is also due to his different objectives in the deliberative and forensic speeches. While his goal in *On the False Embassy* is to convict Aeschines of public misconduct, in the deliberative speeches, he chiefly strives to demonstrate his unique political skills, to

---

15. Plut. *Moral.* 810d has noticed this practice and Demosthenes' extant Assembly speeches bear him out; cf. Trevett 1996, 432. Public speakers in Thucydides, as well as the speakers of And. 3, [Dem.] 7; 11; 17, behave similarly. Hence Sealey's (1993, 233) assumption that Demosthenes' naming his opponents was excised from the Assembly speeches prior to publication is unnecessary. Dem. 10.70–74 and persons no longer living in the city (Dem. 2.19; 5.6–8) are the exceptions.

blame his rivals for the Athenians' disappointments in the peace with Philip, and to warn the demos that Philip poses a present danger.

Since not all of Demosthenes' deliberative speeches have survived, it would be unwise to argue that he sharpened the tone and increased the volume of his conspiracy allegations only starting in 346-4, the dates of Dem. 5 and 6. Yet several considerations make these dates or their proximity likely. In 346, Demosthenes was about thirty-eight years old, still relatively young for a public speaker, and he may have been apprehensive earlier about incurring the resentment of other, more senior, politicians with his charges of conspiracy.[16] In addition, prior to the controversies over the peace with Philip, or before the Athenians showed their disappointment with the peace and were divided on how to interpret Philip's subsequent actions, there were too few occasions to make charges of plotting by Philip's local hirelings seem likely.[17] Demosthenes himself declares in the *Third Philippic,* delivered in 341, that he dates (literally, has marked out) Philip's war with Athens from the destruction of Phocis in 346 (Dem. 9.19). The fact is that he had warned the Athenians that Philip was their enemy and that they might have to fight him close to home starting at least in 352/1 (Dem. 4.50; cf. 2.25). His redating of the conflict to 346, however, suggests that the Athenians had been less apprehensive of a Macedonian threat earlier, and hence less receptive to allegations of plotting.[18]

Thus, up to 346, Demosthenes uses the theme of Philip's machinations and his colluding with local Athenians only sparingly. He has more to say about it in his *Second Philippic,* delivered in 344, where he discusses Philip's plots against Greece, and in particular Athens, and charges nameless politicians with cooperating with the Macedonian king

---

16. In 346, Demosthenes was the youngest of the ten envoys sent to Philip to discuss peace terms in the first Athenian embassy to the king (Aes. 2.22). Cawkwell's (1996, 101-4) conclusion that Demosthenes' "obsession" with Philip's corrupting politicians began with his prosecution of Aeschines in 343 underestimates the occurrence of the charge in earlier deliberative speeches and of the theme of bribed politicians in Demosthenes' public and forensic speeches of the 350s (Dem. 15.30-33; 23.201; 24.146-47). See also Buckler 2000, 133.

17. See above for Aeschines' failure to persuade the Greeks about Philip's threat following the fall of Olynthus in 348. Buckler 1996, 77-85, thinks that Philip had no intention of damaging Athens' interests outside northeastern Greece before his settlement of the Sacred War in 346. It should be said in fairness that it is unknown how many Athenians shared this view. For Philip's attempts to reconcile with Athens in the late 340s: Ellis 1976, 143-56; Cawkwell 1978b, 123-26.

18. See also Ryder 2000, 45, 50, 58. Fisher 2001, 62-67, detects a drive to strengthen Athens' institutional and moral fabric in 346. Wallace 2000, 590, dates the turning point in Athenian public opinion against Philip to the summer and fall of 343.

(6.29–34). Demosthenes' aim is to persuade an audience still doubtful as to whether Philip is indeed their enemy that the king's military and diplomatic activities are geared primarily against them, and that they should play the role of Philip's staunch and unselfish foe that Demosthenes wants them to. It should be noted, however, that the speaker's charges against bribed speakers occupy a relatively small space in the speech.

Demosthenes *On the Chersonese* (Dem. 8), delivered in 342/1, resembles the *Second Philippic* in its treatment of the topic.[19] The speaker reiterates his warning that Athens and its democracy are the chief object of Philip's plots and implies that those who oppose fighting Philip and offer to recall the Athenian general Diopeithes from Thrace and thereabouts, where he had clashed with Philip, have colluded with the king (8.4–20; cf. 8.40–43; 10.11, 15). He also harps on the theme of missing opportunities when he reproaches the Athenians for warning other Greeks of Philip's designs while taking no action to frustrate them (8.34–37). As in Dem. 6, however, his plotting charges do not constitute a major theme in the speech.

Demosthenes' *Third Philippic* (Dem. 9), delivered in 342/1 as well, is more hostile to local politicians than any other public speech discussed hitherto. The reason is unclear; it may have to do with temporary intensification of political rivalry in the city. Demosthenes commences the speech by identifying the chief culprits responsible for Athens's plight with speakers trying to curry favor with the people, but not, as in his earlier speeches, with Philip or the complacent demos (9.1–3). To explain Philip's success, he contrasts the past, when those who had taken bribes from the Persians had been severely punished, with the present, when individuals take bribes openly and are even envied for doing so (9.36–39; cf. 19.259, 268–72). At the same time, he greatly expands on Philip's aggression toward Greeks in general and Athens in particular, and how he secures allies and power on the Greek mainland through local traitors (9.7, 27–28, 56–63). The last point aims to show the demos what happens when they do not listen to men (i.e., Demosthenes) who say what is best for the city.

---

19. Since Dem. 8.38–67 and 10.11–27, 55–70 largely duplicate each other, scholars have debated which speech was delivered first, and if one of them was delivered at all. See note 22 below and Adams 1938; Daitz 1957; Sealey 1993, 232–33; Trevett 1996, 429–30, 438–39; Hadjú 2002, esp. 44–49, 451–72. For the purpose of this discussion I accept the view that only 8.1–37 was delivered on this occasion, while the rest of the speech better fitted Dem. 10, which was given shortly afterward. The analysis offered here, however, should not offend those who believe in the integrity of Dem. 8 (myself, till recently, included).

One of the examples that Demosthenes uses to illustrate this point also shows how he handles the theme of shared responsibility and culpability between external and internal plotters. He reports on a power struggle in the city of Oreus in Euboia (in 343–32) between Philistides and his comrades, who were acting for Philip, and one Euphraeus, who stood for the people's freedom. The people, however, treated Euphraeus with contempt. A year before the Macedonians captured Oreus, Euphraeus had indicted Philistides as a traitor. Then many men had come together, with Philip as their financial backer (*chorēgos*), and taking charge, they had imprisoned Euphraeus for causing troubles in the city. The demos, far from helping Euphraeus and punishing his opponents harshly, rejoiced in Euphraeus's lot and thought that he deserved it. Consequently, Euphraeus's rivals were free to plot the city's capture, because no one dared oppose them for fear of suffering Euphraeus's fate. Some offered resistance only when the enemy was already at the gates, while others betrayed the city. The result was that Philistides and his friends became tyrants of Oreus, and those who opposed Euphraeus for selfish reasons were exiled or executed. Euphraeus himself committed suicide, thus showing the justice of his opposition to Philip. Lest the audience fail to grasp the implications of this warning tale for Athens, Demosthenes equates speaking for Philip with the search for popularity and saying what is best for the city with the need to tell the demos things they do not care to hear (9.59–65).[20]

Demosthenes' aims in this quasi-allegorical story are to cast himself as a patriotic democrat and malign those who oppose confronting Philip as either the king's intentional or unwitting collaborators in pandering to their audience. He also wishes to warn and rebuke those in the audience who have failed to support him and gullibly trusted his rivals. Noteworthy, however, is the relatively secondary role that he allows Philip in the affair. The king is the underwriter of the conspiracy, but the plotting is mostly the work of local conspirators, who are less his puppets than his partners (cf. 10.4–5; 19.136). This construction has less to do with Demosthenes' wish to reconstruct events in Oreus accurately than with attaining the rhetorical ends just mentioned. Indeed, elsewhere in this speech, Demosthenes makes Philip's dispatching of troops responsible for Philistides' tyranny, because the point there is to illustrate the king's

20. For the affair, see Cawkwell 1963, esp. 201–3 = Perlman 1973, 166–68; 1978a; 1978b, 132; Ellis 1976, 164, 282 nn. 22–29; Sealey 1993, 175–77, 261–62.

ubiquitous intervention in Greek affairs.[21] It appears, then, that Demosthenes focuses on Philip's machinations when he wishes to explain his policy and to scare the Athenians into fighting him. When he strives to convince them of his own patriotism and the superiority of his advice over competing recommendations, however, he marginalizes the king and dwells on his opponents' corrupt policies. The space he allots to each of these themes or to their combination in his deliberative speeches may have also been a function of his need to respond to attacks on him and his policy.

Demosthenes' *Fourth Philippic* (Dem. 10), perhaps delivered in 341/0, adds its own nuances to the themes of Philip's schemes and his Athenian hirelings.[22] As in the previous speeches, Demosthenes makes Athens the main target of Philip's hostile designs and actions, although he adds a war against the Persian king to Philip's plans (10.15, 32). When he comes to deal with Philip's Athenian agents, he asserts that while the worthy political advisor (such as he) urges the city to check Philip's aggression, those in Philip's pay accuse the good speaker of warmongering, of trying to deplete the city's wealth, and of ignoring the sufferings caused by war. The purpose of their scheme (*to kataskeuasma*) is to put those who speak best for the city on trial, win popularity, protect their source of income from Philip, and allow the latter to wage his campaign uninterrupted (Dem. 10.55–60). Demosthenes thus delegitimizes any credible opposition to a war with Macedonia as a conspiracy.[23] Shortly afterward, he allows himself an untypical outburst. Claiming that Athens faces a life-and-death battle with Philip, he calls upon his hearers to deliver to public execution those who have sold themselves to the king, because it is impossible to overcome the external enemy before punishing the enemy within (10.62- 63; cf. 8.60–61; 9.53). Yet this impassioned call pales in comparison to the centrality of other points in the speech, such as that the peace with Philip is not a real peace, that Philip poses a

---

21. Dem. 9.33; cf. 8.18, 36 with scholia, 59; 9.12, 10.9, 61; 18.71, 81. It is noteworthy that the second-century historian Carystius reports that Philip's general Parmenion executed Euphraeus: Athenaeus 508e.
22. On the scholarly debate over the authenticity and delivery of Dem. 10, see note 19 above. Worthington 1991, and Trevett 1996, 429–30, 438–39, think that the extant version of Dem. 10 is a draft, while Sealey 1993, 182, 233, argues for its actual delivery; *contra*: Usher 1999, 241; Milns 2000, 205.
23. The comparable passage in Dem. 8.52–58 has identical charges, though their conspiratorial dimension is toned down. The difference indicates the license speakers enjoy in making these charges.

great danger, and that the Athenians should do something about it before they come to regret their inaction.

All in all, Demosthenes does not privilege the rhetoric of conspiracy by, or with, Philip in his deliberative speeches. Although he uses it to warn the Athenians of the king and to make sense of his policy, he seems to have judged it less effective in stirring them into action than his appeals to their competitive and manly ideology, their opportunism and self-interest, and their tradition of patriotic sacrifice for the city and other Greeks.

Yet both he and other speakers are well aware of the traducing quality of the accusations of plotting with Philip. Thus, we find the author of *On Halonnesus* ([Dem.] 7), delivered possibly by the politician Hegesippus in 342, asserting that Philip allows himself to demand concessions from Athens because he relies on local friends, who are loyal to him rather than to the polis, take his bribes, and instruct him as to what to tell the Athenians ([Dem.] 7.17–18, 23). The author of the speech *Regarding Philip's Letter* ([Dem.] 11), possibly the historian Anaximenes of Lampsacus, perhaps writing for delivery in 340, makes similar charges. Among the reasons he enumerates for Philip's success in his conflict with Athens are hired rhetors, who shamefully serve him and gullibly trade his bribes for the state. He also discusses Philip's deceit, plotting, greed, and violence in an effort to present him as a giant with feet of clay, ready to collapse at the first sign of failure ([Dem.] 11.7, 18, cf. 3).[24] The charge of plotting with Philip for profit was so common that Philip himself used it against his Athenian detractors, reportedly saying that Athenian sycophants both asked him for money and slandered him ([Dem.] 7.21; cf. 12.20).

Isocrates, however, alludes to an additional incentive for making such charges. In the same passage in which he alludes to the "word makers" who attribute plans to take over Greece to Philip, he also discusses the consumers of their rhetoric. He divides the latter into those "who covet" the pessimistic scenarios of Macedonian occupation described by the speakers, fools who are grateful for those who pretend to fear for them, and men who admire Philip's hegemonic ambitions (Isoc. 5.73–75). Isocrates' criticism aside, this attests to the popular appreciation of those who expose plots to harm the polis and its government.

---

24. [Dem.] 7: Libanius's *Hypothesis to Dem. 7;* Sealey 1993, 177–78. [Dem.] 11: Sealey 1993, 239–40, but see Trevett 1996, 440, on the possibility that this speech was composed by Demosthenes, though not delivered in its extant form.

Politicians, then, were motivated to detect conspiracies and harmful designs, because in addition to earning public gratitude, they showed by doing so that they were better and smarter than other politicians, and even the demos (cf. Thuc. 3.82.5). Aeschines is reported to have boasted that he was the first and only speaker to realize that Philip was plotting against the Greeks and to have alerted the Athenians, Arcadians, and other Greeks about the king's designs, albeit unsuccessfully (Dem. 19.9–12; 302–6). Demosthenes, as we have seen, claimed the unique distinction of having perceptively exposed the actor Neoptolemus as Philip's accomplice (Dem. 5.6–9). In his speech *On the Crown*, he reminds his audience of how he had caught (ca. 343) the former Athenian citizen Antiphon, who had promised Philip to burn the dockyards of the Piraeus, and of the fact that Antiphon had been executed notwithstanding the demos's initial error of failing to convict him and Aeschines' efforts to rescue the spy by complaining about Demosthenes' hubristic treatment of him. As this shows, the discovery of a plot moved the public detective's rivals to dispute its validity and discredit his motives and conduct. According to Aeschines' biased account, Demosthenes had contrived (*kateskeuasas*) to charge one Anaxinus of Oreus with spying for Philip when Demosthenes himself was about to be impeached by Aeschines (some time between 343–340). Following Anaxinus's execution, Aeschines charged Demosthenes in the Assembly with torturing and proposing the death penalty for Anaxinus, even though he had been Demosthenes' friend (*philos* and *xenos*). Aeschines adds that Demosthenes tried afterward to fabricate a charge of revolution against Aeschines based on forged letters, arresting spies, and torturing informants (Aes. 3.223–25). Demosthenes responds by accusing Aeschines of meeting privately with Anaxinus, which made him no less a spy and an enemy (Dem. 18.137). The mutual recriminations attest to the high value Athenians set on exposing plots, which explains the integration of charges of conspiracy into contests over political supremacy and survival.[25]

It is no wonder, then, that the rhetoric of averting dangerous plots and countering it by calling the plot detector an abuser of conspiracy charges survived the feud between Demosthenes and Aeschines. In 324/3, about seven years after Aeschines had left Athens to go into exile, Demos-

---

25. For the Antiphon's affair and its date: Dem. 18.132–34; Din. 1.63; Plut. *Dem.* 14; Carlier 1990, 180–81; Worthington 1992, 227–28; Harris 1995, 121, 169–70, 205 n. 32; Wallace 2000, 574–75, 590, 592. For Anaxinus's trial: Hansen 1975, 103 no. 111. See also note 27 below.

thenes' adversaries recycled his accusation that Demosthenes made conspiracy allegations to save his skin. According to a speech written by Dinarchus, Demosthenes had preempted his own trial on bribery charges by impeaching one Callimedon for conspiring with exiles in Megara to overthrow the Athenian democracy and then dropped the charge, and he had falsely informed the Assembly about a conspiracy against the Piraeus dockyards on this or a different occasion (Din. 1.94–95).[26] It is permissible to assume that Demosthenes protested the charge as a debasement of a patriotic act or countered it with plotting allegations of his own, as he had done in the case of the spy Anaxinus.

The fact that Demosthenes had a long record of unmasking spies and foiling plots, or of alleging conspiracies, does not mean that all of his accusations were unfounded. The extant evidence is too scanty or tendentious to allow us to come to a reliable conclusion one way or other.[27] But regardless of the merit of his charges, he was surely aware that they might enhance his image as the people's guardian. In this, he was no innovator but rather showed his affinity to Aristophanes' Cleon/Paphlagonian, who describes himself as the demos's best friend, who alone put a stop to conspiracies, knew about every conspiracy in town, and immediately "hollered" about them (Aristoph. *Knights* 860–63). The detector of plots performed a valuable public service, which gave him a political advantage, especially when he did it exclusively or first.[28]

---

26. For the case against Callimedon, see Hansen 1975, 111 n. 129; Worthington 1992, 264–65; Rubinstein 2000, 121 n. 107.

27. For the likelihood of the truth of Demosthenes' charges against Antiphon, see Usher 1993, 217–18; *contra,* Harris 1995, 121, who thinks that Demosthenes was "fomenting a witch-hunt against Philip's supporters." Cf. Carlier 1990, 181; Wallace 2000, 590. See Din. 1.62–63 for Demosthenes' direct and indirect involvements in other trials against men charged with treason.

28. Cf. Hesk 2000, 239.

CHAPTER 7

International Conspiracies

The idea that individuals, and especially associations or organizations, conspire to cause harm from afar by playing nation against nation or creating divisions within a nation, is common in modern conspiracism and growing more popular with the advance of globalization. The closest one comes to this notion in fourth-century Greece is Demosthenes' portrayal of Philip of Macedon as constantly interfering in Greek affairs, and another speechwriter's charge that Cleomenes of Naucratis in Egypt was attempting to control the international grain trade.

PLOTTING WAR: PHILIP AND THE FOURTH SACRED WAR

The perception of Philip as an international plotter inspires Demosthenes' account of the outbreak of the so-called Fourth Sacred War. Briefly, the war grew out of a violent clash between the Amphictyonic League, which administered and protected the temple of Apollo at Delphi, and the Locrian state of Amphissa in early 340/39. It ended with Philip's punishing Amphissa in 339, after he had been asked by the Amphictyonians to lead the war against it. Philip's Amphissan campaign was preceded by his capture of the Phocian city of Elatea, an act that greatly alarmed the Athenians, who had been in a state of war with him since 340 and expected him to continue his march from there to Athens. The two powers eventually clashed in the battle of Chaeronea in 338, which ended in an Athenian defeat, but many Athenians believed that the Amphissan war had allowed Philip to move his forces into central Greece and eventually against their city and against Thebes, their ally.[1]

The Amphissan war furnished material for mutual recriminations between Aeschines and Demosthenes. In the course of a trial in 330, initiated six years earlier by Aeschines against a proposal to crown Demosthenes for his public service, Aeschines blamed Demosthenes for preventing Athens from joining this just holy war. Demosthenes, for his part, accused Aeschines of conspiring with Philip to instigate the war and, hence, with responsibility for its adverse effects on Athens and Greece. The purpose of the following examination is to discuss the rhetoric of conspiring war and to establish its validity.[2]

Aeschines, who as a prosecutor enjoyed the right of presenting his version of the events first, places the story of the war at the outset of what he describes as the third period of Demosthenes' destructive career. He begins by impressing upon the jurors the grave sacrilege committed by the Amphissans when they cultivated the plain of Cirrha and collected dues from a nearby harbor, both consecrated to Apollo. In order to check any action against them in the Amphictyonic Council or in Athens, the Amphissans retained Demosthenes' services. Some time later (340/39), the Athenians sent a three-member embassy, including Aeschines, to the Amphictyonic Council in Delphi. The Amphissans, instigated by Thebes, charged Athens before the council with having improperly dedicated shields in the new Delphic temple of Apollo prior to its consecration and moved to fine the Athenians fifty talents and to ban them from entering the temple. Since the two other Athenian envoys fell sick, the chief Athenian envoy asked Aeschines to speak for Athens, which Aeschines was determined to do in any case. His impatient entrance into the council allowed an Amphissan delegate to launch a bitter attack on Athens. Aeschines, full of patriotic indignation, retorted with a speech, which he recounts in loving detail to the audience, that succeeded in turning the tables on the Amphissans and making their sacrilege the target of an Amphictyonic action. The next day, a crowd consisting of Amphictyonic delegates and residents of Delphi descended on the plain of Cirrha and the harbor and destroyed and burned some structures, but was put to flight

---

1. On the Fourth Sacred War see, e.g., Wankel 1976, 821–22; Sealey 1978, 310–16; Londey 1990; Harris 1995, 126–32; Sánchez 2001, 227–45; Buckler 2003, 489–96. Its chronology: Londey 1995, 240–41; Buckler 2003, 490 n. 1, who is exceptional in dating Philip's Amphissan campaign prior to his capture of Elatea; cf. Plut. *Dem.* 18.1.

2. [Plut.] *Moralia* 840b–c and perhaps Strabo 9.3.4 also report on the conflict, but their information has no independent value: Sánchez 2001, 236 n. 60.

by an Amphissan armed force. The following day, Cottyphus, the Thessalian representative to the Amphictyonic Council and its presiding officer, moved in the Amphictyonic Assembly to convene a special meeting in Thermopylae in order to discuss how to punish the Amphissans for their sacrilege.

According to Aeschines, when the Athenian embassy had returned home from Delphi and reported what had happened, the people were ready to act reverently (i.e., join the anti-Amphissan action) in spite of the opposition of the Amphissan hireling Demosthenes. Unable to mislead the people openly, this speaker opted for clandestine means. He went to the Council, arranged for it to meet in secret, and, taking advantage of the inexperience of a certain councilman, had him draft a proposal that effectively made Athens neutral, which was brought to the Assembly. Demosthenes then managed to pass it in the Assembly when it was adjourning and after most people, including Aeschines, had already left. The decree read well but was in fact shameful. Aeschines cites it as instructing the Athenian representatives to the Amphictyonic Council to go there at the time designated by the Athenian ancestors and forbidding them from joining other delegates in word, decision, or action. The speaker interprets the motion as aiming to prevent the Athenian delegates from attending the special Amphictyonic meeting and Athens from acting piously. The outcome was that representatives of Athens and Thebes did not attend the Amphictyonic Council. The Amphictyonians decided against Amphissa and elected the Thessalian Cottyphus as their general. In an aside, Aeschines remarks that Philip was far away in Scythia at that time, even though Demosthenes would argue that Aeschines had been responsible for bringing him down on Greece. The Amphictyonians' campaign against Amphissa resulted in the imposition of a fine, the expulsion of those responsible for the sacrilege, and the restoration of Amphissan exiles. The Amphissans, however, did not pay the fine or allow the exiles to return, and even banished those restored by the Amphictyonians. Because of this conduct, the Amphictyonians later launched a second campaign against them under the leadership of Philip, who had returned from Scythia by now. Aeschines concludes his account with a dramatic statement that the gods had granted Athens the leadership of the pious cause, but that Demosthenes' bribe-taking had prevented the city from assuming it (Aes. 3.106–129).

Aeschines' purpose is to discredit Demosthenes' sensible (and successful) attempt to keep Athens out of the Amphissan war as an evil conspiracy. But he also wishes to justify his own conduct in the affair, and to account for his failure to persuade the Athenians to follow his anti-Amphissan and anti-Theban policy. Indeed, his charge against Demosthenes of bribe-taking is conventional, unproven, and does not become more credible just because he repeats it several times. In a variant on his depiction of Demosthenes' collaboration with Philocrates, discussed in chapter 6, he describes the standard legislative practice of cooperation between a public actor and a councilman in producing an item for the Assembly's agenda as a trick played by a clever politician on a naïve man who lacked the former's expertise and experience.[3] He seeks to prove that Demosthenes' decree was deceptive and harmful on the basis of what the decree did *not* say and by relying on people's search for a hidden agenda. Variations of the charge that the orator had taken advantage of the sparse attendance in the Assembly to pass his proposal recurs in other speeches with a frequency that makes it border on a rhetorical topos.[4]

Yet Aeschines' portrayal of Demosthenes as a mighty trickster is also designed to explain his own failure to stop him. For example, Demosthenes' arranging for a secret Council meeting to discuss his proposal enabled him to dupe the people and to prevent any nonmember, including Aeschines, from attending and finding out about it. The same holds true for Demosthenes' waiting for the members of the Assembly, Aeschines included, to disperse before voting on his decree. One is struck by the orator's manipulative powers that enabled him to induce one councilman to move his proposal and the chairman of the Assembly, whom Aeschines neglects to include in the conspiracy, to place it at the end of the session. Moreover, Aeschines' departure prior to the introduction of the decree is somewhat puzzling, given that the proposal, in one form or another, had most likely been put on the Assembly's agenda, which was normally posted prior to its meeting. It appears that this public watchdog fell asleep. His version of events exonerates the people of having passed an allegedly bad decree, and especially himself of having failed to oppose it.[5]

---

3. On legislative cooperation, see Rhodes 1985, 57; Hansen 1987, 59, 80, 163 n. 488. Cf. Dem. *Pr.* 52 for associating politicians who deceive the demos with contriving, craftiness, trickery, and hiring their services to others.
4. See Dem. 18.149; 24.47; 57.8–10; cf. Aristophanes *Eccless.* 376–94. Calhoun 1913, 124, 129–30 regards this ploy as common practice, and too readily ascribes it to the working of political clubs. The verb *diaprattō* that Aeschines uses for effecting the trick is characteristic of plotters and deceivers.
5. On administering the Assembly and drafting the agenda: *Ath. Pol.* 43.4, 44.2–3; Hansen 1987, 27, 99. Publication of the Assembly's agenda in advance: *Ath. Pol.* 44.2;

In addition to depicting Demosthenes as a corrupt politician and legislative plotter, Aeschines presents the origins of the Amphissan war in such a way as to show an attempt to exclude the possibility that he had been involved in any plot to provoke it on Philip's behalf. This was Demosthenes' contention, and even though he spoke after Aeschines, the latter's remark that Demosthenes will say that he was responsible for bringing Philip down on Greece shows that he was familiar with it either prior to the trial or certainly following it and before his speech was circulated in public.[6] Accordingly, he highlights the motifs of divine intervention and spontaneity, which run counter to plotting. Thus, after stressing the Amphissans' sacrilege and Demosthenes' ignoble collusion with them, he prefaces his role in the affair by proclaiming that divine power (*daimōn*) and fortune (*tukhē*) had prevailed over the Amphissans' impiety (Aes. 3.115). He reports that he entered the Council meeting angrily and impatiently, that is, not with a plotter's cold calculation.[7] His description of the debate in the Amphictyonic Council and the subsequent march to the Cirrhan plain evinces not a plan but a frenzy of emotions and actions (3.117–23).

In addition, Aeschines' arranges the events in Delphi in a tight chronological and causal sequence that leaves no room for a plot or for Philip's involvement. In his account, the Athenian embassy learned about the Amphissans' anti-Athenian motion not in advance but upon their arrival in Delphi. This led to Aeschines' speech against Amphissa, which had not been planned but was the result of the Amphissan provocation and the other envoys being disabled. The discussion in the Council on punishing the Amphissans had lasted until late in the day, which was the reason for the Delphian herald's call for the Delphians to march on the plain the day after. The march began at dawn, ended in a flight, and was followed the day after by a meeting and a resolution to call a special Amphictyonic meeting to deal with Amphissa. These hectic activities and the crowded timetable are framed in a way that makes each event the outcome of the one that preceded it, rather than of a guiding hand.

The narrative then moves to Athens and to the Amphictyonians' later clashes with Amphissa, but Aeschines takes care to point out that Philip

---

45.4; cf. *IG* II² 206. The Byzantine scholar Photius, s.v. *propempta,* as well as *lex Seg.* 296.8–11, mention four days' advance notice for a regular meeting. See Hansen 1987, 24; 1991, 133.

6. Aes. 3.128. The odds are even for each of these possibilities. See [Dem.] 53.14 for an example of a disclosure of arguments to an adversary.

7. Cf. Roux 1979, 32–33; Usher 1993, 225.

was in distant Scythia at the time, and that his campaign against Amphissa took place only much later (3.128–29). Both assertions intend to exclude the possibility of the king's having orchestrated the conflict or of Aeschines' having had anything to do with it. Indeed, Aeschines is careful to delineate his role in the affair as merely redirecting the Amphictyonians' wrath from Athens to Amphissa. He states that he left the Council after making his speech and let other people, be they the Delphian herald or the Thessalian Cottyphus, initiate later events and actions.[8] He reports taking part and even risking his life in the march on Amphissa, but the herald's proclamation that failure to join the march would put a polis under a curse and bar its citizens from entering Apollo's temple had justified his doing so (Aes. 3.122–23). The subsequent events were outside his control, thanks to Demosthenes' decree. Thus, rather than privileging Demosthenes' conspiracy theory with detailed refutation or close attention, Aeschines construes his tale so as to make a conspiracy scenario unthinkable.

The speaker fails to mention, however, that when Philip answered the call to fight Amphissa, he did not lead his army there but first seized Elateia. He also does not report that Philip had tried unsuccessfully to entice Thebes to be his ally against Athens, and that his advance was blocked by a joint Athenian-Theban army. The omissions are partly because of the Athenians' familiarity with these events and partly because they do not serve his position that Athens could have joined Macedonia against Amphissa and Thebes rather than follow Demosthenes' advocacy of a coalition with the latter against Philip. Like most Athenians, he must have acknowledged that the Fourth Sacred War occasioned Philip's capture of Elateia, forced Thebes to decide between an alliance with Macedonia and one with Athens, and eventually led to Athens's defeat at Chaeronea. He thought, however, that these developments were preventable, while Demosthenes saw them as inevitable.[9] Indeed, Demosthenes' version of the outbreak of this war makes it the outcome of a well-planned plot and shows that it led to Macedonian domination of Greece.

Demosthenes discusses the Fourth Sacred War in the part of his

---

8. As *pulagoras*, an elected representative to the Amphictyonic meeting, as opposed to the *hieromnēmōn*, an appointed state representative for one year, Aeschines could not participate or vote in the meeting: see Lefèvre 1998, 210, and generally, Sánchez 2001, 496–509.

9. Cf. Londey 1990, 254 n. 76. For these orators' different views of the state of the Athenian-Macedonian conflict at this stage, see Buckler 2000, 142–45.

speech dedicated to an attack on Aeschines' background, character, and career. He prefaces it by asserting Aeschines' mendacity and by calling on the gods to witness that he, in contrast, is telling the truth. After warning the audience not to underestimate Aeschines' wickedness, Demosthenes lays out his major thesis: that the Amphissan War was jointly contrived (*sunkataskeuasas*) by Aeschines and Philip, that it had brought the destroyer of the Greeks to Elateia as the Amphictyonians' leader, and that Aeschines was the source of the Athenians' great evils (18.143). But before discussing the preliminaries to the war, Demosthenes reminds the Athenians that when he had tried to warn them at that time that Aeschines was bringing war into Attica, he had been silenced or disbelieved.[10] In this way, the orator reconfirms his credentials as a public watchdog, as well his superior foresight and powers of observation, which render his version of the events credible, or at least should move the people not to heckle him again. He then introduces his audience to the plot by promising them that he will enlighten them about how the affair had been jointly prepared (*suneskeuasthē*) and coordinated (*suntethen*), as well as about Philip's cleverness (*deinotēs hen*).[11]

Demosthenes links the Amphissan conflict to Philip's great difficulties in his war against Athens and because of piracy. The king needed the Thessalians' or the Thebans' aid to contend with Athens, but realized that he would fail to persuade them to join him precisely because of his private feud with the Athenians.[12] He thought, however, that if he found a common cause and was chosen as its leader, he might succeed either by deception (*parakrousesthai*) or by persuasion. So he set out skillfully to get the Amphictyonians involved in a war and to confound their meeting, surmising that they would promptly ask him to take over. He realized that a representative of his or of his allies would raise the Thebans' or the Thessalians' suspicions, but that if the proposer were an envoy of his enemy, Athens, the king would easily escape notice. He managed this by hiring this man (Aeschines). As usual, no one in Athens was monitoring the situation, and Aeschines was elected as an envoy by three or four hands.

---

10. Dem. 18.143. Aeschines confirms this statement in a way when he mentions Demosthenes' initial failure to convince the demos that Aeschines had done wrong in Delphi: Aes. 3.125.
11. Dem. 18.144. For the negative meaning of these Greek words: Wankel 1976, 781, 789; cf. Yunis 2001, 196.
12. Dem. 18.147. Usher 1993, 224, sees the work of local agents in the prefix of *sumpeithoi* (lit., to persuade with) used in relation to the aforementioned potential allies; but see Wankel 1976, 791–92.

Arriving at the Amphictyonic meeting, Aeschines dedicated himself to the job for which he had been hired. He gave the Amphictyonic delegates, men unused to oratory and with little foresight, a fine speech that persuaded them to inspect land that the Locrian Amphissans claimed as their own, but that he presented as consecrated to Apollo. Demosthenes denied Aeschines' assertion that Amphissa had made any charges against Athens. His proof: they could nòt bring charges without a summons, but no such summons had been served on any magistrate or institution in the city, so Aeschines' contention was just a lie and an excuse (18.148–50). Guided by Aeschines, the Amphictyonians had toured the plain, but the Locrians surprised them and even captured some sacred delegates; hence, the complaints and the war against Amphissa. At first, the Thessalian Cottyphus had led an Amphictyonic army, but as some failed to rally to it and nothing was accomplished, those "who had been suborned" (*kateskeuasmenoi*) among the Thessalians and other cities immediately proposed electing Philip as commander at the next meeting (18.151–52). They gave reasonable grounds for their motion by contrasting it with the far less attractive options of paying taxes to finance a war, maintaining a mercenary force, or fining those who refused to contribute. In this way, Philip was elected as commander. He immediately collected forces, bade the people of Cirrha and Locris a warm goodbye, and went to seize Elateia instead. Demosthenes notes that if the Thebans had not been quick to change their minds (in favor of an alliance with Athens), Athens would have been overrun, but thanks to the gods and Demosthenes, Philip's advance was checked (18.153–54).

Demosthenes thus involves both Aeschines and Philip in an international conspiracy that included major and minor states all the way from Macedonia to Athens. He is not particularly consistent, however, in assigning the responsibility for the plot and its consequences. At first, he focuses almost exclusively on Aeschines' role in the affair and makes him chiefly responsible for the conspiracy's ruinous effects (18.140–43). Later, however, he portrays him as Philip's tool and the king as the prime plotter and the bane of Greece (18.147–57). Toward the end of his account, he brings Aeschines back to center stage and argues that Philip concealed his personal goal behind the common Amphictyonic cause, and that Aeschines had provided him with the means and the excuses and "jointly prepared" (*sumparaskeuasas*) all these. He also calls Aeschines the curse of everything that was destroyed: men, places, and cities (18.156, 158–59; cf. 163). Demosthenes' oscillation is probably owing to his wish to augment Aeschines' culpability, on the one hand,

and his concession to the communis opinio that held Philip as primarily responsible for anything that resulted in sufferings for the Greeks, on the other (18.158). The elasticity of the rhetoric of conspiracy, which allowed identifying an individual both as an agent and as the master plotter in the same plot, helped him to reallocate the blame within a short narrative span.

In addition to displaying many of the familiar marks of conspiracy tales, Demosthenes' plotting scenario includes some new ones. Philip is something of an exception among plotters in that he schemes from a position of relative weakness rather than strength vis-à-vis his intended victims. Yet the king's alleged plight makes his resorting to intrigues believable.[13] Demosthenes then maintains that the king had colluded with Aeschines based on their record of plotting together and by detecting a preconceived plan behind three loosely related facts: Aeschines' election to represent Athens (not Macedon) in what promised to be an uneventful meeting of the Amphictyonic Council, his initiating there of an anti-Amphissan action, and Philip's later march into central Greece.[14] Moreover, the orator recasts the entire affair as a plot against Athens, rather than as an Amphictyonic conflict that later escalated into a Macedonian-Athenian confrontation, thus showing a deterministic and Athenocentric interpretation of the events, as well as deducing motives from results—and, in this case, hardly anticipated results.[15]

Hindsight also allows Demosthenes to describe the plot as failure-proof. For example, the entire plot hinged on Aeschines' election as an envoy, which was neither predestined nor assured. Demosthenes accordingly uses Athenian apathy to account for this troublesome possibility. To enhance his plot scenario, he uses the same technique as

13. Harris 1995, 130, who rejects Demosthenes' version of the Amphissan affair, thinks, nevertheless, that Philip's difficulties were real. The possibility of a reuse of earlier Demosthenic material should not be excluded: Dem. 19.315-25 (including problems of piracy); cf. also 18.294-97; Griffith in Hammond and Griffith 1972, 2: 523-24; Wankel 1976, 786-87, 794; Yunis 2001, 195. Philip's difficulties also augment the villainy and treachery of his Athenian partner.

14. Aeschines and Philip's previous collaboration: e.g., Dem. 19.230; 18.31-41; cf. 19.144; 18.61. Georges Roux, inspired by Demosthenes' account and Parke's interpretation of it (1939), thinks that Aeschines knew in advance what would happen in Delphi, that he had planned to make charges against Amphissa, and that he may even have had a hand in provoking Thebes to incite Amphissa to propose the anti-Athenian motion following the dedication of Persian and Theban shields in the new Apollo temple: Roux 1979, 32-34; Parke 1939. Except for accusing Amphissa, not even Demosthenes makes such claims.

15. See, e.g., Schaefer 1856-58, 2: 539 n. 3; Wankel 1976, 794. Aristotle *Rhet.* 2.24.8 1401b29-34 complains against Demades for fallaciously using similar tactics against Demosthenes when he blamed the latter's prewar policy for subsequent evils, including the war.

Aeschines of arranging events in a tight logical and chronological order. He has Aeschines' speech in the Amphictyonic Council followed by what he calls their "tour" of the Cirrhan Plain, the Locrians' counterattack, and Cottyphus's unsuccessful campaign, but skips over events recorded by Aeschines such as the Amphictyonians' decision to reconvene after they had been repelled by the Locrians, the decisions of that meeting, and Cottyphus's punishment of Amphissa. Demosthenes says that following Cottyphus's failure, the move to elect Philip general was "immediately" contrived, and that after the Amphictyonians had been persuaded to give the king command, Philip "immediately" assembled an army, which he led to seize Elateia. At a minimum, the events just described spanned over six months.[16] Yet a plot scenario is intolerant of lags, interruptions, and digressions, because it draws its appeal from its neat logic and structure and from having everything in it fall into place.

Plotting tales also make the unpredictable predictable and the unlikely likely. Philip could tell that the Amphictyonians would request his help in a war that he had yet to provoke, because like other master planners, he could see two steps ahead of everybody. This skill and his corrupt agents also explain why he did not have to be on the spot when the Amphictyonians decided to march against Amphissa or later to make him their leader. Even though Athens was his enemy, his using an Athenian representative to instigate the war was not incredible but ingenious, because it fooled everybody, that is, the Thessalians, the Thebans, the Amphictyonians, the Locrians, and even the Athenians, except for Demosthenes (cf. Dem. 19.37–38, 324).

Throughout the account, the speaker labors both to slander Aeschines and to refute his version of the affair. Either because conspiratorial minds think alike or, no less likely, because he borrows motifs from Aeschines' version, he replaces Aeschines with himself as the gods' ally, gives him his role as Amphissa's hireling by changing it to Philip's employee, and substitutes Aeschines' election as a delegate thanks to the people's indifference for his own passing of a decree with only few men present. Conspirators, indeed, often take advantage of other people's negligence and ignorance. Demosthenes then implies that the Amphissans might have committed no crime and goes on to smartly use Aeschines' rendition of his rhetorical triumph at the Amphictyonic

---

16. This is Wüst's chronology (1938, 153–55), challenged by Griffith (Hammond and Griffith 1972, 2: 717–19), and defended by Sealey (1993, 311 n. 112); cf. Sánchez 2001, 228.

Council against him by converting it into the successful duping of a naïve audience. Thus, he can belittle Aeschines' accomplishment and saves himself the need to deal again with the irksome possibility that Aeschines' rhetorical success, and consequently that of the plot, was not self-evident or sufficient to create a war with Amphissa. He then tries to demolish Aeschines' main justification of his conduct in Delphi by claiming that Athens was never charged with sacrilege, as attested by the fact that no summons had been served in Athens on that charge. But Aeschines never said that the Amphissans had lodged a formal complaint or used any legal procedure against Athens, only that they had moved in the Council to punish Athens, and that he had nipped their attempt in the bud (Aes. 3.116).[17] Demosthenes also makes Aeschines a prime actor in the raid on the Cirrhan plain and harbor by depicting him as its guide. Aeschines, we recall, tried to minimize his role in the conflict following the conclusion of his speech.

Demosthenes' decree that allegedly shackled Aeschines' hands prevented the orator from linking him to the Amphictyonians' later decision to ask Philip to champion their cause. So he expands the circle of plotters to "wicked men" from Thessaly and other places. He converts their otherwise sensible assessment of the Amphictyonians' limited capacity to launch a second campaign and wish to use Philip's army against Amphissa into a rhetorical trick that cornered the Amphictyonians into inviting Philip to fight for them. Demosthenes must have hoped that his audience remembered his earlier depiction of the Amphictyonians as unused to oratory and lacking in foresight, because it was the second time that they had been tricked. Lest the court find these Thessalian and other plotters chiefly responsible for Philip's campaign, Demosthenes hastens within a few sentences to produce decrees that will show "the extraordinary trouble that this disgusting person [*miara kephalē*; i.e., Aeschines] stirred up" (18.153). He cites decrees and a letter from Philip to his Peloponnesian allies, whose contents are now lost (18.153–58). His interpretation of Philip's letter, however, raises doubts about its evidentiary value, because he focuses on what Philip has tried to conceal from those he addressed and on his pretending to act in a common Amphictyonic cause, rather than on what the king explicitly says.[18]

In sum, Demosthenes' account of the Amphissan war asks the Athe-

---

17. See, in addition, Harris 1995, 128, 206 n. 8; Sánchez 2001, 231–32.
18. For the spurious decrees and letter in the text: Yunis 2001, 29–31. Sealey 1993, 191 accepts Demosthenes' evidence, but Harris 1995, 128, 206 n. 6 thinks that his proofs are worthless.

nians to regard it as a grand conspiracy. For this purpose, he simplifies a complex story involving a large number of states, each with its own interests, as well as events that were often unpredictable and that stretched over a considerable span of time, into a compact, easily intelligible tale. He establishes the plot's aim and the plotters' identities according to the ultimate outcomes of the affair guided by the reductive question "Cui bono?" He also turns what might easily be Philip's opportunistically taking advantage of the invitation to fight Amphissa in order to seize Elateia into a premeditated act. In depicting Philip, he uses the conspiratorial topos of the wirepuller who from his hideout sets events and people in motion, and who is aided by his uncanny ability to predict events and human reactions, as well as by collaborators disguised as local patriots. Equally familiar are the logographer's basic assumptions that, except for the plotters and the plot detector, no one else who experienced the events was able to tell their true purpose, although they unwittingly aided the conspiracy, and that the plan or the plot had no room for mishap, chance, or conduct that was disinterested and honest.

Scholars have been divided about the merits of Aeschines' and Demosthenes' accounts of the outbreak of the Fourth Sacred War. Although these speakers' mutual charges of bribe-taking or of working for foreign states have been given little credence, some interpreters have largely followed Demosthenes' view that Philip's long hand can be discerned in the affair, while others, and especially more recently, have rejected Demosthenes' plot scenario in favor of a modified version of Aeschines' account. They have argued that Philip had no wish for, or interest in, fomenting a war in central Greece or marching on Athens; that championing a campaign against Amphissa was the wrong way to entice Thebes to become his ally; that he had no effective means of communicating with, or guiding, conspirators from Macedonia; that the conflict with Amphissa made perfect local sense without outside provocation; and that if there was a man who should be blamed for the war and its consequences, it was the Thessalian Cottyphus, or, alternatively, Aeschines, respectively acting in the interests of their homelands or Delphi, but not those of Philip. They also have argued that neither Philip nor Aeschines could have planned the latter's speech in the Amphictyonic Council, which was occasioned by the accident of the other Athenian delegates' falling sick.[19]

19. See the literature cited in note 1 above. Carlier 1990, 210, 212, and Ryder 2000, 80, are among the fairly recent scholars who imply or suggest Philip's involvement in the affair.

I share the skepticism regarding Demosthenes' account but wish to point out that it is largely based on speculative reconstructions, sensible as they may be, of Philip's intentions or of what his best interests at that time might have been. Aeschines' version is by and large more likely than Demosthenes' but may not be used to refute it because of the high likelihood, discussed above, that it was designed to achieve this very purpose. Demosthenes' account is faulty because it is inherently improbable and on a matter that both he and Aeschines agree upon. The two speakers report that Philip was called to fight Amphissa because of Cottyphus's failure to punish that city. There was no way that Philip could have known in advance that the Thessalian's campaign would prove ineffective (and ironically thanks in part to Demosthenes' decree and policy).[20] Demosthenes' version puts the worst possible conspiratorial face on the relations between cause and effect. It should be said to his credit (?), however, that he is the first attested orator to create what might today be called a world-class conspirator.[21]

PLOTTING IN INTERNATIONAL TRADE

Perhaps it was the Macedonian expansion into Greece and Asia that contributed to an increase in allegedly international plots in the second half of the fourth century. In addition to Philip's intrigues reported by Demosthenes and other speakers, one speech, delivered sometimes between 323 and 322 and around the time of Alexander's death, recounts a plotting tale that spans across the eastern Mediterranean at least and alleges an attempt to corner the market in Egyptian grain. In the period under discussion, grain was a staple much in demand, whose importance and shifting availability make the need for it somewhat resemble our dependence on foreign oil.

Against Dionysodorus, which has been wrongly attributed to Demosthenes, involves a damage suit concerning a maritime loan.[22] The lenders were Pamphilius and his partner, the speaker, who is identified by Liba-

---

20. Cf. Sánchez 2001, 237.
21. Cf. Hammond 1994, 142. That Philip allegedly had prearranged for his invitation is stated in 18.143, 147, and indicated by the use of the past perfect in relation to the plotters who proposed him as a leader against Amphissa: *oi kateskeuasmenoi kai palai ponēroi* (those who had been suborned and men of long-standing wickedness: 18.151).
22. [Dem.] 56. Hansen in Isager and Hansen 1975, 200–213; Carey and Reid 1985, 195–235, and Harris 2003 comment on the case. For the speech's authorship and date, see, in addition, Worthington 2002. Athenians and grain: Garnsey 1988, 87–164, and grain supply at the time of the speech: ibid., 151–64; Reed 2003, 16–19, 43–51.

nius in the fourth century C.E. as Darius (*Hypothesis to Dem. 56*). The two men had loaned money to the traders Dionysodorus and Parmeniscus on the security of a grain ship going to Egypt. According to the speaker, the borrowers wanted to use the ship to transport grain from Egypt to Rhodes or to Athens, but the lenders insisted, and put it in a contract, that the ship would import grain only to Athens and that the loan would be repaid with interest upon arrival at the Piraeus. The speaker stresses this stipulation because of the lenders' alleged violation of it, and because it was illegal for Athenian citizens and alien residents to import grain anywhere but to Athens or to give loans for grain shipments destined elsewhere. The civic status of the parties involved in this dispute is unclear, and it is possible that at least one of the borrowers was a foreigner unbound by the Athenian import regulations. Yet the expectation of honoring these rules seemed to have been universal, especially in times of shortage, which accounts for the speaker's emphasizing that the borrowers were engaged in financing and importing grain to Rhodes, while he was concerned not even to be suspected of financing such transactions.[23]

The ship, as it happened, never made it to Athens, but was used instead to traffic between Egypt and Rhodes and elsewhere. The reason, according to the speaker, had to do with an elaborate plot involving these grain traders and Cleomenes of Naucratis, an appointee of Alexander's who had been in charge of administrative and financial affairs in Egypt up to sometime prior to this trial.

Darius argues that after taking the loan, Parmeniscus sailed with the ship to Egypt, while Dionysodorus stayed in Athens. They were all, however, underlings and accomplices (*hupēretai kai sunergoi*) of Cleomenes, who had harmed the Athenians and other Greeks by buying and selling Egyptian grain, setting its price, and that these two were "with him" (*met' autou*) in the business. There were some people who sent the grain out of Egypt, others who transported it, and still others who stayed in Athens to sell it. The latter would advise the traffickers through letters to bring the grain to Athens when the price was high and to sell it elsewhere when it was low. It was by means of these letters and this collaboration (*sunergiōn*), the speaker explains, that the price of grain in Athens was manipulated. Indeed, when the said ship had left Athens,

---

23. Dem. 56.11, 13, 17, 47–48. For the laws regulating grain import and the status of the disputants, see Hansen in Isager and Hansen 1975, 213; Carey and Reid 1985, 197–98; Garnsey 1988, 139–42; Todd 1993, 320–21; Reed 2003, 119–20.

grain was expensive, but following a drop in price, Dionysodorus sent a messenger to Rhodes to inform his partner of the situation, knowing that the ship would stop there. Parmeniscus consequently sold the grain in Rhodes, even though it was in violation of the contract.

When the lenders found out about this transaction, they approached "the architect of the entire plot" (*arkhitektoni tēs olēs epiboulēs*), namely, Dionysodorus, protested the breach of contract, and complained that people would suspect them of being partners in shipping the grain to Rhodes. Their demand to get back the loan and the agreed-upon interest was answered with an insolent ploy: Dionysodorus offered to pay the portion of the loan and interest that would cover the trip from Egypt to Rhodes, well knowing that the lenders would refuse, because it would make them suspect of importing grain to Rhodes instead of Athens. Later, when they reconsidered and were ready to a compromise based on Dionysodorus's offer, he demanded the voiding of the contract in return, but the speaker and his partner would hear nothing of it ([Dem.] 56.1–17). Elsewhere in the speech, Darius tries to refute the defendant's claim that the ship had been damaged and could go no further than Rhodes, contending that it was a lie and that the ship was used to go back to Egypt and everywhere but to Athens (56.21–23).

I shall avoid discussing the merit of the speaker's suit, which has been rightly questioned, especially because he produces no corroborative evidence or testimonies in support of his allegations, except for the contract. Indeed, the defendant may have been within his rights not to honor the agreement if the ship was damaged.[24] My interest is rather in the depiction of the plot and its likelihood. There are several factors that could have made Darius's story fall on ready ears. The author of Ps. Aristotle's *Oeconomica* reports that because of hunger in Egypt, Cleomenes forbade the export of grain or allowed limited exports, on which he imposed heavy duties. He also bought grain cheaply and then sold it for more than three times its cost. According to Peter Garnsey, Athens suffered five food shortage crises between 338/7 and 323/2.[25] As with other conspiracy theories, then, Darius's tale uses a plot to explain events and interpret conditions that his audience had experienced. Their distress,

---

24. Harris 2003, 9, 13, notes also that neither the borrowers' initial intention to sail to Rhodes, nor the ship's sailing from Rhodes to Egypt are proven; cf. Carey and Reid 1985, 199. For the defendant's case: Hansen in Isager and Hansen 1975, 210–21; Harris 2003, esp. 13, and see note 22 above.

25. [Arist.] *Oec.* 1352a16–23; 1352b 14–20. Garnsey 1988, 157–62, and see Hansen in Isager and Hansen 1975, 200–206; Carey and Reid 1985, 204–5.

and the overwhelming presence of non-Athenians among maritime traders, who were perceived as more interested in personal profit than in the welfare of the community, made the idea of international plotters being responsible for the Athenians' sufferings quite attractive. The speaker, accordingly, links the defendant and his partner to Cleomenes in the hope that the latter's unpopularity in Greece will rub off on them, make their involvement in an unscrupulous profit-making scheme seem credible, and turn their action against the lenders into a plot against the city.[26] Since stereotypes and rhetorical topoi make a story familiar and hence plausible, the speaker adds to his description a number of conspiratorial motifs, such as the plotters' greed, brazenness, and insolence, their seizing of opportunities and taking advantage of people's vulnerability, their willingness to honor agreements only when it suits their interest (56.9), and their ability to foresee events and predict human reactions, as evinced by Dionysodorus's expectation that the lenders would reject his "shameful" offer to pay part of the loan (56.2-3, 12-13, 16, 20). No less common is the speaker's assigning of the role of chief plotter to Cleomenes in one place and elsewhere to Dionysodorus.

Darius also tries to impress the court with the magnitude of the plot when he construes it as an operation involving an unknown number of faceless men who export, transport, and sell grain in Athens when the price is high (56.8). Yet this allegation is a mere expansion to other traders of the presumed cooperation between Cleomenes and the borrowers, because when he comes to demonstrate the working of this "international conspiracy," he details the transactions of Cleomenes and his legal adversaries. Indeed, the likelihood that such scheme existed is small, notwithstanding Ps. Aristotle's report on Cleomenes' activities. Ps. Aristotle describes an attempt to control the export and price of Egyptian grain rather than an enterprise that detects where the best price for grain is through a network of commercial spies. The only information produced in support of such operation is the speaker's claim that one merchant in Athens wrote another in Rhodes to sell the grain on the island because of declining prices.[27]

---

26. Foreign maritime traders: Reed 2003, 82–85, who may be going too far in downplaying the "otherness" of these traders (ibid., 54–61). Unpopular men and plots: cf. Is. 8.40–42; Isoc. 18.11, and in this case, Gernet 1959, 3: 134; Carey and Reid 1985, 205, 211. The defendants harming the city: cf. Carey and Reid 1985, 210; Christ 1998, 190.

27. See also Carey and Reid 1985, 205, 212. Erxleben 1974, 489–90, and Hansen in Isager and Hansen (1975, 206), however, credit Cleomenes with a network of Greek informants; cf. Garnsey 1988, 157.

It may be worthwhile by way of conclusion to compare Philip's and Cleomenes' alleged machinations with modern global conspiracy theories. After all, for the Greeks, divided into separate city-states and ethnic groups, such plans were not unlike the alleged ambitions to take over our fragmented world or to monopolize essential resources. Ancient and modern plot scenarios also share some attributes. Philip and even Cleomenes, like modern global conspirators, be they the United Nations, business conglomerates, secret government agencies, or ethnic or religious groups, are often portrayed as moral outsiders. Both ancient and modern conspirators are active practically everywhere, unfettered by geographical and national boundaries or by loyalties other than to themselves. Both pursue either profit or power, are very skilled in planning and taking advantage of other people's gullibility and weakness, and are assisted by agents and efficient communication channels. Yet as world-class plotters, Cleomenes, and especially Philip, also differ significantly from their modern counterparts. Philip may be secretive and underhanded, but his takeover plots depend in the final analysis on his ability to prevail over his chief opponents in open military confrontations, rather than through deceit and conspiratorial networks. Unlike many modern global plotters, too, he and Cleomenes are not anonymous but clearly identified. Finally, both his and Cleomenes' opponents feel less impotent or resigned than many modern conspiratists and their followers do.

Conclusion

Conspiracy Theories, Ancient and Modern

To what extent are the conspiracy scenarios described in this book no more than rhetorical ploys? It is impossible to answer this question with certainty because we do not know to what extent the speakers believed their own stories. What is more feasible and even useful is to examine the mind-set that made such tales both common and acceptable and the role that conspiracy played in ancient Athenian private and public psychology and discourse.

Conspiratorial outlooks are amply attested by both oratorical and nonoratorical evidence, both inside and outside the environments of the Athenian courts and assemblies. On the Athenian stage, for example, to take the case of political conspiracies, one finds Sophocles' Oedipus refusing to believe Creon's assertion that Laius, the former ruler of Thebes, had been killed by robbers, and suggesting instead that his death was the outcome of a domestic political plot.[1] It is an observation worthy of Thucydides' Cleon, who evokes the Athenians' fear of conspiracy in order to justify treating the Mytilenaean rebels harshly on utilitarian, legal, and moral grounds. In Aristophanes' comedies, Cleon warns against or accuses citizens of plotting and tyrannical ambitions and is joined in this by persons from all walks of life.[2] The pervasiveness of

---

1. Sophocles *OT* 120–25. Newton 1978–79 suggests that his suspicion is based on earlier indications in the play, and see also Ahl 1991.
2. For Thucydides' and Aristophanes' testimonies, see chapter 4 above.

these allegations cannot simply be attributed to the historical circumstances attending these works, because they appear with equal frequency in the orations of fourth-century Athenians. The speakers charge politicians with designs to overthrow the democracy because it stands between them and uninhibited power, gratification of desires, or the preservation of ill-gotten gains. They also describe them as members of cabals or as paid agents of Persia, of Philip, or even of fellow citizens.

The plotting charges can be attributed only in part to their abuse by the politically active in their partisan or legal feuds, because the evidence suggests that both the masses and the elite were concerned about political conspiracies and took them seriously. Councilmen and jurors took oaths to remain alert to the threat of revolution, usually envisioned as the product of conspiracy. Meetings of the Council and the Assembly commenced with evocations of such threats. Legislation against attempts to overthrow the democracy was prolific during and after the Peloponnesian War. In 410, Demophantus initiated a decree giving immunity to anyone who killed men seeking to overthrow the democracy to establish a tyranny. Between 410 and 404, an eisangelic law criminalized a series of public offenses, including conspiring against the demos. Two highly restored decrees from 362/1 and 361/0 record Athenian alliances with Peloponnesian and Thessalian peoples that appear, among other things, to have protected Athens from overthrow of its democracy and attempts to establish tyranny. In 336, Eucrates reintroduced the outlawing of such attempts.[3] Some of the these initiatives were justified by the historical circumstances attending them, but together with the other evidence, they suggest an anxiety about the safety of the political regime that is not easily reconcilable with the political and social stability enjoyed by Athens after the Peloponnesian War.[4] In addition, this concern was not born of the oligarchic experiences of 411 and 404–3 but preceded them and was

---

3. Councilmen and jurors' oaths and alerting councilmen and assemblymen of subversive threats: Dem. 24.144–48; Aristophanes *Thesmophoriazousae* 335–39, 360–66; Rhodes 1985, 36–37. Demophantus's decree: And. 1.96–98; Dem. 20.159; Lyc. 1.124–27; Ostwald 1986, 409, 414–15. The eisangelic law: Dem. 46.26; Hyp. 4.7–8, 29–30; Hansen 1975, 13–20; Rubinstein 2000, 52–53. Athenian alliances: Tod 1948, nos. 144.25–26; 147.28–29 = R&O 2003, nos. 41, 44. Eucrates' proposal: *SEG* 12.87 = Harding 1985, no. 101. It is easy to imagine that there were other similar laws now lost to us. Hansen 1975, 49, surmises that legal charges against treason and overthrowing democracy were mostly directed against the politically active and during their *eisangeliai* and *euthunai*.

4. Athenian stability: Ober 1989, esp. 96–97, 102–103; 1996, passim; Hansen 1991, esp. 304; Rhodes 1995, 318–19. While Ober ascribes the stability to the Athenians' ideology, Hansen and Rhodes attribute it to their institutions. See Roisman 2005, 194–99, for the related Athenian anxiety about the soundness of their civic order.

associated with their aftermaths only to a limited degree. The rhetoric of alerting Athenians to political conspiracy was common, because it found a receptive audience. What made the Athenians so concerned about intrigues against their state?

I wish to argue that accusations and fears of political plots should be viewed in the larger context of the Athenians' anxiety about conspiratorial activity in general. This is suggested by the shared vocabulary, perceptions, and themes in depictions of political and nonpolitical conspiracies and in a way that goes beyond general similarity. Conspirators, be they men coveting other people's property, planning murder or revenge, aiming to defeat a legal action, or politicians, distinctly resemble one another in character, means, the structure of their plots, and the attributes of their victims. I have tried to highlight these similarities throughout this work, but the following examples may serve as an illustrative reminder.

The choregus in Antiphon's speech who accuses his prosecutor in a homicide trial of pressing charges against him in the interest of others resembles Demosthenes, who at one point charges Thrasylochus with having challenged him to exchange estates in collusion with Demosthenes' guardians, and at another accuses Aeschines of conspiring with Philip to provoke a war in central Greece.[5] In all these cases, the speaker detects behind the seemingly legitimate conduct of a legal adversary an ulterior motive and a hidden puppet master. In all of them, he forges a causal link between events based on their (at times, presumed) temporal proximity and the premise that this proximity cannot be accidental. Since tales of plotting exclude chance, it was by design that Herodes and the man accused of killing him sailed on the same boat, just as it was not by accident that Aeschines fell ill when a third Athenian embassy went to Philip. According to Demosthenes, Aeschines feigned sickness as part of a plot to leave someone in Athens in order to prevent Demosthenes from sabotaging the peace while the embassy was away.[6] Andocides' observation, in relation to the men who allegedly framed him for impiety, that plotters lay their plans carefully, secretly, and without risk to themselves, and then surprise their victim when he is most vulnerable (And.1.6), is not far removed from Lysias's portrayal of the Athenian oligarchs prior to Athens's defeat in 404. The latter waited for the right opportunity to execute their scheme and used deceit, secrecy, and a well-coordinated plan against a weak and ignorant demos (Lys. 13; cf. 5.2). Their designs, like

5. Ant. 1; Dem. 21.78–80; 18.140–59.
6. Ant. 5.20–22; Dem. 19.121–30; Aes. 2.94–96.

Philip's plans to take over Greece, or Diocles' schemes against his rivals to Ciron's estate, evince the perception of plotters as all-powerful and able to direct events to suit their purposes (Isoc. 5.73–74; Is. 8.36–43). Finally, political conspirators and those who plot to appropriate other people's possessions are greedy and brazen, while those who unmask them either implicitly or explicitly claim personal and communal rewards. In short, charges of political conspiracy belonged to a larger conspiratorial environment, while the many plotting accusations and their different articulators suggest less their conventionality than the Athenians' broad concern about conspirators, as well as their propensity to be suspicious of others. The concept of distrust as a useful self-defense mechanism must have contributed to this state of mind.[7]

Such attitudes, as well as personal or collective experiences of being victimized by (real or imagined) plotters that appeared to validate them, were likely to encourage a search for and detection of conspiracies.[8] It is tempting, for example, to attribute Demosthenes' fondness for conspiracy scenarios to his youthful experience. We have seen that upon reaching maturity, he sued his guardians for misappropriation and mismanagement of his father's estate and abuse of trust. Demosthenes describes several schemes that his guardians concocted in an effort to make him drop his suit and let them keep the family property. These include subjecting him to an *antidosis* challenge shortly before he was about to sue the guardians, suborning false witnesses, and feigning marriage, divorce, and payments of dowry and mortgage in order to deprive him of a piece of land. Demosthenes ended up losing much of his inheritance, including his mother's dowry, in the process.[9] Even if, as shown above, there is no need to accept his version of these events verbatim, it is likely that his experience of facing a group of ill wishers alone, who had tried, he believed, to take away his property by fair means or foul, instilled into him a suspicious worldview populated by schemers who colluded in secret to harm individuals or the state. It also taught him to play the role of a conspiracy spoiler.

---

7. On Greek suspiciousness, see Rosen 1992; Sagan 1991; Hesk 2000, 248–58. On suspicions in Xenophon's *Anabasis:* Wencis 1977; Hirsh 1985, 16, 26–28. For advocating distrust, see, esp., Dem. 6.24; cf. Lys. 32.18; Dem. 23.122; Aes. 3.234.
8. For treasonable conspiracies during siege warfare, see Aeneias Tacticus, esp. 1.1.1–15; Whitehead 1990, 25–29.
9. The schemes: Dem. 28.17; 21.78–80; 29.28; 30.6–19. Loss of property: [Plut.] *Mor.* 844d; Pomeroy 1997, 175; Burke 1998, esp. 45–51; Rowe 2000, 283–86. Hunter (1989, esp. 46–47) thinks that Demosthenes' mother was a full partner in Demosthenes' legal battles, and Foxhall (1996, 144) that she was the driving force behind them.

Conclusion

Eli Sagan would have found Demosthenes' career useful for his observations on Athenian conduct and attitudes. As noted in the introductory chapter, he links suspicions of conspiracy to paranoia, which he detects in the Athenian psyche. Although some of Sagan's conclusions concur with the findings of this work, I cannot share his attribution of the Athenian conspiratorial outlook to their presumed paranoia. I have indicated as much in some of the previous chapters, but will state here briefly my main variances with his interpretation.

1. In recent times, and especially among therapists, Freudian psychology appears to have fallen out of grace, but I presume that even among Freudians, some will be disturbed by the application of Freud's theory of developmental stages of personality to the ancient Athenians, not to mention its extension to the classification of governments, societies, and cultures.

2. Sagan finds paranoid tendencies and a wish to defend the self in the form of a *libido dominandi* in classical Athens, which made her resort to acts of aggression, especially abroad. Consequently, his most prominent examples refer to wartime situations, which are too special and cannot serve to demonstrate the quotidian applicability of these psychic forces.[10]

3. Since Sagan uses the oratorical evidence only sparingly and focuses chiefly on politics, he fails to see that aggression was only one potential outcome of Athenians' anxieties. The same holds true of Athenian conspiracies, actual or suspected, which involved more than politics and included goals that had little to do with greed, power, or the wish to control.

4. For Sagan, the powerful use suspicions and especially charges of conspiracy to obtain control. Often, however, accusations of plotting are made by the (supposedly) powerless, whose exposure of the conspiracy empowers them.[11] In addition, identifying unfavorable circumstances as due to a plot does not neces-

---

10. Sagan 1991, e.g., 16–19, 27–29, 155–58, 176–85, 362–70. Cf. Goldberg 2001, passim, who protests against the psychological explanation of conspiracism as based on private paranoia and fantasies. Pagán, who deals primarily with political conspiracies in Rome, thinks that the Roman attitudes toward conspiracy were largely concerned with violation of boundaries (2005, 107).

11. Cf. Goldberg 2001, 240, and the contributors in West and Sanders, 2003, who regard conspiracy theories as responses to "modernity," i.e., what are perceived as undesirable political, social, and economic processes (but see Harding and Stewart 2003).

sarily suggest a psychological malfunction or fantasy but may be an attempt to make sense of these circumstances. Similarly, characterizing an opponent and his supporters as co-conspirators may be due not to fanciful paranoia but to an interpretation of a dispute grounded in social realities, such as the cooperation expected of friends and kin.

Studies of modern conspiracy theories may be more useful in accounting for the Athenian phenomenon. Even though some of them associate conspiracism with paranoia, they are less committed than Sagan to the universal application of Freudian psychology and present patterns of conspiracy theorizing that, mutatis mutandis, bear a significant resemblance to, and offer more insights regarding, their ancient Athenian counterparts.[12]

Scholars of conspiracy theories, many of them sociologists, anthropologists, communication experts, and social psychologists, deal with their forms, contexts, and functions. Generally, conspiracy theorists offer reconstructions of events or actions whose logic is (too) impeccable and that free the plotters from mistakes, failures, or spontaneous and ambiguous conduct. Their tales may also include wondrous elements or clever puzzles.[13] Conspiracists claim that there are hidden hands or agendas at work and explain the success of the conspirators by portraying them as more powerful, clever, and efficient than the average person, and at times as displaying a kind of solidarity that is the opposite of normative solidarity.[14] Conspirators' power is overwhelming, especially in relation to plots that occurred in the past. Present or future plots can still be defeated by exposing the plotters' weak spot or by taking appropriate countermeasures, which often depends on the possession of exact knowledge of the plotters' aims and plans.[15]

12. Owing to the range of these studies and their occasional irrelevance to the subject at hand, my use of them is necessarily eclectic.
13. Hofstadter 1967, 36; Zukier 1987, 89; Marcus 1999, 2–5; cf. Pipes 14. Marcus argues that postmodern conspiracy theories give up on plausibility in favor of the telling of a wondrous story; and cf. Stewart and Harding 1999, 293–96, on conspiracy theories, apocalypticism, and millennialism. Wondrous elements also existed, however, in earlier tales. The distinction made, by, e.g., Pipes 1997, 21, between "real" conspiracies and "fantastic" conspiracy theories is not theoretically helpful, because some of the "real" conspiracies may be imagined, while for the theorists, conspiracies are very real; cf. Goodnight and Poulakos 1981, 301–2.
14. Knight 2001, 20–21; Zukier 1987, 97, and Groh 1987, 1–5. Groh discusses mostly blaming groups with plotting harm; cf. Goldberg 2001, 20, 260.
15. Groh 1987, 3–4; Kruglanski 1987, 219–20; Graumann 1987, 248. According to West and Sanders, adherents of more recent conspiracy theories "seek to reveal and steer

Conclusion

Allegations of conspiracy appear to flourish and to be adopted with greater frequency during crisis situations.[16] Such situations create a state of anxiety, which the conspiracy allegations deal with by blaming misfortunes on individual scapegoats or shadowy cabals. In this way, they also "restore a sense of agency, causality, and responsibility" to what otherwise seems to be an "inexplicable play of forces over which we have no control" (Knight 2001, 20–21). In other words, by linking together disparate elements, conspiracy interpretations order chaotic or incomprehensible situations into structures of cause and effect.[17] The act of bringing people into a seemingly better understanding of the workings of the world functions well in particular for those who think that they have unfairly suffered injustice or disaster, and who look for groups or individuals whom they regard as responsible for their being punished, rather than being rewarded for being and doing good. Leaders who articulate such theories and identify culprits are often protecting, not only traditional values and institutions, but their own power.[18]

The above survey shows the affinities of modern conspiracy theories with Athenian tales of conspiracy, but it should not conceal their differences. The modern experiences of charging Jews, freemasons, imperialists, communists, and large corporations and institutions with conspiratorial plans have inclined their investigators to focus on collective plotting accusations, the wide scope of the plots, and the anonymity of the plotters.[19] The classical Athenians, however, tended to personalize conspirators, be they citizens or foreigners, and to limit their objectives to individual or local harm, and only occasionally, and late in the period, do they refer to individuals or faceless groups with far-reaching aims. In-

---

the hidden forces that they believe animate the world, to explore the nuances of power and to take advantage of its ambivalence" (2003, 16).

16. Graumann 1987, 247; Groh 1987, 7. Graumann and the contributors in West and Sanders 2003 discuss chiefly political, economic, and spiritual crises on the collective level, but following Groh 1987, 5 (and the orators), I would add personal crisis or distress as well. Kruglanski (1987, 225–28) suggests that normative confusion, a sense of urgency, and coherence between conspiracy theory and the groups' strongly held beliefs increase receptivity to warnings of conspiracy. These, of course, are not the only, or necessary, conditions.

17. Hofstadter 1967, 36; Parish 2001; Poper 1965, 123–25, 341–42; Graumann 1987, 224. For conspiracies as explanatory devices: Groh 1987, 1–9; Moscovici 1987; Zukier 1987, 97–98; Craig and Gregory 1999 (who argue that conspiracists offer complex, rather than simplistic, explanations). Moscovici (1987, 156–57), perhaps thinking of the Holocaust, argues that conspiracy theory reveals the danger in order to eliminate it, not just to explain it.

18. Goldberg 2001, 20, 64, 149, 188; cf. Harding and Stewart 2003, 260.

19. E.g., Moscovici 1987, 154, 157.

deed, the notion of a single conspirator, a semantic oxymoron, posed no difficulties for the Athenians. Neither did the Athenians ever translate their prejudices and conspiratorial suspicions into systematic and organized mass murders and hateful persecutions of the kind that modern states have perpetrated.[20]

On the other hand, modern and ancient Athenian conspiracies have much in common. They share the perfect logic, causal linking, and the predetermined results of their constructions. They include entertaining and unlikely elements (e.g., Athenian legal entrapments and Philip's controlling events from afar) and discount good intentions and spontaneous actions. They share a search for hidden agendas, for masterminds and their agents, and the granting to them of unfair advantages. They attribute inordinate power and countersolidarity to the plotters (as in the case of Athenian legal adversaries or political cabals). Both modern and ancient conspiracy detectors make exclusive claim to detailed knowledge of the plot and how to deal with it. Lastly, they both use conspiracy charges in defense of their positions, but also of established values and institutions such as Athenian justice or the city's political regime, national heritage, and social order.

There is much in modern conspiracism that can also explain the reasons for the Athenians' energetic production and consumption of conspiracy charges and tales. For example, the link between conspiracies and states of crisis is easily detectable in the oratorical corpus. Although crisis and stress are relative or subjectively defined, many Athenian charges of conspiracy are at least associated with crises on the national and personal levels, as in the cases of litigants' facing trial or Athens's facing external threats. The ability of conspiracy interpretations to restore order by placing destabilizing and unexpected actions in a logical sequence of cause and effect, and to clarify events that otherwise seem inexplicable and uncontrollable, fits Demosthenes' explications of Philip's actions and aims in terms of his plotting against Athens and Greece. Similarly, the Athenians had little control over the cost of grain and its impact, but the story about how Cleomenes and the grain merchants were manipulating the market accounted for their resulting hardship. Like modern conspiracists, the ancient Athenians often concretized anxieties into definable fears and blamed misfortunes on simple scapegoats, such as corrupt politicians. In both the private and the public spheres, accusing a man of plotting made the danger manageable, provided that the

20. *Pace* Sagan 1991, 25.

agency that had the power to deal with it, often the Athenian court, agreed with the speaker.

Yet there was more to the Athenian rhetoric of conspiracy than assigning blame. To understand much of its appeal, let us turn to Cleon, one of the great practitioners of the art, who commences his speech in the so-called Mytilenaean Debate by warning the Athenians not to pity the Mytilenaeans just because "your daily interactions with one another are free from fears and plots" (Thuc. 3.38.1). Judging by the oratorical evidence on the Athenians' "daily interactions," he could not have been more wrong.[21] Yet Cleon refers to a desirable social climate that the Athenians thought they had or wished to have. Alongside suspicion and distrust, there was a yearning in Athens for a tolerant, trusting, and peaceful existence, which democracy was supposed to guarantee.[22] Thus, Thucydidean Pericles, whom Cleon may have sought to echo in the aforementioned statement, says in the funeral orations of 431/0 that in Athenian democracy, the citizens are not resentful or envious and do not seek to supervise the conduct of their neighbors, but let them live as they wish (Thuc. 2.37.2). More than a century later, the prosecutor of the politician Aristogeiton expresses similar sentiments when he commends the Athenians on their leniency (*philanthropia*) and kindred feeling (*sungeneia*) and compares them to a household in which youthful misconduct is either tolerated or discreetly corrected (Dem. 25.87–89). A Lysian speaker protests that his opponents' public conduct is creating suspicion in the city instead of concord (*homonoia*), which has been established with great difficulty following the restoration of the democracy. Demosthenes similarly reproaches the demos with treating the wealthy in a way that makes the latter fear, resent, and distrust the former. He also notes in a speech he wrote for the prosecutor of Leptines that Athens is superior to other cities in prosperity and harmony.[23] Indeed, even speakers' complaints about dysfunctional domestic or foreign affairs draw their power from the Athenians' longing for, and expectations of, a well-managed and prosperous state with a social environment free from harm

---

21. I am aware that the orations tend to ignore peaceful conflict resolutions or sedate circumstances and interactions. At the same time, they also fail to report disputes and plots outside the logographers' knowledge and interest, while the prevalence and variety of plots discussed here in both the private and the public spheres militates against Cleon's contention.

22. Cf. Aes. 1.5; Arist. *Pol.* 4 1295b33–34; Sagan 1991, 88–89, 195. For the following, see also Menu 2000, 202–12.

23. Lys. 25.27–30; Dem. 10.44–45; 20.170; cf. And. 1.140; Dem. 9.38; 18.246; 24.185; [Arist.] *Rhetoric to Alexander* 20 1424b10–13.

and anxiety. In addition, both Athenian speakers and their audience, who upheld communal values and believed that they were good, also expected good returns for their conformity. It was the plotters' fault, then, that good things did not happen to good people. It was thanks to the belief in plots and the plot detectors that faith in the validity of basic values and the existing system could be reaffirmed. Rather than being linked to paranoia or fear-induced aggression, conspiratorial allegations filled a psychological need by helping the Athenians to understand and deal with discrepancies between expectations and reality.

APPENDIX A

Demosthenes 32.
Against Zenothemis

In chapter 2, I recount the story of an alleged plot to defraud Demon of Syracusan grain that secured his loan. M. H. Hansen, who has offered the most detailed commentary on the case, has convincingly shown why Demon's version should be suspected rather than believed.[1] In what follows, I wish to discuss some of Hansen's arguments and perhaps improve upon them.

I agree that Zenothemis, Demon's competitor for the cargo, had a better claim to it. It appears that the grain that he and Hegestratus, the shipowner, bought in Syracuse served as security for several loans: the loan that Protus, the grain importer, took from Demon in Athens, and the loans that Hegestratus and Zenothemis took from Massaliote lenders residing in Syracuse (cf. Dem. 35.21–23).[2] Hanson accepts Demon's contention that Zenothemis and Hegestratus cheated their lenders when they took money to buy grain but remitted it to Massalia instead. This means that the amount of grain actually bought was significantly smaller than it should have been. He sensibly argues that the lenders from Syracuse joined these merchants for the trip to Athens (esp. 32.8) but wonders how they failed to detect the fraud when they were aboard the ship. His solution: Hegestratus and Zenothemis tricked the lenders by paying high custom tolls in Syracuse, which suggested that they had more grain than they actually had. I find it hard to accept, however, that the lenders would have gone to the trouble of accompanying the merchants on board the grain ship but have neglected to check the actual state of their security, or failed to find out about the missing cargo before the ship made it to Cephallenia or Athens. Besides, it is uncertain that the grain was registered with the Syracusan port authorities under

1. Hansen in Isager and Hansen 1975, 138–49.
2. See Reed 2003, 100–101, for views for and against Zenothemis's being a lender. I agree with the former.

Hegesetratus's and Zenothemis's names. According to Demon, he and Protus challenged Zenothemis to go back to Syracuse so that they could prove from the customs records that Protus was the one who owned the grain (32.18).

Hansen thinks that "the only swindler in the case" was Protus.[3] He did not buy grain with Demon's money but thought to claim it after Hegestratus's death. Protus may have been an unsavory character, but the suggestion that he bought no grain is hard to reconcile with the claim that he was the one who paid customs duty on it in Syracuse.[4] Hanson also argues that Protus tried to steal a contract showing Zenothemis's right to the cargo. It is true that Zenothemis charged Protus with stealing and opening a contract (32.27), but we do not really know what it entailed.[5] I think that the difficulties regarding the dispute between Protus and Zenothemis over the ownership of the grain can be better understood if we assume that Protus borrowed money for the transaction not just from Demon but also from Zenothemis. This will account both for the Syracusan records of his ownership of the grain and for his seizing the grain in Athens.[6] Protus did not, however, buy enough grain to cover all of his loans. As for Zenothemis and Hegestartus, they might or might not have sent the money they had borrowed to Massalia, but they and their creditors were likely to make sure that there was enough grain on the ship to cover *their* investments. Protus's debt to Demon was his business or problem, not theirs.

Hansen then questions the story of Hegestratus's making a hole in the ship's hull and suggests instead that the ship was damaged by a storm, alluded to in Zenothemis's charge that Protus had been drunk and had acted insanely during a storm (32.27). Moreover, it is certainly unclear how Hegestratus thought he could get away with cutting a hole in the ship unnoticed and during the night, when any noise is likely to be more audible (32.5).

In Athens, the possession of the cargo was first disputed between Protus and Zenothemis, but soon Protus left Athens because he was concerned about the falling price of grain, which made him liable to Demon for the shortfall between the original loan and the expected sale price of the grain. He was also fearful of Zenothemis's suit against him for damages for stealing the contract. If Protus borrowed money from Zenothemis, the latter had one less contender for the grain to worry about, but also no one to sue for the debt. His situation, however, was better than Demon's, because he had witnesses, namely, his creditors and perhaps also the alleged turncoat Aristophon, to substantiate his claim to the

---

3. Hansen in Isager and Hansen 1975, 143, and argued previously by Gernet 1954, 1: 114–15.
4. It will not do to claim that Protus too paid customs duty on nonexistent grain, for it would have made him a prime suspect in the alleged plot to sink the ship. His daring Zenothemis to go to Syracuse might have been a bluff, but Zenothemis's apparent declining of the dare has left no one, including modern interpreters, to call him on it. For his dare: Johnstone 1999, 157 n. 10.
5. Mirhady 2004, 54–55, prefers the term "written document" rather than "contract" for the lost *sumbolaion*.
6. Against Hansen's (Isager and Hansen 1975, 140) conjecture that the stolen contract was between a Syracusan lender and Hegestratus and Zenothemis, or MacDowell's (2004, 86) hypothesis that it was between Zenothemis and Hegestratus, I would conjecture a contract between Zenothemis and Protus.

grain. Demon, in contrast, had lost his prime witness for his counterclaim.[7] He decided, then, to lodge a countersuit (*paragraphē*), which allowed a defendant to argue that the charge against him was illegal or inadmissible and thus become the prosecutor in the case. He also built his speech on a tale of plotting to account for his inferior case.

It should be admitted, however, that any reconstruction of this affair from Demon's highly tendentious account is bound to be speculative. In addition, there is the knotty problem, which I shall not seek to untangle here, of who exactly had possession of the grain in Athens and when, and what legal procedures were taken in relation to it. The speech at one point makes the grain merchant Protus and his creditors the possessors of the cargo (32.14), at another, Zenothemis (32.17), and yet at another, Demon (32.20), unless the latter was one of the aforementioned Protus's creditors (32.14). The nature of the procedure of ejectment (*dikē exoulēs*), used by the disputants in this conflict, also confuses the picture. This procedure could have been used by the holder of the cargo, but also by the one who tried to oust him. It could also mean a legal suit as well as the use of force in a self-help action.[8] Our ignorance and uncertainty are not necessarily the logographer's fault, but he probably would have been glad if Demon's audience had simplified this complex case into a conspiracy against the speaker.

7. The speech indicates that the speaker produced testimonies to corroborate his narrative (32.13, 19), but there is no telling by whom or what they stated.
8. Hansen in Isager and Hansen 1975, 144–46; Harrison 1968–71, 1: 218–20, 313–14; 2.113–15; cf. Pearson 1972, 264–65; Hunter 1994, 233 n. 48. For different interpretations of the legal procedures and tactics used here, see Harrison 1968–71, 2: 114; Pearson 1972, 267; Hansen 1975, 147–48.

APPENDIX B

The Date and Background of Aristocrates' Decree

In chapter 5, I examine the validity of the plotting charges against Aristocrates' decree that honored and protected Charidemus. The following discussion looks at the historical and chronological setting of his proposal.

Briefly, Charidemus's career before the war between Cersebleptes and his neighbors shows him frequently switching sides between Athens and her opponents, or so the speaker of Dem. 23 would have us believe.[1] Around 360/59, Cotys, king of Thrace and Charidemus's employer, died, and his kingdom was divided (from east to west) among three kings, Cersebleptes, Amadocus, and Berisades.[2] Charidemus entered the service of Cersebleptes, with whom he was linked by marriage. In 357, Athens made a treaty with the three kings (Tod no. 151 = R&O no. 47), and, in that year or slightly later, Charidemus probably became Athenian citizen (Davies 1971, 571). In the summer of 356, Athens signed another treaty with Berisades' heirs, chiefly Cetriporis, as well as with Paeonian and Illyrian rulers, promising them to fight Philip, to regain territory for Cetriporis that he had lost to the Macedonian king, and to help him take Crenides, which Philip had seized earlier that year (Tod no. 157 = R&O no. 53). Philip defeated his Thracian opponents, however, and forced them to become his allies (Diod. 16.22.3). The dating of the next event is more controversial. Dem. 23.183 mentions a meeting in Maroneia between Philip, the Theban general Pamenes (who was on his way with an army to Asia Minor), and an envoy of

---

1. For Charidemus's career, see Höck 1891; Parke 1933, 125–32; Davies 1971, 570–72, no. 15380; Heskel 1997, esp. 53–157; and Hamel 1998, 18, all citing additional studies. The chronology adopted for these events chiefly follows Sealey 1993, 109–32.

2. Only Cersebleptes was Cotys' heir; the other two were regional leaders who assumed independence following Cotys' death: Höck 1891, 100; Archibald 1994, esp. 459–60.

Cersebleptes', who proclaimed Cersebleptes' allegiance to Philip. The other Thracian ruler, Amadocus, however, demanded that Philip leave the area, and the Macedonian obliged. Scholars have dated this event from 356/5 to 354/3.[3] In 353/2, the Athenian general Chares sailed to the Chersonese and captured Sestus. Cersebleptes, fearful of Philip, gave Athens cities in the Chersonese to colonize, except for Cardia (Diod. 16.34.3; *IG* II² 1613, 297). In the autumn of 352, Philip intervened in a conflict between Cersebleptes on the one hand, and Perinthus, Byzantium, and Amadocus on the other. He defeated Cersebleptes, apparently greatly reducing his power.[4] In 351, Charidemus sailed with a small fleet to the region, this time as an Athenian general (Dem. 3.5).

When did Aristomachus propose in the Assembly that Charidemus be elected general and Aristocrates move his decree? Most scholars have followed Dionysius of Halicarnassus's dating of *Against Aristocrates* to 352/1 (Dion. Hal. *Letter to Ammaius* 1.4). Since the speaker suggests that Aristocrates' decree was moved at least a year before his trial (23.92), the decree has been usually dated to 353/2. Robin Lane Fox, however, has argued for an earlier date.[5] He points out that the speaker associates Aristocrates' decree with Cersebleptes' offensive against the other Thracian dynasts in the aftermath of Berisades' death in 357/6 and notes the relative dearth of references in the speech to events after 357/6, as opposed to the wealth of information about events in Thrace before that year. He concludes that the decree was moved and challenged in 356, but that the trial took place only in 353/2, and suggests that Demosthenes wrote a draft of the speech in 356 and updated it slightly for the trial. This should explain the speaker's alluding to events between the draft and the actual delivery, as well as his failure to mention events up to the trial, such as Philip's interventions in Greece and Thrace, that one would expect him to note, given their relevance to the issues he raises.

Because I am chiefly interested in the alleged conspiracy surrounding Aristocrates' decree, I cannot fully join this chronological fray. In my opinion, however, Lane Fox's dating of the decree to 356 has much merit, although I would date the trial later in 352 than he does. Euthycles places the decree in conjuncture with Cersebleptes' beginning of hostilities against the other kings following Berisades' death, and in violation of a treaty with Athens (23.10, 13, 170). Since Berisades died sometime between 357 and 356, and the "violated" treaty was presumably the one made in 357 and involved all three of Cotys' successors (see above), 356 is the most logical date for the conflict in Thrace, Aristomachus's recommendation that Charidemus be made general, and the decree.

The speaker's remarks in 23.178–80 appear to confirm this date. There, he summarizes the history of Charidemus's dealings with Athenian generals in

---

3. For 356/5, see Badian 1983, 57–60; for 355, see Buckler 1989, 177–80, whose assumption that Cersebleptes cooperated with Philip against Athens since 356 and even later is unsupported by the evidence. For 354/3, see Sealey 1993, 123, 298 n. 88.

4. Schol. Aes. 2.81; Aes. 2.81; Theopompus *FGrH* 115 F 101. See Badian 1983, 59 n. 31, against the identification of this Amadocus with his son. Lane Fox 1997, 186–87, dates Philip's invasion to autumn 351.

5. Lane Fox 1997, 183–87. Dating the decree to 353/2, see, e.g., Badian 1983, 60–61; Sealey 1993, 130. Cawkwell 1978, 76, dates it to 352.

Appendix B

chronological order, starting with Cephisodotus (359/58), through Chabrias (358/7), up to Chares (early 357/6).[6] He adds that "after these [events]" (*meta tauta*), as long as Athens occupied the Hellespont, Charidemus ingratiated himself to Athens, but once he had found out that the Hellespont was "empty of forces," he had tried to topple the two kings and take over the entire kingdom, breaking his agreement with Athens. Aristocrates' decree, the speaker alleges, was intended to facilitate his plan. It is likely that the speaker's reference to the presence of Athenian forces in the Hellespont relates to Chares' expedition to the Chersonese in 357 (Dem. 23.173), and that the one about Charidemus's agreement with Athens relates to his agreement with Chares, which might have resulted in the treaty recorded in an Athenian inscription (23.173; Tod no. 151). The statement concerning the absence of Athenian forces in the region probably has to do with their engagement in the Social War and Chares' expedition to Chios in 356 (Diod. 16.21.1; Sealey 1993, 104). Aristomachus's informing the Athenians that Cersebleptes has no intentions of making an enemy of Athens by taking over or plundering the Chersonesus (23.110) fits this chronology as well, because it assured them that the king would not take advantage of their preoccupation with the Social War to overrun this region.[7]

6. Develin 1989, 270–73, and Heskel 1997, 176–81, date each of these generalships one year earlier, but see Sealey's (1993, 254–55) and R&O's (2003, 240–41) chronology.
7. Euthycles' use of the verb "to rob" (*apostereō*) to describe the Thracian's intentions regarding the Chersonese is his own choice of words: cf. 23.3, 107, 162.

Works Cited

Adams, C. D. 1938. "Speeches VIII and X of the Demosthenic Corpus." *CP* 33: 129–44.
Ahl, F. 1991. *Sophocles' Oedipus: Evidence and Self-Conviction.* Ithaca, N.Y.
Archibald, Z. A. 1994. "Thracians and Scythians." In *Cambridge Ancient History*[2], vol. 6, ed. D. M. Lewis, J. Boardman, S. Hornblower, and M. Ostwald, 444–75. Cambridge.
Aurenche, O. 1974. *Les Groupes d'Alcibiade, de Léogoras et de Teucros: Remarques sur la vie politique athénienne avant 415 J.C.* Paris.
Avramovic, S. 1990. "Plaidoyer for Isaeus, Or. IX." In *Symposion 1988*, ed. G. Nenci and G. Thür, 41–55. Cologne.
Badian, E. 1983. "Philip II and Thrace." *Pupudeva.* 4: 51–71.
———. 2000. "The Road to Prominence." In *Demosthenes: Statesman and Orator*, ed. I. Worthington, 45–89. New York.
Bearzot, C. 1997. *Lisia e la tradizione su Teramene: commento storico alle orazioni XII e XIII del corpus Lysiacum.* Milan.
———. 2000. "La terminologia dell'opposizione politica in Lisia: interventi assembleari (*enantioumai, antilegō*) e trame occulta (*epibouleuō*)." In *L'opposizione nel mondo antico*, ed. M. Sordi, 121–34. Milan.
Bers, V. 2002. "What to Believe in Demosthenes 57 *Against Eubulides.*" *Hyperboreus.* 8: 232–39.
Black's Law Dictionary. 2004. 8th ed. Edited by B. A. Garner. St. Paul, Minn.
Blass, F. 1887. *Die attische Beredsamkeit.* Vol. 3.1. Leipzig.
Boegehold, A. 1999. *When a Gesture Was Expected: A Selection of Examples from Archaic and Classical Literature.* Princeton, N.J.
Buckler, J. 1989. *Philip II and the Sacred War.* Leiden.
———. 1996. "Philip II's Designs on Greece." In *Transitions to Empire: Essays in Honor of E. Badian*, ed. R. W. Wallace and E. M. Harris, 77–97. Norman, Okla.

———. 2000. "Demosthenes and Aeschines." In *Demosthenes: Statesman and Orator*, ed. I. Worthington, 114–58. New York.
———. 2003. *Aegean Greece in the Fourth Century*. Leiden.
Burke, E. 1998. "The Looting of the Elder Demosthenes." *C&M* 49: 45–65.
Calhoun G. M. 1913. *Athenian Clubs in Politics and Litigation*. Austin, Tex.
———. 1918. "The Status of Callistratus in the Litigation over the Estate of Conon [Demosthenes] xlviii. 31, 43ff." *CPh* 13: 410–12.
Carawan, E. 1991. "*Ephetai* and Athenian Courts for Homicide in the Age of the Orators." *CP* 86: 1–16.
———. 1998. *Rhetoric and the Law of Draco*. Oxford.
———. 2001. "What the Laws Have Prejudged: *Paragraphē* and Early Issue Theory." In *The Orator in Action and Theory in Greece and Rome*, ed. C. W. Wooten, 17–51. Leiden.
———. 2004. "Andocides' Defence and MacDowell's Solution." In *Law, Rhetoric, and Comedy in Classsical Athens: Essays in Honour of Douglas M. MacDowell*, ed. D. L. Cairns and R. A. Knox, 103–12. Swansea.
Carey, C., ed. 1989. *Lysias: Selected Speeches*. Cambridge.
———. 1992. *Apollodorus against Neaira [Demosthenes] 59*. Greek Orators, vol. 6. Warminster, Wilts., U.K.
———. 1997. *Trials from Classical Athens*. New York.
———. 2004. "Offence and Procedure in Athenian Law." In *The Law and the Courts in Ancient Greece*, ed. E. M. Harris and L. Rubinstein, 111–36. London.
———. 2005. "Propaganda and Competition in Athenian Oratory." In *The Manipulative Mode: Political Propaganda in Antiquity. A Collection of Case Studies*, ed. K. A. E. Enenkel and I. L. Pfeijffer, 65–100. Leiden.
Carey, C., and R. A. Reid, eds. 1985. *Demosthenes' Selected Private Speeches*. Cambridge.
Carlier, P. 1984. *La Royauté en Grèce avant Alexandre*. Strasbourg.
———. 1990. *Démosthène*. Paris.
Cawkwell, G. L. 1963. "Demosthenes' Policy after the Peace of Philocrates." *CQ* 13: 120–38, 200–213 = Perlman 1973, 145–78.
———. 1978a. "Euboea in the Late 340s." *Phoenix* 32: 42–67.
———. 1978b. *Philip of Macedon*. London.
———. 1996. "The End of Greek Liberty." In *Transitions to Empire: Essays in Greco-Roman History, 360–146 B.C., in Honor of E. Badian*, ed. R. W. Wallace and E. M. Harris, 98–121. Norman, Okla.
Chiron, P. 2002. "Lysias démagogue dans le *Contre Ératosthène*. In *Papers in Rhetoric*, ed. L. C. Montefusco, 4: 41–60. Rome.
Christ, M. R. 1998. *The Litigious Athenian*. Baltimore.
Cohen, D. 1991. *Law, Sexuality, and Society: The Enforcement of Morals in Classical Athens*. Cambridge.
———. 2003. "Writing, Law, and Legal Practice in the Athenian Courts." In *Written Texts and the Rise of Literate Culture in Ancient Greece*, ed. H. Yunis, 78–98. Cambridge.
Cohen, E. E. 1992. *Athenian Economy and Society: A Banking Perspective*. Princeton, N.J.

———. 2000. *The Athenian Nation.* Princeton, N.J.
Collart, P. 1937. *Philippes, ville de Macédoine.* Paris.
Cox, C. A. 1998. *Household Interests: Property, Marriage Strategies, and Family Dynamics in Ancient Athens.* Princeton, N.J.
Craig, T., and W. L. Gregory. 1999. "Beliefs in Conspiracies." *Political Psychology* 20.3: 637–47.
Daitz, S. G. 1957. "The Relationship of De Chersoneso and Philippica Quarta of Demosthenes." *CP* 52: 145–62.
Davidson, J. N. 1993. "Fish, Sex and Revolution in Athens." *CQ* 43.1: 53–66.
———. 1997. *Courtesans & Fishcakes: The Consuming Passions of Classical Athens.* New York.
Davies, J. K. 1971. *Athenian Propertied Families, 600–300 B.C.* Oxford.
Develin, R. 1989. *Athenian Officials, 684–321 B.C.* Cambridge.
Dodds, E. R. 1951. *The Greeks and the Irrational.* Berkeley.
Dover, K. J. 1968. *Lysias and the "Corpus Lysiacum."* Berkeley.
———. 1974. *Greek Popular Morality in the Time of Plato and Aristotle.* Berkeley.
Dow, S. 1960. "The Athenian Calendar of Sacrifices: The Chronology of Nicomachus' Second Term." *Historia* 9: 270–93.
Edwards, M. J. 1995. *Greek Orators—IV: Andocides.* Warminster, Wilts., U.K.
———, ed. 1999. *Lysias Five Speeches: Speeches 1, 12, 19, 22, 30.* London.
Edwards, M. J., and S. Usher, eds. 1985. *Greek Orators—I Antiphon & Lysias.* Warminster, Wilts., U.K.
Ehrenberg, V. 1962. *The People of Aristophanes: A Sociology of Old Comedy.* 3d rev. ed. New York.
Ellis, J. R. 1976. *Philip II and Macedonian Imperialism.* London.
Engels, J. 1993. *Studien zur politischen Biographie des Hyperides: Athen in der Epoche der lykurgischen Reformen und des makedonischen Universalreiches.* 2d ed. Munich.
Erxleben, E. 1974. "Die Rolle der Bevölkerungsklassen in Aussenhandel Athens im 4. Jahrhundert v. u. Z." In *Hellenische Poleis*, ed. E. C. Welskopf, 1: 460–520. Berlin.
Faraone, C. A. 1999. *Ancient Greek Love Magic.* Cambridge, Mass.
Fisher, N. R. E. 1992. *Hybris: A Study in the Values of Honour and Shame in Ancient Greece.* Warminster, Wilts., U.K.
———, ed. and trans. 2001. *Aeschines:* Against Timarchus. Oxford.
Fornara, C. W. 1970. "The Cult of Harmodios and Aristogeiton." *Philologus* 114: 155–80.
Foxhall, L. 1996. "The Law and the Lady: Women and Legal Proceedings in Classical Athens." In *Greek Law in Its Political Setting: Justification Not Justice*, ed. L. Foxhall and A. D. E. Lewis, 133–52. Oxford.
Fuks, A. 1953. *The Ancestral Constitution.* London.
Furley, W. D. 1996. *Andokides and the Herms: A Study of Crisis in Fifth-Century Athenian Religion. Bulletin of the Institute of Classical Studies* suppl. 65.
Gabrielsen, V. 1987. "The *Antidosis* Procedure in Classical Athens." *C&M* 37: 99–114.

———. 1994. *Financing the Athenian Fleet: Public Taxation and Social Relations.* Baltimore.
Gagarin. M. 1981. *Drakon and Early Athenian Homicide Law.* New Haven, Conn.
———. 1988. *The Murder of Herodes: A Study of Antiphon 5.* Frankfurt a/M.
———. 1990. "Bouleusis in Athenian Homicide Law." In *Symposion 1988: Vorträge zur griechischen und hellenistischen Rechtsgeschichte,* ed. G. Nenci and G. Thür, 81–99. Cologne.
———. 1996. "The Torture of Slaves in Athenian Law." *Classical Philology* 91: 1–18.
———, ed. 1997. *Antiphon: The Speeches.* Cambridge.
———. 2002. *Antiphon the Athenian: Oratory, Law, and Justice in the Age of the Sophists.* Austin, Tex.
———. 2003. "Telling Stories in Athenian Law." *TAPhA* 133: 197–207.
Gagarin, M., and D. M. MacDowell, trans. 1998. *Antiphon & Andocides.* Austin, Tex.
Garnsey, P. D. A. 1988. *Famine and Food-Supply in the Greco-Roman World: Responses to Risk and Crisis.* Cambridge.
Gernet, L., ed. and trans. 1954–60. *Démosthène: Plaidoyers civils.* 4 vols. Paris.
Goldberg, R. A. 2001. *Enemies Within: The Culture of Conspiracy in Modern America.* New Haven, Conn.
Goodnight, G. T., and J. Poulakos. 1981. "Conspiracy Rhetoric: From Pragmatism to Fantasy in Public Discourse." *Western Journal of Speech Communication.* 45: 299–316.
Grauman C. F. 1987. "Conspiracy: History and Social psychology." In *Changing Conceptions of Conspiracy,* ed. C. F. Graumann and S. Moscovici, 245–51. New York.
Green, P. 1991. "Rebooking the Flute-Girls: A Fresh Look at the Chronological Evidence for the Fall of Athens and *oktamēnos arkhē* of the Thirty." *AHB* 5: 1–16.
———. 1996. "The Metamorphosis of the Barbarian: Athenian Panhellenism in a Changing World." In *Transitions to Empire: Essays in Greco-Roman History, 360–146 B.C., in Honor of E. Badian,* ed. R. W. Wallace and E. M. Harris, 5–36. Norman, Okla.
Gribble, D. 1999. *Alcibiades and Athens: A Study in Literary Presentation.* Oxford.
Groh, D. 1987. "The Temptation of Conspiracy Theory, or: Why Do Bad Things Happen to Good People? Part I: Preliminary Draft of a Theory of Conspiracy Theories." In *Changing Conceptions of Conspiracy,* ed. C. F. Graumann and S. Moscovici, 1–13. New York.
Hadjú, I., ed. 2002, *Kommentar zu 4. philippischen Rede des Demosthenes.* Berlin.
Hall, E. 1995. "Lawcourt Drama: The Power of Performance in Greek Forensic Oratory." *BICS* 40: 39–58.
Hamel, D. 1998. *Athenian Generals: Military Authority in the Classical Period.* Leiden.

―――. 2003. *Trying Neaira: The True Story of a Courtesan's Scandalous Life in Ancient Greece.* New Haven, Conn.
Hammond, N. G. L. 1994. *Philip of Macedon.* Baltimore.
Hammond, N. G. L., and G. T. Griffith. 1979. *A History of Macedonia.* Vol. 2. Oxford.
Hansen, M. H. 1974. *The Sovereignty of the People's Court in the Fourth Century B.C. and the Public Action against Unconstitutional Proposals.* Translated by Jørgen Raphaelsen and Sonja Holbøll. Odense, Denmark.
―――. 1975. Eisangelia: *The Sovereignty of the People's Court in Athens in the Fourth Century B.C. and the Impeachment of Generals and Politicians.* Odense, Denmark.
―――. 1976. Apagoge, Endeixis *and* Ephegesis *against* Kakourgoi, Atimoi *and* Pheugontes. Odense, Denmark.
―――. 1983–89. *The Athenian Ecclesia.* 2 vols. Copenhagen.
―――. 1987. *The Athenian Assembly in the Age of Demosthenes.* Oxford.
―――. 1991. *The Athenian Democracy in the Age of Demosthenes.* Oxford.
Harding, P. 1976. "Androtion's Political Career." *Historia* 25: 186–200.
―――, ed. and trans. 1985. *From the End of the Peloponnesian War to the Battle of Ipsus.* Cambridge
―――, ed. and trans. 1994. *Androtion and the* Atthis: *The Fragments Translated with Introduction and Commentary.* Oxford.
Harding, S., and K. Stewart, 2003. "Anxieties of Influence: Conspiracy Theory and Therapeutic Culture in Millennial America." In *Transparency and Conspiracy: Ethnographies of Suspicion in the New World Order,* ed. H. G. West and T. Sanders, 258–86. Durham, N.C.
Harris, E. M. 1995. *Aeschines and Athenian Politics.* New York.
―――. 2003. "Law and Economy in Classical Athens: [Demosthenes], 'Against Dionysodorus.' " In *Dēmos: Classical Athenian Democracy,* ed. C. W. Blackwell, 2–15. www.stoa.org/projects/demos/article_law_economy (accessed January 2, 2006).
Harrison, A. R. W. 1968–71. *The Law of Athens.* Vol. 1: *The Family and Property.* Vol. 2: *Procedure.* Oxford.
Harvey, F. D. 1985. "*Dona Ferentes:* Some Aspects of Bribery in Greek Politics." In *Crux: Essays in Greek History Presented to G. E. M. de Ste. Croix on His 75th Birthday,* ed. P. A. Cartledge and F. D. Harvey, 76–117. London.
―――. 1990. "The Sykophant and Sykophancy: Vexatious Redefinition?" In *Nomos: Essays in Athenian Law, Politics and Society,* ed. P. A. Cartledge, P. C. Millett, and S. C. Todd, 103–21. Cambridge.
Hellegouarc'h, J. 1972. *Le Vocabulaire latin des relations et des parties politiques sous la république.* Paris.
Henry, A. S. 1983. *Honours and Privileges in Athenian Decrees : The Principal Formulae of Athenian Honorary Decrees.* Hildesheim.
Herman, G. 1987. *Ritualised Friendship and the Greek City.* Cambridge.
Hesk, J. 2000. *Deception and Democracy in Classical Athens.* Cambridge.
Heskel, J. 1997. *The North Aegean Wars, 371–360 B.C.* Historia Einzelschriften no. 102. Stuttgart.

Hirsh, S. W. 1985. *The Friendship of the Barbarians: Xenophon and the Persian Empire*. Hanover, N.H.
Höck, A. 1891. "Das Odrysenreich in Thrakien in fünften und vierten Jahrhundert v. Chr." *Hermes* 26: 76–117.
Hofstadter, R. 1967. *The Paranoid Style in American Politics and Other Essays*. New York.
Humphreys, S. 1985. "Social Relations on Stage: Witnesses in Classical Athens." *History and Anthropology* 1: 313–69.
Hunter, V. 1989. "Women's Authority in Classical Athens." *Échos du monde classique / Classical Views* 8.1: 39–48.
———. 1994. *Policing Athens: Social Control in the Attic Lawsuits, 420–320 B.C.* Princeton, N.J.
———. 1997. "The Prison of Athens: A Comparative Perspective." *Phoenix* 51.3–4: 296–326.
Isager, S., and M. H. Hansen 1975. *Aspects of Athenian Society in the Fourth Century B.C.: A Historical Introduction to and a Commentary on the Paragraphē-Speeches and the Speech Against Dionysodorus in the Corpus Demosthenicum (XXXII–XXXVII, and LVI)*. Translated by J. H. Rosenmeier. Odense, Denmark.
Jaeger, W. 1938. *Demosthenes: The Origin and Growth of His Thought*. Berkeley.
Just, R. 1989. *Women in Athenian Law and Life*. London.
Johnstone, S. 1999. *Disputes and Democracy: The Consequences of Litigation in Ancient Athens*. Austin, Tex.
———. 2000. "Apology for the Manuscript of Demosthenes 59.67." *AJP* 132.2: 229–56.
Kapparis, K. A., ed. and trans. 1999. *Apollodoros "Against Neaira" [D. 59]*. New York.
Kelly, D. 1990. "Charidemos's Citizenship: The Problem of *IG* II^2 207." *ZPE* 83: 96–109.
Kertsch, M. 1971. *Kommentar zur 30. Rede des Demosthenes (gegen Onetor I)*. Vienna.
Knight, P. 2001. "ILOVEYOU: Viruses, Paranoia, and the Environment of Risk." In *The Age of Anxiety: Conspiracy Theory and the Human Sciences*, ed. J. Parish and M. Parker, 1–16. Malden, Md.
Koch, S. 1989. "Verstiess der Antrag des Aristokrates (Dem. 23, 91) gegen die Gesetze?" *Zeitschrift der Savigny-Stiftung für Rechtsgeschichte* 106: 547–56.
Konstan, D. 1997. *Friendship in the Classical World*. Cambridge.
Krentz, P. 1982. *The Thirty at Athens*. Ithaca, N.Y.
Kruglanski, A. W. 1987. "Blame-Placing Schemata and Attributional Research." In *Changing Conceptions of Conspiracy*, ed. C. F. Graumann and S. Moscovici, 219–229. New York.
Lane Fox, R. 1997. "Demosthenes, Dionysius and the Dating of Six Early Speeches." *C&M* 48: 167–203.
Lefèvre, F. 1998. *L'Amphictionie pyléo-delphique: Histoire et institutions*. Paris.
Lintott, A. W. 1982. *Violence, Civil Strife and Revolution in the Classical City, 750–330 B.C.* Baltimore.

Lofberg, J. O. 1917. *Sycophancy in Athens.* Chicago.
Loening, T. C. 1987. *The Reconciliation Agreement of 403/2 B.C. in Athens. Hermes* suppl. 53. Stuttgart.
Londey P. 1990. "The Outbreak of the Fourth Sacred War." *Chiron* 20: 239–60.
MacDowell, D. M. 1962. *Andokides: On the Mysteries.* Oxford.
———. 1963. *The Athenian Homicide Law in the Age of the Orators.* Manchester.
———. 1971. *Aristophanes: Wasps.* Oxford.
———. 1978. *The Law in Classical Athens.* Ithaca, N.Y.
———. 1983. "Athenian Laws about Bribery." *RIDA* 30: 57–78.
———, ed. and trans. 1990. *Demosthenes Against Meidias: (Oration 21).* Oxford.
———, ed. and trans. 2000. *Demosthenes On the False Embassy (Oration 19).* Oxford.
———, trans. 2004. *Demosthenes, Speeches 27–38.* Austin, Tex.
Marcus, G. E. 1999. "An Introduction to the Volume: The Paranoid Style Now." In id., ed. *Paranoia within Reason: A Casebook on Conspiracy as Explanation,* 1–11. Chicago.
Markle, M. M. 1976. "Support of Athenian Intellectuals for Philip: A Study of Isocrates' *Philippus* and Speusippus' *Letter to Philip.*" *JHS* 96: 80–99.
Menu, M. 2000. *Jeunes et vieux chez Lysias: L'akolasia de la jeunesse au IVe siècle av. J.C.* Rennes.
Meyer-Laurin, H. 1965. *Gesetz und Billigkeit im attischen Prozess.* Weimar.
Millett, P. 1991. *Lending and Borrowing in Ancient Athens.* Cambridge.
Milns, R. D. 2000. "The Public Speeches of Demosthenes." In *Demosthenes: Statesman and Orator,* ed. I. Worthington, 205–23. New York.
Mirhady, D. C. 2000. "Demosthenes as Advocate: The Private Speeches." In *Demosthenes: Statesman and Orator,* ed. I. Worthington, 205–23. New York.
———. 2004. "Contracts in Athens." In *Law, Rhetoric, and Comedy in Classical Athens: Essays in Honour of Douglas M. MacDowell,* ed. D. L. Cairns and R. A. Knox, 51–63. Swansea.
Missiou, A. 1992. *The Subversive Oratory of Andocides: Politics, Ideology, and Decision-Making in Democratic Athens.* Cambridge.
Mitchell, L. G. 1997. *Greeks Bearing Gifts: The Public Use of Private Relationships in the Greek World, 453–323 BC.* Cambridge.
Moscovici, S. 1987. "The Conspiracy Mentality." In *Changing Conceptions of Conspiracy,* ed. C. F. Graumann and S. Moscovici, 151–69. New York.
Munn, M. 2000. *The School of History: Athens in the Age of Socrates.* Berkeley.
Murphy, T. M. 1989. "The Vilification of Eratosthenes and Theramenes in Lysias 12." *AJP* 110: 40–49.
Naiden, F. S. 2004. "Supplication and the Law." In *The Law and the Courts in Ancient Athens,* ed. E. M. Harris and L. Rubinstein, 71–91. London.
Newton, R. M. 1978–79. "The Murderers of Laius, again (Soph. *OT* 126–7)." *CW* 72: 231–34.
Ober, J. 1989. *Mass and Elite in Democratic Athens: Rhetoric, Ideology, and the Power of the People.* Princeton, N.J.

———. 1996. *The Athenian Revolution: Essays on Ancient Greek Democracy and Political Theory*. Princeton, N.J.
Osborne, R. 1985a. *Demos: The Discovery of Classical Attika*. Cambridge.
———. 1985b. "Law in Action in Classical Athens." *JHS* 105: 40–58.
Ostwald, M. 1986. *From Popular Sovereignty to the Sovereignty of the People: Law, Society and Politics in Fifth-Century Athens*. Berkeley.
Pagán, V. E. 2005. *Conspiracy Narratives in Roman History*. Austin, Tex.
Page, D. 1962. *Poetae Melici Graeci*. Oxford.
Papillon, T. L. 1998. *Rhetorical Studies in the Aristocratea of Demosthenes*. New York.
Parish, J. 2001. "The Age of Anxiety." In *The Age of Anxiety: Conspiracy Theory and the Human Sciences*, ed. J. Parish and M. Parker, 17–30. Malden, Md.
Parke, H. W. 1933. *Greek Mercenary Soldiers from the Earliest Times to the Battle of Ipsus*. Oxford.
———. 1939. "Delphica: The Persian Shields of the Medes and the Thebans." *Hermathena* 28: 71–78.
Patterson, C. 1994. "The Case against Neaera and the Public Ideology of the Athenian Family." In *Athenian Identity and Civic Ideology*, ed. A. Boegehold and A. Scafuro, 199–216. Baltimore.
Patteson, A. J. 1974. "Commentary on [Demosthenes] LIX: Against Neaera." Ph.D. diss., University of Pennsylvania.
Paulsen, T., ed. 1999. *Die Parapresbeia-Reden des Demosthenes und des Aischines: Kommentar und Interpretationen zu Demosthenes, or. XIX, und Aischines, or. II*. Trier, Germany.
Pearson, L. 1972. *Demosthenes: Six Private Speeches*. Atlanta, Ga.
———. 1981. *The Art of Demosthenes*. Ann Arbor, Mich.
Perlman, S. 1957. "Isocrates' 'Philippus'—A Reinterpretation." *Historia* 6: 306–17 = Perlman 1973: 103–16.
———. 1969. "Isocrates' Philippus and Panhellenism." *Historia* 18: 370–74.
———, ed. 1973. *Philip and Athens*. Cambridge.
Pipes, D. 1997. *Conspiracy: How the Paranoid Style Flourishes and Where It Comes From*. New York.
Pomeroy, S. C. 1997. *Families in Classical and Hellenistic Greece: Representations and Realities*. Oxford.
Popper, K. R. 1965. *Conjectures and Refutations: The Growth of Scientific Knowledge*. New York.
Porter, J. 1997. "Adultery by the Book: Lysias 1 (*On the Murder of Eratosthenes*) and Comic Diegeses." *Échos du monde classique / Classical Views* 16: 422–53.
Pritchett, W. K. 1971–91. *The Greek State at War*. 5 vols. Berkeley.
Reed, C. M. 2003. *Maritime Traders in the Ancient Greek World*. Cambridge.
Renaud, R. 1970. "Cléophon et la guerre du Péloponnèse." *RÉG* 78: 458–77.
Rhodes, P. J. 1985. *The Athenian Boule*. Oxford.
———. 1993. *A Commentary on the Aristotelian* Athenaion Politeia. Oxford.
———. 1995. "Judicial Procedures in Fourth-Century Athens: Improvement or Simply Change?" In *Die athenische Demokratie im 4. Jahrhundert v. Chr.:*

Vollendung oder Verfall einer Verfassungsform? ed. W. Eder, 303–19 Stuttgart.
Rhodes, P. J., and D. M. Lewis. 1997. *The Decrees of the Greek States.* Oxford.
Rhodes, P. J., and R. Osborne. 2003. *Greek Historical Inscriptions, 404- 323 BC.* Oxford.
Rickert, G. 1989. *Ekōn and Akōn in Early Greek Thought.* Atlanta, Ga.
Roisman, J. 2005. *The Rhetoric of Manhood: Masculinity in the Attic Orators.* Berkeley.
Rosen, S. 1992. "Suspicion, Deception, and Concealment." In *Le Miracle grec: Actes du IIe Colloque sur la pensée antique, les 18, 19 et 20 mai 1989 à la Faculté des lettres de Nice,* ed. Antoine Thivel, 59–68. Paris.
Roux, G. 1979. *L'Amphictionie, Delphes et le temple d'Apollon au IVe Siècle.* 1979.
Rowe, G. 2000. "Anti-Isocratean Sentiment in Demosthenes' *Against Androtion.*" *Historia* 49.3: 278–302.
———. 2002. "Two Responses by Isocrates to Demosthenes." *Historia* 51.2: 149–62.
Rubinstein, L. 1993. *Adoption in IV. Century Athens.* Opuscula Graecolatina 34. Copenhagen.
———. 2000. *Litigation and Cooperation: Supporting Speakers in the Courts of Classical Athens.* Historia suppl. 147. Stuttgart.
Ryder, T. T. 1994. "The Diplomatic Skills of Philip II." In *Ventures into Greek History: Essays in Honour of N. G. L. Hammond,* ed. I. Worthington, 228–57. Oxford.
Sagan, E. 1991. *The Honey and the Hemlock: Democracy and Paranoia in Ancient Athens and Modern America.* Princeton, N.J.
Ste Croix, G. E. M. de. 1963. "The Alleged Secret Pact between Athens and Philip Concerning Amphipolis and Pydna." *CQ* 13: 110–19 = Perlman 1973, 35–46.
Sánchez, P. 2001. *L'Amphictionie des Pyles et de Delphes: Recherches sur son rôle historique, des origines au IIe siècle de notre ère.* Historia suppl. 148. Stuttgart.
Sanders, T., and H. G. West. 2003. "Power Revealed and Concealed in the New World Order." In *Transparency and Conspiracy: Ethnographies of Suspicion in the New World Order,* ed. H. G. West and T. Sanders, 1–37. Durham, N.C.
Sartori, F. 1957. *Le eterie nella vita politica ateniese del VI e V secolo a. C.* Rome.
Scafuro, A. 1994. "Witnessing and False Witnessing: Proving Citizenship and Kin Identity in Fourth-Century Athens." In *Athenian Identity and Civic Ideology,* ed. A. L. Bogehold and A. Scafuro, 159–98. Baltimore.
———. 1997. *The Forensic Stage: Settling Disputes in Greco-Roman New Comedy.* Cambridge.
Schäfer, A. 1856–58. *Demosthenes und seine Zeit.* Vol. 3.2. Leipzig.
Schindel, U. 1979. *Der Mordfall Herodes Zur 5. Rede Antiphons.* Göttingen.
Schweizer, A. 1936. *Die 13. Rede des Lysias: Eine rhetorische Analyse.* Leipzig.
Sealey, R. 1955. "Dionysius of Halicarnassus and Some Demosthenic Dates." *REG* 68: 77–120

---. 1965. *Essays in Greek History*. New York.
---. 1978. "Philipp II. und Athen, 344/3 und 339." *Historia* 27.2: 295–316.
---. 1993. *Demosthenes and His Time: A Study in Defeat*. New York.
Sinclair, R. K. 1988. *Democracy and Participation in Athens*. Cambridge.
Stem, R. 2003. "The Thirty at Athens in the Summer of 404." *Phoenix* 57.1–2: 18–34.
Stewart, K., and S. Harding. 1999. "Bad Endings: American Apocalypses." *Annual Review of Anthropology* 28: 285–310.
Strauss, B. S. 1986. *Athens after the Peloponnesian War: Class, Faction and Policy, 403–386 B.C.* London.
Thompson, W. E. 1976. *De Hereditate Hagniae: An Athenian Inheritance Case. Mnemosyne* suppl. 44. Leiden.
Tod, M. N., ed. 1948. *A Selection of Greek Historical Inscriptions*. Vol. 2. Oxford.
Todd, S. C. 1990. "The Purpose of Evidence in Athenian Courts." In *Nomos: Essays in Athenian Law, Politics and Society*, ed. P. A. Cartledge, P. Millett, and S. Todd, 19–40. Cambridge.
---. 1993. *The Shape of Athenian Law*. Oxford.
---. 1996. "Lysias Against Nicomachus." In *Greek Law in Its Political Setting: Justifications Not Justice*, ed. L. Foxhall and A. D. E. Lewis, 101–31. Oxford.
---. trans. 2000. *Lysias*. Austin, Tex.
---. 2004. "Revisiting the Herms and the Mysteries." In *Law, Rhetoric, and Comedy in Classsical Athens: Essays in Honour of Douglas M. MacDowell*, ed. D. L. Cairns and R. A. Knox, 87–102. Swansea.
Too, Y. L. 1995. *The Rhetoric of Identity in Isocrates: Text, Power, Pedagogy*. Cambridge.
Trevett, J. 1992. *Apollodoros the Son of Pasion*. Oxford.
---. 1996. "Did Demosthenes Publish his Deliberative Speeches?" *Hermes* 124: 425–41.
Usher, S. 1999. *Greek Oratory: Tradition and Originality*. Oxford.
Wallace, R. W. 2000. "'Investigations and Reports by the Areopagus Council and Demosthenes' Areopagus' Decree." In *Polis & Politics: Studies in Ancient Greek History Presented to Mogens Herman Hansen on his Sixtieth Birthday, August 20, 2000*, ed. P. Flensted-Jensen, T. H. Nielsen and L. Rubinstein, 581–95. Copenhagen.
Wankel, H. 1976, ed. *Demosthenes, Rede für Ktesiphon über den Kranz*. 2 vols. Heidelberg.
Wencis, L. 1977. "Hypopsia and the Structure of Xenophon's *Anabasis*." *CJ* 73: 44–49.
West, H. G., and T. Sanders, eds. 2003. *Transparency and Conspiracy: Ethnographies of Suspicion in the New World Order*. Durham, N.C.
West, W. C. 1995. "The Decree of Demosthenes against Leptines." *ZPE* 107: 237–47.
Whitehead, D. 1986. *The Demes of Attica 508/7–ca. 250 B.C.* Princeton, N.J.
---. 1990. *Aeneas the Tactician: How to Survive under Siege*. Oxford.
---, trans. and ed. 2000. *Hypereides: The Forensic Speeches*. Oxford.

Wilson, P. 2000. *The Athenian Institution of the Khoregia: The Chorus, the City and the Stage*. Cambridge.
Wohl, V. 1999. "The *Eros* of Alcibiades." *Classical Antiquity* 18: 349–80.
Wolff, H. J. 1943. "The *dikē blabēs* in Dem. 55." *AJP* 64: 316–24.
———. 1966. *Die attische Paragraphē: Ein Beitrag zum Problem der Auflockerung archaischer Prozessformen*. Weimar.
Wolpert, A. 2002a. "Lysias 18 and Athenian Memory of Civil War." *AJP* 132.1–2: 109–26.
———. 2002b. *Remembering Defeat: Civil War and Civic Memory in Ancient Athens*. Baltimore.
Worthington, I. 1991. "The Authenticity of Demosthenes' Fourth Philippic." *Mnemosyne* 44: 425–28.
———, ed. and trans. 1992. *A Historical Commentary on Dinarchus: Rhetoric and Conspiracy in Later Fourth-Century Athens*. Ann Arbor, Mich.
———, ed. 2000. *Demosthenes: Statesman and Orator*. New York.
———. 2002. "Who Is Demosthenes at the End of Demosthenes 56, Against Dionysodorus? An Exercise in Methodology." *Scholia* 11: 18–24.
Wüst, F. R. 1938. *Philipp II. von Makedonien und Griechenland*. Münchener Historische Abhandlungen 14. Munich.
Wyate, W. [1882] 1979. *Demosthenes Against Androtion and Against Timocrates*. New York.
Wyse, W. 1904. *The Speeches of Isaeus*. Cambridge.
Yunis, H., ed. 2001. *Demosthenes: On the Crown*. Cambridge.
Zukier, H. 1987. "The Conspiratorial Imperative: Medieval Jewry in Western Europe." In *Changing Conceptions of Conspiracy*, ed. C. F. Graumann and S. Moscovici, 87–103. New York.

General Index

Acarnania, 29
Adultery, 16–18, 58–62
Aegospotamoi, 73, 79, 83
Aenus, 14
Aeschines, 51, 114, 120–21, 131, 153.
  See also Demosthenes, and Aeschines
Agamemnon, 13
Agasicles, 91n50
Agoratus, 7, 72–83, 84, 85
Agyrrhius, 87
Alce, 20
Alcibiades, 70, 80n26
Alexander the Great, 8, 118, 145, 146
Amadocus, 96, 165–66
Amnesty, 52, 72
Amphictyonic league, 133–45
Amphipolis, 97, 100, 101, 102, 103, 125
Amphissa, 133–45
Anaximenes, 130
Anaxinus, 131, 132
Andocides, 51–54, 55, 69–70, 87, 153
Andros, 58
Androtion, 104–12
Antidosis (exchange), 45–47, 153–54
Antigone, 32–34
Antiphilus, 92
Antiphon (spy), 131
Apaturius, 38–40, 41
Apagōgē (summary arrest), 15
Apographē, 111
Aphidna, 56
Aphobus, 23–27, 45–47
Apollo, 133, 134, 138, 140

Apollodorus, 42, 44, 56–57, 58–64
Apollophanes, 56
Arbitration and reconciliation, 38–40, 50–51, 52–54, 55, 57, 59–62
Arcadia, 120–21, 131
Archebius, 104–12
Archippus, 38–39
Archon, 48–50
Areopagus, 12
Arethusius, 63–64
Argos, 121
Aristocles, 38–40
Aristocrates, 96–103, 165–67
Aristogeiton, 88, 159
Aristomachus, 97–98, 100, 103, 166, 167
Aristophanes (playwright), 66–68, 88, 123, 151
Aristophanes (plotter), 80
Aristophon of Piraeus, 36–38, 58, 162
Aristophon (politician), 105, 108
Arrybas, 99n8
Artemis, 74
Assembly, 4, 74, 75, 78, 79, 81, 85, 95, 96–103, 105–6, 109–11, 115, 132, 135–36, 152, 166
Athene, 93, 105
Athenogenes, 32–34, 63

Berisades, 96, 165, 166
Black's Law Dictionary, 2
Blass, F, 107
Boeotia, 125

181

Boeotus, 54–55
Borrowing and Lending, 35–42, 62–64.
  See also Grain; Trade, maritime
Bosporus, 40
Byzantium, Byzantines, 38–39, 166

Callias, 52–54, 55, 69
Callimachus, 56–58
Callimedon, 132
Callipus, 28–31
Callistratus, 28–31
Cardia, 166
Carey, C., 61
Caria, 104, 105
Carystius, 129n21
Cephallenia, 36, 161
Cephisius, 52
Cephisodotus, 167
Cephisophon, 56
Cersebleptes, 96–103, 115, 165–67
Cetriporis, 165
Chabrias, 167
Chares, 166–67
Chaerestratus, 19–20
Chaeronea, battle of, 88, 120n5, 133, 138
Charidemus, 96–103, 165–67
Chersonese. See Thrace
Chios, 167
Choregus, 47–51, 153
Chremdon, 83, 84
Chrysippus, 40–41
Ciron, 20–22, 153
Cirrha, 134, 140, 142, 143
Cleomenes, 133, 146–49, 158
Cleon, 66–67, 86, 88, 132, 151, 159
Cleophon, 73, 74, 77, 79, 80, 83–85
Clytemnestra, 13
Comon, 28–31
Conspiracism, 13, 76, 133, 149, 151–60.
  See also Conspiracy, and conspiratorial mindset
Conspiracy: and agents, 13–14, 18, 20–22, 35, 37, 40, 45, 46, 48, 63, 76, 88, 116, 118–49, 122–31, 134–45, 158; and Athenian democracy, 6, 7, 66–117, 123, 127, 152–53, 155–56, 158–60; and bribes, 8, 44–45, 47–51, 52, 66, 86–87, 91, 92, 98n5, 106, 114, 118–19, 120, 122, 123, 125, 126n16, 127–32, 134–36, 139–45; and chance, 4, 14, 16, 18, 47, 49, 90, 113, 114, 141, 153; and causal linking 24, 47, 48, 49, 50, 97, 113, 141–42, 145, 153, 157, 158; and changeable plotters, 32n26, 37, 46–47, 76n19, 98, 140–41, 148; and conspiratorial mindset and theories,

2, 6, 15, 16, 24, 43, 65, 93–94, 113, 117, 121, 124, 138, 149–60; and conspirators' attributes, 4–5, 15, 20, 21, 28, 31, 37, 40n38, 54, 56, 57–58, 70, 77, 93, 99, 114, 115, 139, 142, 144, 148, 149, 153, 156; and the courts, 3–5, 13, 22, 27, 28, 29–31, 35, 42, 43, 44–45, 46, 54, 56, 57–58, 64, 74, 75, 81–82, 83–85, 91, 93, 105, 116, 152, 159; and deceit, fraud, and trickery 1, 3–4, 14, 15, 21, 23, 27, 30, 31–34, 36–37, 45, 48, 65n37, 69, 125, 130, 136, 139, 140, 142–43, 149, 153, 161–63; definition of, 2; and desires and love, 11–12, 31–34, 54, 58–62, 63, 68, 85, 122, 152; and dropping suits, 15, 45–54, 56, 60–63, 131–32, 154; as explanatory device, 7, 18, 28, 37–38, 79, 89, 93–94, 139, 141, 147–48, 156–60, 163; and fairness and justice, 4–5, 18, 22, 28, 34, 54, 85, 90, 93, 158; and fear of, 5, 6, 20, 21, 42, 53, 68, 70, 85–86, 119–20, 121, 126, 129, 152–60; and foreign and international plots, 8–9, 96–103, 118–49, 153, 157–58; and framing, 51–65, 93; and friendship, 24, 42, 62–64, 70, 71–72, 131, 156; against Greece (see Grain; Persia; Philip II); and greed, 6, 15, 18, 20, 21, 31, 34–35, 41, 42, 43, 58, 66, 68, 85, 94, 114, 122, 125, 130, 148, 149; and homicide, 11–18, 21, 47–51, 55, 56–58, 64, 96–97, 100, 102, 151, 153; and kinship, 3, 20, 22, 35, 54–55, 57, 156; legal plots, 27, 30, 35, 44–65, 83–85, 88; and legislation, 77, 95–117; and logic, 4, 12, 13, 16, 18, 48–49, 77, 91, 142, 156, 158; models and themes of, 1–5, 13–14, 18, 20, 21–22, 26, 30–34, 37, 43, 45, 58, 64–65, 77–78, 79–80, 82, 84, 88, 93–94, 97–98, 103, 113–14, 116–17, 121, 128–29, 136, 138, 141–42, 148, 153–60; and motives, 4, 12, 14, 15, 17, 28, 92, 103, 104, 114, 117, 123, 129, 136, 141–45, 155; and oligarchy, 68–85, 153; and opportunity, 5, 13, 15, 20, 30, 77, 79, 90, 91, 144, 153; and paranoia, 6–7, 18, 43, 94, 156–60; and planning, 4–5, 13, 13n4, 14, 15, 30–31, 77, 97, 115, 121, 138–45, 149, 153; and plot detectors, 4–5, 56, 67, 95, 97–98, 119, 125, 130–32, 144, 154, 156, 158, 160; political plots, 44,

General Index

66–118, 151–55, 158; and power, 4, 6, 15, 18, 21, 22, 31, 42, 94, 99, 121, 136, 141, 149, 154–56; and property and inheritance, 3–4, 15, 19–43, 57–58, 85, 116–17, 154; regarded positively, 7–9; in Rome, 2, 2n2, 155n10; and sycophancy, 15, 15n8, 34, 37n34, 38, 41, 43, 50, 53, 55n23, 56, 57–62, 63, 85, 86, 91, 116, 130; and treason, 66, 68, 84, 84n37, 86–87, 123, 128, 131–32; and tyranny, 7, 67–68, 71, 73, 128, 152; and victims of, 5, 17, 20, 26, 28, 31, 32–35, 42, 46, 47, 53, 56, 64, 67, 68, 76, 78, 82, 87–88, 90, 93, 98, 117, 120, 123, 153, 154; vocabulary and terms of, 2–3, 27–31, 69–70, 97, 119, 128, 139; and wealth, 42; and witnesses and evidence, 3, 12, 14–15, 18n15, 23–27, 39, 40–41, 42–43, 56, 57, 62–65, 84, 90–91, 117, 131, 143, 147, 154, 162, 163n7. *See also* Decrees; Intentionality; Philip II
Contract, 32–34, 146–47, 162
Corinth, 80n27
Cottyphus, 135, 138, 140, 142, 144–45
Cotys, 96, 102, 102n16, 103, 165, 166
Council, 44, 50, 52, 74, 76–77, 80–82, 83–85, 86, 88, 95, 96, 97, 105, 106, 109–10, 112–13, 115, 134–36, 152
Cratinus, 57–58
Crenides, 102n14, 165
Creon, 151
Critias, 71, 79, 82n32
Ctesiphon, 114
Cyrene, 56

Damage, 31–35, 41, 47
Darius, 145–48
Davis, J. K., 165
Decrees (*psēphismata*), 52, 77, 81, 82, 89, 93, 95–117, 136, 143, 165–67
Delphi, 133–34, 138, 143, 144
Deme (township), 88–94
Demon, 35–38, 41, 161–63
Demophantus, 152
Demosthenes, 51, 101n13, 103, 114, 117, 153, 154, 166; and Aeschines, 71, 114–16, 118, 122–24, 125, 131–32, 134–45, 153; and his family and inheritance, 22–27, 38n35, 45–47, 114, 154; as political actor, 8, 87–88, 104, 115–16, 118–45, 131–32. *See also* Philip II
Diadikasia (judgment between), 3, 27–28, 29–31, 106n24

Dikai emporikai (maritime cases). *See* Trade, maritime
Dike blabēs. *See* Damage
Dikē exouēs (ejection suit), 23, 163
Diocles, 20–22, 58, 154
Diodorus, 103–14
Diopeithes, 127
Dion, 40
Dinysodorus (general), 72, 73, 79, 80
Dionysodorus (merchant), 146–48
Distrust. *See* Conspiracy, and conspiratorial mindset
Divorce, 23–27
Dowry, 23–27, 59–62, 154

Eisangelia (impeachment), 47–48, 84n37, 86, 104, 152, 152n3
Egypt, Egyptians, 32, 104, 108, 145–49
Elatea, 133, 134n1, 138, 139, 140, 142, 144
Eleusinion, altar of, 52, 54
Eleusis, 7
Endeixis (denouncement), 15, 88
Epaenetus, 58–62, 63
Epichares, 116–17
Epicrtaes (councilman), 112–13
Epicrates (prosecutor), 32–34, 63
Eratosthenes (adulterer), 16–18
Eratosthenes (oligarch), 7, 79
Ergocles, 86–87
Eryxias, 39–40
Eubilides, 89–94
Euboia, 125, 128
Eubulus, 98, 120
Eucrates, son of Niceratus, 79
Eucrates, son of Aristotimus, 152
Euctemon of Cephisia 19–20
Euctemon (politician), 104–12
Euphiletus (in And. 1), 69
Euphiletus (in Lys. 1), 16–18
Euphraeus, 128, 129n21
Euthycles, 96–103, 166
Euthunai (giving account), 92, 152n3
Euxitheus, 88–94

Freudian psychology, 6, 155, 156

Garnsey, P., 147
Glaucestas, 104–12
Grain, 35–38, 85n39, 133, 145–49, 158, 161–63. *See* Trade, maritime
Graphē nomon mē epitēdeion theinai, 95, 103, 104n19, 107n26
Graphē paranomōn, 95, 96, 99n7, 104n19, 106, 111n38, 114, 116, 117

Guardians, 20, 22–27, 45–47, 114, 118, 153–54

Hagnias, 3, 27–28, 38
Halimus, 88–94
Hansen. M. H., 36, 161–63
Harmodius and Aristogeiton, 7
Harpalus, 118
Hegesippus, 130
Hegestratus, 35–38, 161–2
Hellespont, 167
Heracles, 8
Herms and the Mysteries affairs, 52–54, 69–70, 87
Herodes, 13–16, 153
Hetaira (courtesan), 32, 58–62
Hetaireiai (lit. companionships), 44, 69–72, 74, 77, 79, 117
Honoring, 93, 96–103, 114–17, 134
Hubadai, 116
Hubris, 22, 42, 45–46, 63, 71
Husbands and wives, 11–13, 16–18, 21, 23–27
Hyperides, 118

Illyria, 165
Imprisonment, 6, 104, 107, 110, 111
Intentionality, 5, 5n6, 11, 12, 31–32, 47
Iphicrates, 102–3
Ischomachus, 116
Isocrates, 111

Kurios (head of household), 16, 60

Lampis, 40–41
Lane Fox, R., 99, 166–67
Laius, 151
Leitourgia, 45, 47
Leptines, 159
Lesbos, 14
Locris, 133, 140, 142
Lycidas, 62–63
Lycinus, 14, 16
Lysander, 74, 78, 79, 80n26, 83
Lysitheides, 104–12

Macedonia. See Philip II
Manhood, 8, 16, 20, 54, 63, 130
Mantitheus, 54–55
Maroneia, 165
Massalia, Massaliotes 35–38, 161–62
Megalopolis, 121
Megara, 25, 132
Meidias, 1, 45–47, 50n11
Melanopus, 104–12
Meletus, 69
Menecles, 55, 58

Menestratus, 82
Messene, 121
Milocythes, 102, 102n16
Mistress, 11–13
Munychia, 74, 81
Mytilene, Mytileneans, 13–14, 67, 99n8, 151, 159

Naucratis, 104, 105
Neaera, 56, 58–62
Neoptolemus, 125, 131
Nicias, 68n5
Nicobolus, 41–42
Nicomachus, 79, 83–85
Nicostratus, 62–64
Nomothetai, 106, 112–13

Oath, 13, 29–30, 32, 74, 80, 86, 92
Oedipus, 151
Olympiodorus, 28–31
Olynthus, 120, 124, 126n17
Onetor, 22–27
Oreus, 128–29

Paeonia, 165
Palladium, 56
Pamenes, 165
Pamphilius, 145–48
Panathenaean festival, 106, 112–13
Pancleon, 89n45
Pantaenetus, 41–42
Paragraphē (counter-prosecution), 35, 38, 40, 41, 163
Parmeniscus, 146–48
Parmeno, 38–39
Parmenion, 129n21
Pasion, 42
Pasiphon, 25
Pericles, 85, 159
Perinthus, 166
Persia, Persian King, 8, 119–21, 127, 129
Phano, 58–62, 63
Phanus, 23
Phasis, 111
Philip II of Macedon, 8–9, 71, 88, 100, 102n14, 103, 115–16, 118–45, 153, 154, 158, 165, 166
Philistides, 128
Philocrates, 47–51, 71, 115, 122, 123, 125, 136
Philoctemon, 20
Phocis, 121, 122, 123, 126, 133
Phocritus, 38–39
Phormio (Apollodorus's stepfather), 62
Phormio (merchant), 40–41
Phrynichus, 7, 72
Physicians, 25, 39, 55

General Index

Piraeus, 11, 37, 39, 74, 131, 132, 141n13
Piracy, 122, 139
Poison, 12–13, 13n5
Pōlētai, 109
Polyeuctus, 116
Prostitutes, 20, 32, 68. *See also* Neaera
Protus, 35–38, 162

Revenge, 12, 16, 18, 30, 84, 116
Rhodes, 82n34, 146–48
Rowe, G., 111

Sacred War: Third, 123, 126n17; Fourth, 133–45
Sagan, E., 6, 18, 43, 155–56
Samos, 78
Satyrus, 83, 84
Scafuro, A., 63
Schäfer, A., 107
Scrutiny, 88–94
Scythia, 135, 138
Sealey, R., 100, 104, 167
Sestus, 166
Sicily, 35–38, 69
Slaves, 12, 13–15, 17, 18, 20, 25, 29, 32–34, 38, 39, 40, 41, 42, 57–58, 62–64, 76, 84n36
Social War, 82n34, 100, 105n23, 167
Socrates, 71
Solon, 34, 85
Sositheus, 27
Sparta, 8, 73–74, 75n16, 77, 78, 80, 81, 82–83, 119n2, 121
State debtors, 41, 62–64, 88, 103–14, 116–17
Stephanus of Eroeadae, 56–57, 58–62, 63
Stephanus, son of Menecles, 42, 44
Supporting Speakers, 19, 43, 44, 53, 89, 115

Sureties, 38–40, 59–62, 74, 80–81, 86, 103
Syracuse, 35–38, 161–62

Tenedos, 99n8
Thebes, 80n27, 122, 134–36, 138, 139, 140, 142, 144, 151
Theocrinus, 116–17
Theocritus, 74, 76–77, 80, 80n26, 81
Theomnestus, 56
Theopompus, 27
Theramenes, 73, 74, 77, 79–80, 82n32
Thermopylae, 122, 135
Thesmothetai, 44, 59
Thessaly, 121, 135, 139, 140, 142, 143, 152
Thirty, the, 7, 70, 72–85
Thrace, Thracians, 96–103, 127, 165–67
Thrasybulus, 86
Thrasylochus, 45–47, 153
Thucydides, 67–68, 69, 125n15, 151
Timarchus, 71
Timocrates, 23–27, 98, 103–15
Todd, S., 31
Torture, 12, 12n3, 25, 42, 74, 77, 80, 131
Trade, maritime, 35–41, 145–49. *See also* Grain
Troizen, 32n27

Whitehead, D., 92
Women, 13, 13n5, 20, 25, 28. *See also* Husbands and wives; Mistress
Wyate, W., 107, 110
Wyse, W., 21, 28

Xenotimus, 57–58

Zenothemis, 35–38, 161–63
Zētētai, 105

Index Locorum

Aeneas Tacticus		7	116n45
1.1.1–15	154n8	58	123
		62–63	115
Aeschines		64–68	51n15
1, *Against Timarchus*		66	8n16
5	95, 159n22	73–74	115n44
62–64	40n38	106–29	135
78	89	116	143
110	71n12	122–23	138
115–15	91n50	125	139n10
173	71	126	90n49
2, *On the Embassy*		128–29	138
1	54n19, 116n45	193	116n45
8	88	212	55n22
19	71	223	13n4
22	123, 126n16	223–25	131
43	123	233	86n40
54	123	234	154n7
76	75n17	242	114
79	120n6	255	72n13
81	166n4	Schol. Aeschines	
82–90	115n44	2.81	166n4
93	55n22		
94–96	153n6	Andocides	
97	123	1, *On the Mysteries*	
123	123	And. 1	51–54
124–25	123n13	1	53n18
138	123	4	52
148	13n4	6	54, 153
154–55	65n37, 86n40	11–12	72
181	88	15	72
3, *Against Ctesiphon*		27–28	72
1	54n19, 65n37, 116n45	54	71n11
2	113n41, 115	73	107n26

187

Index Locorum

Andocides
1, *On the Mysteries (continued)*
92–99	15n8, 53
96–98	152n3
100	71n12
110	54
110–16	52
110–36	53
117–21	52
122–23	52, 53
124–31	53
132	52
133–35	53, 87
140	159n23

2, *On His Return*
4	54n20

3, *On the Peace with Sparta*
And. 3	125n15
10–11	83
11–12	78

[4], *Against Alcibiades*
4	72n13
15	13n4

Antiphon
1, *Against the Stepmother*
Ant. 1	11–13, 14, 153n5
3	13
5	13
5–12	12
9	12n2, 14
15–16	13n4
17	13
19	12
19–20	13n4
20	12
21	13
25–27	13
28	13

2, *First Tetralogy*
1.1–2, 13n4	
1.5–6	13n4
2.3	13n4
2.8	13n4
2.12	5n7
3.7	13n4
4.3	13
4.4	13n4
4.7	13

4, *Third Tetralogy*
2.4	13
13	
3.4	13
4.4–5	13

5, *On the Murder of Herodes*
Ant. 5	13–16, 17n14, 51
1–7	15
10	15
16	15n8
16–18	15
19	15
20–22	14, 153n6
25	15
26–27	14
34–35	15
35	15
39–42	14
45	14
46	15
55–56	15
57	14n7
57–60	14
62–63	14
64–70	16
74–80	15
79–80	15
85	15

6, *On the Chorus Boy*
Ant. 6	47–54
7	48, 54
9	48
16	47n6
19	47n6
20–22	48
35	48
37	49
33–38	48
36	48
38–40	50
41–43	49
43	50
44–50	50
48	48, 50

Fragments (Thalheim)
1a	68n3

Aristophanes
Birds
1074	68n5

Ecclesiazusae
376–94	136n4

Knights
235–39	66, 68n4
255–57	67
434–81	66
451–52	67, 68n4
461–81	67
860–63	132
847–66	67, 68n4, 88

Lysistrata
618–23	68n5
630	68n5

Plutus
569–70	68n5, 87n43

Index Locorum

Thesmophoriazusae		19	125n15
331–37	68n5	25	126
335–39	152n3	3, *Third Olynthiac*	
360–66	152n3	Dem. 3	124
Wasps		5	166
340–45	68, 68n4	30–32	124
418	68n2, 68n4	4, *First Philippic*	
463–65	68n2	Dem. 4	124
474–76	68n2	18	124
480–83	68n2	50	124, 126
488–507	68, 68n2	5, *On the Peace*	
493–502	68	Dem. 5	125, 126
		5	125
Aristotle		6–8	125n15
[*Athēnaiōn Politeia*]		6–9	125, 131
(*Constitution of Athens*)		9–12	125
28.3	85	6, *Second Philippic*	
34.2–35.1	78	Dem. 6	122, 125, 126, 127
34.3	75n16	2	122n9
35.1	82n32	6–8	122n9
43.4	109n33, 136n4	12	122n11
44.2	136n5	13	122n9
44.2–3	136n5	16–19	122n9
45.4	137n5	24	154n7
47.2–3	109n33	26–27	122n9
47.3–4	107n26	29–34	125, 127
52.1	109n33	35	122n9
Generations of Animals		[7], *On Halonnesus*	
608a35–b13	5n7	Dem. 7	125n15, 130
Magna Moralia		17–18	130
1188b29–38	12n2	21	130
Nicomachean Ethics		23	130
7 1149b14–20	32n27	45	8n16
[*Oeconomica*]		8, *On the Chersonese*	
1352a16–23	147n25, 148	Dem. 8	127, 127n19
1352b14–20	147n25, 148	1–37	127n19
Politics		4–20	127
4 1295b33–4	42n44, 159n22	13	122n12
5 1313b20–21	43n45	18	8n12, 129n21
5 1314a14–18	43n45	20	122n12
Rhetoric		32	8n16
1.7.13	1364a 13n4	34–37	122n10, 127
2.24.8	1401b 141n15	35	120
[*Rhetoric to Alexander*]		36	129
15 1424a23–24	43n45	36–67	127n19
20 1424b10–13	43n45, 159n23	40–43	127
32 1426b33–27a3	32n24	47	122n10
75 1437a10–14	117n47	52–58	129n23
		59	129n21
Athenaeus		60–61	129
508e 129n21		9, *Third Philippic*	
		Dem. 9	122n10
Demosthenes		1–3	127
1, *First Olynthiac*		7	127
Dem. 1	124	12	129n21
2, *Second Olynthiac*		16	122n10
Dem. 2	124	19	126

Demosthenes
9, *Third Philippic (continued)*
25–62	122n10
27–28	122n9, 127
33	129n21
36–39	120n4, 127
38	159n23
53	129
56–63	127
59–65	128
69–72	122n10

10, *Fourth Philippic*
Dem. 10
	127n19, 129n22
2	122n9
4–5	128
9	129n21
11	122n10, 127
11–27	127n19
12–13	122n9
15	127, 129
15–16	122n10
32	129
44–45	159n23
49–50	122n10
55–60	129
55–70	127n19
60–61	122n10
61	129n21
62–63	129
70–74	125n15

[11], *Regarding Philip's Letter*
Dem. 11
	123n15, 130
3	130
7	130
18	130

[12], *Philip's Letter*
| 9 | 103n17 |
| 20 | 130 |

14, *On the Symmories*
Dem. 14
4–5	119
12–13	119
36–37	119

15, *For the Liberty of the Rhodians*
2–3	119n2
15–16	82n34
23–24	120n4
30–33	86n40, 126n16

16, *For the Megalopolitans*
Dem. 16
| | 101n13 |

[17], *On the Treaty with Alexander*
[Dem.] 17
| | 125n15 |

18, *On the Crown*
25	122n11
31–41	122n11, 141n14
38	122
61	122n11, 141n14
66	122n10
71	129n21
81	129n21
131–59	5in15
132–34	131
137	131
140–43	140
140–59	153n5
143	139, 139n10, 145n21
144	139n11
147	139n12, 145n21
147–57	140
148–50	140
148	136n4
150–51	140
151	145n21
153	143
153–54	140
153–58	143
156	120n5, 140
158	141
158–59	140
163	122n11, 140
246	159n23
248–49	88
294–97	141n13
294–98	122n12
322	88

19, *On the False Embassy*
Dem. 19
9–12	120n6, 131
13	123
16	5in15
19–28	125
21	13n4
27–28	5in15
36	23n13
37–38	142
41–46	125
68–69	124
110	123
121–30	153n6
122–25	124
136	124, 128
144	122n11, 141n14
174	115n44
175	123, 123n13
179–81	115n44
188	123
202	123
230	122n11, 141n14
259	127
268–72	127
294–95	123
297–99	118

Index Locorum

302–6	120n6, 131*	92	166
315–25	122n11, 141n13	93	98
324	142	102–3	101
20, *Against Leptines*		103	100n12, 102
159	152n3	107	167n7
170	159n23	110	97, 98, 167
21, *Against Meidias*		114–17	101
Dem. 21	46	119	102n16
20	71n13	122	154n7
78	40n39, 46	123	101n13
78–80	46, 153n5, 154n9	130	103n17
83–88	65n37	143	102n15
88	1	144–83	101
104	50n11	145	99n9
104–5	54	146–47	98n5, 99
104–22	48n7	162	167n7
106	1, 65n37	164	101
112	53n17	165–67	101
115	1	168–78	102
116	50n11	170	166
126	1, 5n7	173	167
131	65n37	178–80	166
139	1, 71n13	180	102
140	72n13	183	165
22, *Against Androtion*		184	99n9, 100n10
Dem. 22	99n7	184–86	98n5, 99
1	108n29	185	99n8
1–2	65n37	188	99n8
5–20	107	189	101n13, 103
37	86	189–90	98
23, *Against Aristocrates*		190	97
Dem. 23	86n40, 96–103, 165–67	201	98n5, 99, 126n16
3	98, 167n7	208–10	99
5	97, 101	24, *Against Timocrates*	
6–7	99n9	Dem. 24	86n40, 99n7, 103–14
8	96	3	104n19
8–17	97n4, 98	7	65n37, 108n29
9	96, 98	7–8	105
10	96, 100, 166	7–10	110
11	97, 98, 103	8–9	105
12	97, 101n13, 102	9	105, 110n34, 111, 111n38, 112
12–14	98	10	105, 108n30
13	97, 97n4, 99n9, 166	11	105, 109
13–18	97	11–16	104
14	97, 100	12	105, 105n23, 109, 110
15	97, 98	12–13	110
16	102n15	13	106
19	99n9	14	104n19, 111
22–99	98	14–15	106
27	102n15	15–16	106, 112
50	102n15	26–27	113, 114
60	102n15	26–32	112
75	102n15	27	112, 113
84	102n15	28	113
89	99n9	38	113
91	102n15	39–40	107n25

Index Locorum

Demosthenes
24, *Against Timocrates (continued)*

47	136n4	28, *Against Aphobus II*	
47–49	114	Dem. 28	46
48	114	16	45n3
60–65	107n25	16–17	45
63–64	104n20	17	152n9
65	114n42	29, *Against Aphobus III*	
65–67	104n19	3	25, 26n14
67	112, 114	22–23	72n13
71–90	107	28	24, 114n43, 154n9
110	113, 114	36	65n37
110	114n42	30, *Against Onetor I*	
112	104n19	Dem. 30–31	22–27
117	108n29	3–4	26
120	104n19	5–7	27
121	104n19	6–9	154n9
124	112	8	27, 83
137	104n19, 106	9	23n7, 114n43
138	114n42	17	24
144	86n41	18	27
144–48	152n3	18–20	23n7
145	24	19–21	23
146	106	24	27
146–47	86	25–26	24
155	126n16	26	27
157	114n42	26–27	24
159	114	27	25
166	114n42	29	26
153–54	104n19	31	26
157–59	95	31–32	24
170	114	33	25
174	114n42	33–36	25
176	114n42	35	25n8
185	106	35–36	25, 26n11
186	159n23	38	24, 27
187	106	31, *Against Onetor II*	
187–89	112	1	27
187–217	112	2	27
190	107	6	27
191	112	10	27
195	112	10–11	24
196	114n42	12	27
196–97	106, 107, 114	14	26
200–3	113	32, *Against Zenothemis*	
201	104n19	Dem. 32	35–38, 46, 58, 93, 161–63
206	114	2	36
25, *Against Aristogeiton I*	95, 114	3	37
40	88	4	36, 37
53	17	5	36, 162
64	88	7	37
87–89	159	8	161
27, *Against Aphobus I*		9	37
13	26n12	10	37n34
16	26n12	11	36, 37, 40n39
32	26n12	12	37
46	26n12	13	163n7
		14	163
		15	37

17	163	43	55
18	162	56–57	55
19	163n7	41, *Against Spudias*	
20	163	1	50n11
24	37	14	50n11
24–27	37	42, *Against Phaenippus*	
26	37	1–2	86
27	162	[43], *Against Macartatus*	
27–28	38	[Dem.] 43	3, 93
30	36	1–10	3, 27
33, *Against Apaturius*		7	28
Dem. 33	38–40	30	27n16, 28
2–3	38	32	27, 65n37
3	39	37	28
9	38	38	28
15–16	38	39–40	28
16	38	42	28
16–17	39	81	3
17	39	44, *Against Leochares*	
19	40n38	3	53n17, 65n37
22	40n38	3–4	42n44
24	38	36	42n44, 65n37
34, *Against Phormio*		56	43n45
Dem. 34	40–41	45, *Against Stephanus I*	
1	40	5–6	65n37
12	40n41	13	43n45
18	40n41	22	65n37
21	40n38	41	65n37
28	40n41	67	27, 42
34–35	40n41	[46], *Against Stephanus II*	
38	40	11	65n37
41	40n41	18	65n37
48	40n41	25	27
35, *Against Lacritus*		26	44n2, 152n3
Dem. 35	34n28	47, *Against Evergus and Mnesibulus*	
21–23	161	75	48n7
27	34n28	48, *Against Olympiodorus*	
37, *Against Pntaenetus*		Dem. 48	28–31, 34n28
Dem. 37	41–42	1	31
8	41	1–4	30
21	41	6	29n19
23–24	41	9	31
35	41	9–10	29n19
39	42	17–19	29n19
48	42	22	29
49–50	41	23–26	29
38, *Against Nausimachus*		27	30
3	15n8	28	29n19
3–6	65n37	29	30
39, *Against Boeotus I*		29–30	29
Dem. 39–40	55n21, 58	31	29, 29n20, 30
2	55n23	32	29n19
34	5n7	36	31, 53n17
40, *Against Boeotus II,*		39	31
9–10	55n23	40	31
32	55	41	29
32–34	55n22	42	29

Demosthenes
48, *Against Olympiodorus (continued)*
   43   29
   43–44   29n20
   45–46   31
   46–51   30n21
   51   31
[49], *Against Timotheus*
   67   86n41
[52], *Against Callipus*
   14   71n11
   30–31   40n38
[53], *Against Nicostartus*
   [Dem.] 53   62–64, 110n35
   1–13   62
   2   111n37
   13–15   62
   15   63
   15–16   63n36
   16   64
   17   64
   18   63, 64
   29   64
54, *Against Conon*
   14–17   72n13
   31–40   72n13
55, *Against Callicles*
   Dem. 55   34–35
   1–2   34
   31–33   34
   34–35   35n31
[56], *Against Dionysodorus*
   [Dem.] 56   34n28, 145–48
   1–17   147
   2–3   148
   8   148
   9   148
   11   146n23
   12–13   148
   13   146n23
   16   148
   17   146n23
   20   148
   21–23   147
   47–48   146n23
57, *Against Eubulides*
   Dem. 57   88–94
   2   90n47
   6   89
   7   90n47
   8   86n40, 92
   8–10   136n4
   9   89
   9–10   89
   10   90
   11–13   90
   12   90
   13   90
   14   90
   16   90, 91
   17   90n47
   24–25   91
   48   90, 92
   48–49   91
   53–54   91
   57   91
   58   92
   59   92n52
   60–61   92
   61   92
   62   89, 91
   63   92, 93
   64   93
   65   92, 92n53, 93
58, *Against Theocrinus*
   22–23   48n7, 117n47
   30   117
   34   117
   29–31   116
   40–41   116n45
   42   72n13
   61–65   86
[59], *Against Neaera*
   [Dem.] 59   56
   7   111
   9–10   56
   10   54
   41–42   58
   55–56   26n11
   64–70   59
   64–71   63
   71   60
   66   59n26
   67   59n27
   71   60
Preambles
   2.2   86
   52   136n3

Dinarchus
1, *Against Demosthenes*
   30   3n4
   63   131n25
   94–95   132
   112   116n45
Fragments (Burtt)
   7   91n50
Diodorus of Sicily
   13.2.3   70n8
   14.3.1   75n16
   14.3.1–5   78

Index Locorum

16.21.1	167	47	165
16.22.3	165	53	165
16.34.3	166	Tod	
16.84.1	120n5	79	70n9, 99n8
		86	98n5
Dionysius of Halicarnassus		109	99n8
Ad Ammaeum		110	99n8
1.4	124n14, 166	116	99n8
1.10	124n14	117	99n9
		131	99n8
Harpocration		132	99n8
Bouleuō 31n22		135	99n8
		143	99n8
Hyperides		144	152n3
1, *For Lycophron*		147	152n3
12	95	151	165
3, *Against Athenogenes*		157	165, 167
Hyp. 3	32–34, 63	167	99n8
1–3	32	170	99n8
1–5	50n11	173	99n8
2	33	175	99n8
2–3	32n25	178	99n8
3	32n27	181	99n8
4	33		
5–6	33	Isaeus	
7	32n25	1, *On the Estate of Cleonymus*	
8	33	6–8	22n5
11	32n25	7	53n17
12	32n25, 34	35	50n11
18	32n25, 33	2, *On the Estate of Menecles*	
21	32n25, 34	28–35	50n11
23–25	33	38	50n11
24	32n25	51	50n11
26	32n25, 33	4, *On the Estate of Nicostratus*	
29–32	32n27	5	65n37
35	32n25	30	48n7
4, *Against Euxenippus*		5, *On the Estate of Dicaeogenes*	
3	91n50	7–8	40n39
7–8	44n2, 86n41, 152n3	31–33	40n38
29–30	152n3	6, *On the Estate of Euctemon*	
30	44n2	Is. 6	19–20
5, *Against Demosthenes*		19–26	20
14–15	118	29	20
Inscriptions		35–37	20
IG I³		36	20
102	72	38	20
IG II²		43	20
206	137n5	45–46	20
1613	100n12, 166	48	20
R&O		50	20
2	99n9	54	20
41	152n3	8, *On the Estate of Ciron*	
44	152n3	Is. 8	20–22, 58
70	99n8	1–2	21
SEG		2	22
12	152n3	3–4	21

Isaeus
8, *On the Estate of Ciron (continued)*
4	21
6	22n4
25	21
27	21
30–34	22n4
36	21
36–43	154
37	21, 22, 53n17
40	21
40–42	21, 148n26
41	21
42	21
43	21
44	21
43	21

9, *On the Estate of Astyphilus*
22–26	22n5

10, *On the Estate of Aristarchus*
1	22n5
7	22n5

11, *On the Estate of Hagnias*
8–10	28
14	22n5
15–18	28
20–22	22n5
24–25	29n19
32	22n5
36	22n5

12, *For Euphiletus*
12	89n46

Isaeus, Fragments (Forster)
1	22n5, 72n13
6	89
7–8	22

Isocrates
4, *Panegyricys*
34	42n44
67	8n14, 119n2
136	8n14, 119n2
155	8n14, 119n2
183	8n14, 119n2

5, *To Philip*
73–74	121n7, 154
73–75	130
73–77	8
76	119n2
79	8n15
103	119n2

7, *Areopagiticus*
24	43n45

8, *On the Peace*
22	100n12
97	119n2

11, *Busiris*
19	43n45

12, *Panathenaecus*
102	8n14, 119n2
114	119n2
159	8n14, 119n2
163	8n14, 119n2

15, *Antidosis*
24	43n45
198	43n45, 85
226–34	85
230	43n45
318	72n14

16, *On the Team of Horses*
5–7	70n8

17, *Trapeziticus*
8	43n45
17–19	50n11
46	43n45

18, *Against Callimachus*
Isoc. 18	56–58
6	57
11	57, 148n26
13	40n38
51	58, 86n40
51–52	57
52–54	57
55	57
55–57	58
57	58
63	58

20, *Against Lochites*
10–13	72n14

21, *Against Eutynus*
15	43n45

Justin
5.8.1–11	78
5.8.5–8	75n16
9.1.1	120n5

Lexicon Rhetoricum Cantabrigiense
 Eisangelia 86n41
Lexica Segueriana
296	137n5

Libanius
Dem. 7	130n24
Dem. 23	96n2, 100
Dem. 24	104n20, 109, 112
Dem. 24	II 109n33
Dem. 34	40n41
Dem. 48	29
Dem. 56	146

Lycurgus
1, *Against Leocrates*
25–26	86n41

Index Locorum

124–27	152n3	4	73
138	53n17	7	77
		7–11	73
Lysias		12	73, 75
1, *On the Death of Eratosthenes*		13–16	73
Lys. 1	16–18	15–16	75
4	17n14	17	77
6	17n13	18	76
6–14	17n13	19	76
11–14	17	20	76
15	17	21	80, 80n26
16	17	20–29	74
16–21	17n13	24–28	80
21–22	18	25	77
21–28	17	27	72, 77
27	17	28–29	81n29
28	17, 17n12	29	74, 81, 81n30
30	17	31–33	81
37	17	34–35	77
37–38	18	34–37	82n32
38	17n12	35	82
39–40	18	36	73
39	17	38	73, 82
41–42	18	30–39	74
42	17	36	82
43–46	17n14	48	74, 77n21, 80n26
44	14n7	50	82
3, *Against Simon*		51	80n26
2	65n37	52	72
14	13n4	55–56	72, 82
16	65n37	58	80
28–29	13n4	58–61	81n28
33–34	13n4	59	81
41–43	13n4	61	76n19
4, *On a Premeditated Wounding*		64	76
1–4	50n11	72	7
9–10	13n4, 55n22	77–79	72
5, *For Callias*		84	80n26
2	153	14, *Against Alcibiades I*	
[6], *Against Andocides*		25–26	5n7
[And.] 6	54, 70n9	18, *On the Property of Nicias' Brother*	
34	87n43		
7, *On the Olive Stump*		4–5	79
3	54n19	19, *On the Property of Aristophanes*	
10, *Against Theomnestus I*			
5	14, 17n15	1–3	54n19
11, *Against Theomnestus II*		2–3	43n45
2	17n14	48	85n38
12, *Against Eratosthenes*		22, *Against the Grain Retailers*	
Lys. 12	72n14	Lys. 22	85n39
43–45	79	15	85n39
44	8n16	15–17	42n44
62–78	79	17	5, 85n39
80	7	21	85n39
13, *Against Agoratus*		23, *Against Pancleon*	
Lys. 13	72–83, 153	3	89n45
1	77n21	5–8	89n45

Lysias *(continued)*
24, *For the Disabled*
   1   65n37
   19   43n45
   27   4
25, *Against the Charge of Overthrowing the Democracy*
   27–30   159n23
26, *Against Euandros*
   4   86n40
   13   72n13
   15   86n40
28, *Against Ergocles*
   Lys. 28   86n42
   5–8   87
   11   75n17, 87
29, *Against Philocrates*
   Lys. 29   86n42, 110n35
30, *Against Nicomachus*
   Lys. 30   72n14, 90n47
   1   84, 84n36
   4   84
   5–7   84n36
   9   85
   9–14   79
   10   83
   10–14   83
   11   85
   12   84, 84n37
   12–13   84
   13   85
   14   76n20, 84, 85
   15   85
   26–30   84n36
31, *Against Philon*
   16   43n45
32, *Against Diogeiton*
   18   154n7
Fragments (Thalheim)
   2   110n35

Papyrus Michigan
   5982   77n22

Plato
Laws
   856b–c 67

Photius
  Propempta 137n5

Plutarch
Alcibiades
   19   70n8
Demosthenes
   6–8   103
   7   26n13
   10   103
   14   131n25
Lysander
   14   75
   14–15   78
Moralia
   810d 125n15
   840b–c 134n2
   844d 154n9

Pollux
   8.52   86n41

Polybius
   18.14   122n12

Sophocles
Oedipus Tyrranos
   120–25   151n1

Strabo
   9.3.4   134n2

Theopompus (*FGrHist* 115)
   30   100, 102n16
   101   166n4

Thucydides
   1.2.4   42n44
   1.122.1   67
   1.133.4   8n12
   2.37.2   159
   3.12.3   67n1
   3.20.1   8n12
   3.37.1–2   67n1
   3.37.2   43n45
   3.38.1   159
   3.39.1–2   67n1
   3.40.1   67n1
   3.40.5   67n1
   3.82.4   8n12
   3.82.4   131
   4.86.6   48
   4.118.6   58
   6.11.7   68n2, 68n5
   6.27.3   70n8
   6.28.2   70n8
   6.37–40   67n1
   6.60.1   70n8
   6.60.4   70n8
   6.61.1   70n8
   6.86.3   8n12
   6.87.5   8n12

Xenophon
Hellenica
   1.7.18   65n37

Index Locorum

1.7.35	85n38	2.3.28	82n32
2.2.3–3.14	78	2.4.8–10	82n32
2.2.12–15	75n17	*Hipparchicus*	
2.2.16–17	77n22	9.8.9	8n13
2.2.22	75	*Memeorabilia*	
2.3.11	82n32	2.9	48n7

Text: 10/13 Sabon
Display: Sabon
Compositor: Binghamton Valley Composition, LLC
Printer and binder: Thomson-Shore, Inc.